T0192847

Chinese and Indian Medicine Today

Md. Nazrul Islam

Chinese and Indian Medicine Today

Branding Asia

Md. Nazrul Islam
United International College
Beijing Normal University–Hong Kong
Baptist University
Zhuhai
China

ISBN 978-981-13-5011-5 ISBN 978-981-10-3962-1 (eBook)
DOI 10.1007/978-981-10-3962-1

Printed on acid-free paper

This Springer imprint is published by Springer Nature
The registered company is Springer Nature Singapore Pte Ltd.
The registered company address is: 152 Beach Road, #21-01/04 Gateway East, Singapore 189721, Singapore

All the respondents those spent many hours voluntarily to pursue my research projects
And
My parents
Mosharrof Hossain
Nurunnahar Hossain

Preface

China and India are the world's two oldest medical civilizations. One of the unique features of this book is comparison of medicinal approaches between China and India. The journey of this book began 13 years ago when I started my Ph.D. at the University of Hong Kong. Since then I have completed three projects and included data from all these projects in this book. The first project was my Ph.D. thesis titled "Repackaging ayurveda in post colonial India: Revivalism and global commodification" (2003–2008) undertaken at the University of Hong Kong where I received a postgraduate studentship/scholarship. The next project titled "Globalization and wellness health tourism in China: Paradigm, prospect and challenges" (2010–2012) was carried out after I joined as a faculty in the United International College, Beijing Normal University–Hong Kong Baptist University. The latest project titled "The business of Chinese medicine today: Commodification and paradigm" (2011–2014) was also pursued during my tenureship in the United International College. Both the above two projects were funded by College Research Grant (CRG). I sincerely acknowledge the University of Hong Kong and the United International College for providing resources for pursuance of these projects.

I acknowledge my Ph.D. supervisor Prof. Dr. K.E. Kuah-Pearce the then Department of Sociology, University of Hong Kong for her sincere supervision and guidance. She spent a lot of time enlightening me on this field and helped me in diversifying intellectual horizon.

This book is dedicated to all the respondents those participated and spent valuable time. I particularly acknowledge those ayurvedic and Chinese medicine practitioners who were the last generation apprentice practitioners from their family. I had an opportunity to interview them and record their views, although some of them passed away. Kabiraj Arun Gupta from Tarok Chaterjee Lane of Kolkata city had a family tradition of practicing ayurveda for several generations and allowed me interviewing him and his patients. Kabiraj Goti Proshad Gupto from G.P. Mukherjee Road of Kolkata city who called me as "son"—a traditional way of greeting in Bengali society—was the third and last generation ayurvedic practitioner from his family. I spent many hours and days with him and he always welcome me whenever I visit his home or chamber, introduced me to his junior physicians. Kabiraj Sri Chandranath Chakrobarti from Bidhan Sharoni of Kolkata city was 88 when I interviewed him in 2005 but was still attending patients. He was also the third and last generation ayurvedic practitioner from his family and one of the few practitioners still alive who learned ayurveda exclusively from *toll* (Traditional schooling system of ayurveda). Kabiraj Krishna Nanda Gupta from Sri Aurobinda Sorani of Kolkata city whose grandfather founded the famous Shyamadas Vaidya Shastra Pith, which is now an institute for postgraduate ayurvedic education in Kolkata, was very enthusiastic about my research. Dr. Ganxiang Zhang from Zhuhai city whose father learned Chinese medicine from a famous master of Hunan province of China and founded polyclinic also admired my research and spend many hours voluntarily. I truly appreciate and acknowledge these apprenticeship practitioners.

Professor Pratip Kumar Debnath who was the then Vice-Principal of J.B. Roy State Ayurvedic College and Hospital in Kolkata helped to find students from his college to interview and also provided valuable comments and information on the practice of ayurveda in India. Dr. Mrs. Suraksha Kohli, a retired assistant director of CCRIMH (Ayurvedic physician) and the then living in Ballygunj Place East in Kolkata city was very enthusiastic and encouraging for my study. She also helped finding many respondents for interview. Professor B. Chaudhuri from the Ballygunj Science College, University of Kolkata, acted as my fieldwork supervisor and arranged my accommodation and other technical and logistic support to live in Kolkata during conducting fieldwork. Dr. C. M. Pradyumna, the then director of Sanjeeva Ayurveda Medical Spa at Vedic Village, allowed me to do fieldwork in Vedic Village and interview his patients. Dr. Atreye Karmokar from the Dabur Ayurvedic Medicine shop of Raza Bazar and the same shop owner Mr. Dayanand Gupta supported all the time to pursue fieldwork and conduct survey at his shop. Mr. Buddihimanta Mallick from the Central Research Institute (Ayurveda) in Kolkata also helped in various occasion during conducting fieldwork at his institute. This book never could come in reality without their kind cooperation. I truly acknowledge their contribution and sacrifice.

The research projects in China which contributed this book could not have been carried out without the support and sincere effort of my student assistants. I acknowledge my student assistants Chen Jingyi from 2007 cohort who pursued graduate study later at the City University of Hong Kong; Huang Lei from 2007 cohort who pursued graduate study later at the University of Macao; Wang Jieyu from 2008 cohort who pursued graduate study later at Chinese University of Hong Kong; Tan Yue from 2010 cohort who pursued graduate study later at University of Exeter in UK; Lin Weitong from 2011 cohort who is currently pursuing her graduate study in University of California, Davis; and Feng Zhanjun from 2011 cohort for their sincere cooperation and hard work during data collection, transcription and translation. My colleague Ms. Zhang Katy from the United International College, Zhuhai, China and friend Ms. Huang Qiuyan also helped as translator during visiting various Chinese Medicine outlets in Zhuhai. I appreciate their sincere support.

Dr. Mark Perry, Assistant Professor in the General Education Office, United International College, Beijing Normal University–Hong Kong Baptist University, and Dr. Victor J. Rodriguez, a Lecturer in History, Wenzhou–Kean University spent many hours voluntarily reading the manuscript and provided valuable feedback during their busy times. I truly appreciate their sincere effort and sacrifice. I was offered a sabbatical leave for the spring semester 2015–2016 by the United International College, and I was hosted by the School of Population and Public Health, University of British Columbia where I resided at Green College and completed this book manuscript. I acknowledge all these institutions for their kind support. I also acknowledge my UBC academic collaborator Dr. Farah Shroff for her cooperation to bring me at UBC.

This book targets both undergraduate and postgraduate student audience who are taking courses on Asian medicine. Particularly in my institution, hundreds of students are taking general education courses and interdisciplinary courses on Asian medicine and globalization, Asian health and wellness, environment, food and psychological health from an Asian perspective, etc. and those students can use this book as a primary reference. Graduate students majoring in Asian medicine, health, medical sociology, medical anthropology, community health, public health, medical history, political science, philosophy, health psychology, biology and other majors related to global health, humanities and social sciences can also use this book as reference for their course work and dissertation. Academics, scholars and policymakers will also find this book helpful for their scholarly work as well as policymaking. However, this book also has several limitations. First, this book is unable to incorporate comprehensive empirical data from China for various reasons including lack of accessibility to the Chinese patients for interview, unwillingness to sit interview in front of a foreign researcher, poor language skills of the principal investigator on Chinese. Second, as noted earlier in this Preface that this book started its journey a decade back and some of the data from India are old.

Zhuhai, China
October 2016

Md. Nazrul Islam

Contents

About the Author

Md. Nazrul Islam is Associate Professor in the General Education Office, United International College, Beijing Normal University–Hong Kong Baptist University. He worked as a Visiting Associate Professor (2015–2016) in the School of Population and Public Health, University of British Columbia during which time he has completed this book manuscript. He received Ph.D. in Medical Sociology from the University of Hong Kong; M.Sc. in Community Health and Health Management from Heidelberg University; and Bachelor in Anthropology from Jahangirnagar University. He also studied at Pabna Cadet College, Faridpur Zilla School, and Tarar Mela Ishan Memorial School. He teaches interdisciplinary course on Asian perspective of food, environment and psychological health; foundation course on Indian civilization and society, Silk road heritages in South Asia; and General Education Free Elective courses on Asian medicine and globalization, Introduction to public health, Globalization and society, Asian health and wellness, and Gender and sexuality. His research interest focuses on Chinese herbal medicine, Indian ayurvedic medicine, Silk Road heritages in South Asia, and health tourism. He was a JIRS Fellow (2011–2016), German Academic Exchange Service (DAAD) Fellow (2002–2003), The United Nations University (Tokyo) Fellow (2001), a Visiting Research Associate at the Ateneo de Manila University (2003), attached to University of Calcutta (2004–2005), and a Visiting Scholar at the Center of Asian Studies (2008), University of Hong Kong. He is the editor of the book Public Health Challenges in Contemporary China: An Interdisciplinary perspective by Springer (2016). He has also produced dozens of high impact journal articles in top-notch journals including Current Sociology, Health Sociology Review, South Asia: Journal of South Asian Studies, Indian Journal of Gender Studies, and so on.

Abbreviations

ASF	Ayurvedic State Faculty
AYUSH	Ayurveda, Yoga and naturopathy, Unani, Siddha, Homeopathy
BAMS	Bachelor of Ayurvedic Medicine and Surgery
CCIM	Central Council of Indian Medicine
CHC	City Health Center
CM	Chinese Medicine
MASF	Member of Ayurvedic State Faculty
MBBS	Bachelor of Medicine and Bachelor of Surgery
MD	Doctor of Medicine
OTC	Over The Counter
PHC	Primary Health Care
TCM	Traditional Chinese Medicine
WHO	World Health Organization
WM	Western Medicine

List of Tables

Chapter 1
Introduction

1.1 Introduction

China and India, the world's most thickly-populated countries, have rich medical and health practice, some of which date back to several thousand years B.C. Pluralism and co-existence of a variety of medical traditions within a selected context is a common feature in these two countries. Some medical and health traditions existed as family or ethnic practices, others in organized institutional form. Medical systems in China and India in general were developed as a knowledge based science and relatively dissimilar to a laboratory based Western medical science. The classical medical texts in China such as *Huang Di Nei Jing* (黄帝内经) and *Bencao Gangmu* (本草纲目); and *Caraka Samhita* (चरकसंहिता), *Susruta Samhita* (सुश्रुतसंहिता), and *Astanga Hrdayam* in India put enormous emphasis on prevention and preservation of health. However, contemporary Chinese medicine schools and ayurvedic[1] institutions are ignoring the prime objective of Chinese medicine and ayurveda by emphasizing a curative focus. This book investigates this scenario through ethnographic fieldwork and finds that modern students and graduates from both the countries perceive the theories and methodologies of Chinese medicine and ayurveda similar to Western medicine. There is a growing tendency to integrate Chinese medicine and ayurveda with Western medical thought in the academic curriculum that has led to a gradual decline of the theories and methods written in the classical texts. At the same time, there has been a massive rise of patent drugs being sold under the brand names of Chinese medicine and ayurvedic companies. Most of these drug and health products do not follow the classical formulas found in the medical texts. This book analyses these texts and concludes that contemporary practice of Chinese medicine and ayurveda rarely follows classical texts, and in fact uses Chinese medicine and

[1]Ayurveda is the oldest and largest among all other systems of indigenous medicine practiced in India.

M.N. Islam, *Chinese and Indian Medicine Today*,
DOI 10.1007/978-981-10-3962-1_1

ayurvedic brands and natural/herbal contents to sell Western health products or practices.

This book particularly focuses on the formal and professional sector of Chinese herbal medicine and Indian ayurvedic medical practice in the urban area. Informal sector of Chinese medicine and ayurveda, especially apprenticeship education and the registration of practitioners were restricted after the formation of the Central Council of Indian Medicine (CCIM) in 1970s in India and the foundation of Chinese medicine colleges according to Western line in 1950s in China. In contemporary Indian, only the graduates from the ayurvedic institutions with Bachelor of Ayurvedic Medicine and Surgery (BAMS) degree are allowed to get registration under the council. Similarly, graduates from the modern Chinese medicine colleges and Universities with Bachelor of Chinese medicine and Bachelor of Integrated Chinese medicine degree or above are allowed to get registration for medical practice although middle schooling education and non-schooling education exist in parallel and have their own regulatory systems.[2] Informal practice also exists in the rural area, which this book ignored because of the lack of regulatory framework. As I noted in the preface that this book is an outcome of three different but mutually interrelated research project carried on in India and China. The purpose of this introduction chapter is to provide an understanding on the historical background; theoretical issues and debates; and the conceptual tools used in the research projects. The methodologies used in these researches and the major techniques for collecting empirical and thematic data are also discussed in this chapter.

1.2 Medical Tradition in China: From Historical Time to Date

Huang Di Nei Jing (The Yellow Emperor's Classic of Medicine or Canon of Medicine) a combination of two classics *Su Wen* (The Basic Questions) and *Lingshu* (The Spiritual Pivots) is a collection that best represents the ancient theories and methods in the practice of Chinese herbal medicine and acupuncture. It was also one of the earliest classical texts of this kind which systematically documented the etiology, physiology, diagnosis, treatment and prevention of disease (Dong and Zhang 2002: 17). The book came to modern readers as a conversation or dialogue between the legendary Chinese emperor *Huang Di* and his minister or vassals *Qi Bo* (Zhu 2009: 265). *Huang Di Nei Jing* was not written during the period of emperor *Huang Di* nor was it written by a single person at a single period. It contains materials from the "Warring States period, along with passages inserted during the Wei and Jin period" (Zhang 2012: 486). However, the current outlook of the book was finalized in the Han period of Chinese history (Ibid). Critics also said

[2]Detail discussion on Chinese medicine education in contemporary China could be found in Chap. 3.

that *Huang Di Nei Jing* has no relation with emperor Huang Di but the medical practitioners from the Han dynasty used the name of Huang Di to receive greater acceptance. There are several English translations of *Huang Di Nei Jing* currently available in the academic arena. This book used two major translations: (1) Yellow Emperor's Canon of Internal Medicine, Original Note by Wang Bing, and translated by Wu Liansheng and Wu Qi and published by China Science & Technology Press; (2) The Medical Classic of the Yellow Emperor, translated by Zhu Ming and published by Foreign Language Press, Beijing. According to *Huang Di Nei Jing* various form of healing practices in China originated in different parts of the country because of the variation of landscape. For example, the use of healing stone in *gua sha* (scraping) has come from eastern China, oral herbs or Chinese herbal medicine from western China, moxibustion from north China, use of nine needles or practice of acupuncture from south China, and *qigong* and massage or *tuina* from central China (*Huang Di Nei Jing*, Twelfth Article 2009: 271–272).

Another master piece in the practice of Chinese herbal medicine is *Bencao Gangmu* (Compendium of Materia Medica) completed by Li Shizhen in 1578 (Li 2012: 33). Like *Huang Di Nei Jing* there is also several English translation of *Bencao Gangmu* available for academic and professional readers. This book uses Condensed Compendium of Materia Medica which is edited by Li Jingwei and Translated by Luo Xiwen and published by Foreign Language Press, Beijing. The *Bencao Gangmu* comprises 52 volumes, describing 1892 drugs, and with 1109 illustrations. This epic classifies drugs and treatments into 16 categories and 62 sub-categories. The 16 categories include: water, fire, earth, metals and stones, herbs, cereals, vegetables, fruits and wood, utensils, insects, animals with scales, shells, fowls, animals, and humans. 62 subcategories include mountain herbs, fragrant herbs, herbs from swampland, toxic herbs, creeping herbs, aquatic herbs, herbs from rocky land, mosses, miscellaneous herbs, and herbs not yet in use. The book also recorded 1094 floral drugs, 444 fauna drugs and 354 mineral drugs (Li 2012: 33–34).

From historical time to date Chinese medical knowledge and practices were transmitted through three different modes: 'secret'; 'personal'; and 'standardised' (Hsu 1999: 1). "Secretly transmitted knowledge is intentionally made secret" and most of the time it is kept as family secret transmitted through one member to another from that particular family (Ibid). This secret has preserved and transferred from one generation to another and crucial to maintain a stable social relationship among those who are involved. Personal transmission of knowledge followed an apprenticeship mode where a Master and his disciples "maintain a personal relationship of mutual trust within which the follower acquires medical knowledge and practice" (Ibid: 2). Professionalised mode of transmission is labelled as standardised transmission which generally requires to follow certain rules and regulations adopted by the modern state (Ibid: 2). This book emphasises the standardised form of practice which could be tracked back during Tang Dynasty (598–907 A.D.) through the establishment of *Taiyishu* to train imperial physicians and supervised by the state. *Taiyishu* was also favoured by the Song dynasty and survived with slight modification until the Ming dynasty (1368–1644 A.D.) (Huard 1970: 367).

The Mongols those founded Young dynasty in China also valued Chinese physicians and re-established *Taiyishu.* They gave physicians a levy privileges and created the taxation and judicial category "Medical Households" in China (Shinno 2013: 140). *Taiyishu* taught various medical specialities such as internal medicine, material-medica, ophthalmology, forensic medicine, dietetics, sexual hygiene, paediatrics, gynaecology, and dermatology (Gaggi 1979: 14–15).

"Family education" and "apprenticeship education" were the other major forms of education in Chinese medicine existed until recent decades (Wangzhong 1996). Under the family education system, medical knowledge and skills were kept as a family secret and transferred from one generation to another among the members of that particular family. Although apprenticeship education is also a part of family education there are some boundaries between the two. In family education, external members are generally excluded from gaining medical training and skill from the senior practitioner while apprentice education allowed external members to learn. Generally under the apprenticeship education system, a senior practitioner has a small school where several students could enroll and learn medical training and expertise from him. Often these junior students live at their master's house as a junior member of the family and accompany him when he attained patients. Apprentice education system in Chinese medicine dramatically declined in China after the foundation of Chinese medicine colleges according to the Western line (Islam 2016: 59–60).

After the 1949 revolution and the foundation of the People's Republic of China Chinese government formulated official policies to revive Chinese medicine and stipulated integration of Chinese medicine with Western medical professionals which caused the rise of a new form of standardized education and practice (Ibid). In 1950s Mao Zedong the founder of the People's Republic of China declared that "Chinese medicine is a great treasure-house, and efforts should be made to explore and raise it to a higher level" (Xie 2002: 119). Followed by that declaration four colleges were established in four different parts of China in 1956 to teach Chinese medicine according to the Western line. These are: Beijing College of Traditional Chinese medicine in North China; Guangzhou College of Traditional Chinese medicine in South China; Shanghai College of Traditional Chinese medicine in East China; and Chengdu College of Traditional Chinese medicine in West China. The goals were to professionalize and standardize Chinese medicine education according to Western line. The government founded State Administration of Traditional Chinese medicine of the People's Republic of China to supervise and regulate the education, practice and drug manufacturing of Chinese medicine (Islam 2016: 61). Most of the Chinese medicine colleges and Universities are currently offering undergraduate programs on Chinese Herbal Medicine, Integrated Chinese medicine, Acupuncture and moxibustion, and Tuina.[3] One of the common features of these

[3]Beijing University of Chinese medicine offer courses such as Chinese medicine, specialization in research and experimental training (7-year combined program leading to Bachelor and Master in Medicine), Chinese medicine (5-year program leading to Bachelor of Medicine), Acupuncture-Moxibustion and Tuina (5-year program leading to Bachelor of Medicine), etc.

Chinese medicine colleges/Universities is to combine Chinese medicine with Western medicine and develop an integrated medical practice. The Chinese constitution promulgated in 1982 and declared that the state should develop both modern/Western medicine and indigenous Chinese medicine which fuelled this trend (Xie 2002: 119). Present constitution also advocates that Chinese medicine and Western medicine should unite and learn from each other, mutually complement each other and improve together (Ibid). There are more than 33 Universities offering Chinese medicine courses, enrolling 48,000 students every year. There are also 53 secondary schools with 50,800 enrolment each year offering Chinese medicine courses (Dutta 2009: 387). However, integrated education and practice has caused various challenges which has been discussed detail in Chap. 3 of this book.

1.3 Historical Preview of the Medical Tradition in India

In India, various outsiders have invaded throughout its history for their own political, economic and religious interests. The first invasion was that of the Aryans, followed by the Persians and the Europeans. All the ethnic outsiders introduced their own conceptions of health, and medical traditions in India from a religious inspiration. For example, the Aryans introduced Vedic medicine from Sanskrit liturgical knowledge of the Veda. Vedic medicine was systemised as ayurveda and was promoted by Brahmanic religious practitioners. The word ayurveda consists of two Sanskrit terms: 'veda' means 'knowledge' or 'science', while *'ayu'*, means 'life' or 'duration of life'. Ayurveda thus refers to the knowledge of life or the science of life. Ayurveda defines *ayu*, or life, as a combination and coordination of four parts: *atta* (the soul), *mona* (the mind), *indrio* (the senses) and *sharer* (the body) (Joshi 1997: 15). Each of these parts has a specific function in maintaining the balance of the body. Whenever there is a disconnection among these four elements an immediate physical, mental or spiritual imbalance arises.

The sacred scriptures, the vedas, reflect a total worldview that includes aspects of creation, metaphysics, philosophy, ethics, religion, magic, medicine, dietary rules, and guidelines for the activities of daily living (Ninivaggi 2001: 7). The most famous two classical ayurvedic epics, the *Caraka Samhita* and the *Susruta Samhita*, were written in Sanskrit and are part of the Brahmanic tradition. There is a third text, the *Astanga Hrdayam* written by Vagbhatas which came much later than the previous two and currently popular in South India. The Sanskrit word *samhita* means 'compendium', and *Caraka* and *Susruta* are the proper names of the authors —thus these titles may be translated as '*Caraka's* Compendium' and '*Susruta's* Compendium' (Wujastyk 1995). It has been stated in the *sutro sthana*[4] of the *Caraka Samhita* text that Agnivesh was the best of Atreya's students and that he

[4]Both the Caraka and Susruta Samhita texts are divided into different parts such as sutro sthana, nidan sthana, uttor sthana, etc.

documented his "preceptor's methodological exposition" and prepared a text under the title *Agnivesa Tantra*, which is another name for the *Caraka Samhita* (Subbarayappa 2001: 14).

Apart from Hinduism's influence, ayurveda has also been subjected to Buddhist influence. While Buddhism did not develop its own medical systems, Buddhist monasteries began medical treatments of the lay community, generally using ayurvedic principles (Tucker 2001: 375). Many Buddhist scholars made positive contributions for the medicinal preparations and development of ayurveda. Nagarjuna, an alchemist, was one of the pioneers among them, having made remarkable contributions in the preparation of medicinal mineral substances (Ninivaggi 2001: 20). The Nagarjuna School developed various techniques to purify toxic substances, such as mercury, and render them non-toxic and suitable for human consumption (Ibid). Buddhists scholars set up one of the most famous ancient Indian universities, 'Nalanda', which continued in prominence until the 12th century. It was later arguable destroyed by the Muslim occupier and only recently revived by the Indian government through establishing a new Nalanda University campus in the Indian state of Bihar within the 10 km distance from the original sight of Nalanda. Although the exact timeframe of the establishment of Nalanda University is debatable, it was between the third and seventh centuries A. D. Some scholars claimed that Nagarjuna was affiliated with that university during his experiments in ayurvedic mineral preparation.

The first Muslim ruler to lead a regular army into India was Muhammad-bin-Qasim, who was sent by Hazzaz-Bin-Yusuf from Iraq. Muhammad-bin-Qasim came by land along the Persian coast and defeated the local Indian king Raja Dahir in the year 711 A.D. The Arabs ruled over the part of India known as Sind for about 300 years without any further expansion. India was ruled by several other Muslim rulers afterwards and finally fell under the 'Sultan regime' until Jahir Uddin Babur founded the great Mughal Empire in 1526 A.D.

One of the noteworthy contributions made by Muslims in the medical field, under these Muslim rulers, was the introduction of the *unani* medical system, widely known as Persian-Arab medicine. The word unani is an Indian version of the name of Ionia, in Greece, where the unani system originated. The unani system was founded by Hippocrates (460–377 B.C.) and further developed by some famous Muslim scholars such as Galen, Ibi-Sina, etc. Unani medicine is based on the 'humoural' theory, according to which there are four humours (*akhlat*) in the human body: blood (*dam* or *khun*), phlegm (*balgham*), black bile (*al-mirra as-sawda*) and yellow bile (*al-mirra as-safra*) (Liebeskind 1995). According to Hippocratic thought, health depended on all the humours being in complete balance with each other. Any change in this balance brings about a change in the state of the body. *Hakim* is a title given to unani medical practitioners in India. There were two major categories of *hakim*. Some came from the Arabian Peninsula or Persia and were employed by an Indian government on a contract basis. A few of them returned to their home countries after their contract had expired, while others permanently settled down in India (Goggi 1981: 102). From the Sultan Regime to the great Mughal Empire, Muslim rulers patronised the unani medical system in

India (Liebeskind 1995). Gradually unani medicine became the main mode of treatment for the urban elite class because of this state patronage (Ibid). Under the Mughal Empire many hospitals, clinics and other medical infrastructure was established. Akbar the Great (1556–1605) was the pioneer among Mughal emperors in establishing hospitals in various locations of Delhi and Agra. During the latter part of the Mughal Dynasty, Aurangzeb (1658–1707) also built hospitals in the provinces, and in small towns.

There are several similarities between unani and ayurvedic medicine, especially in the fields of philosophy and diagnostic principle. Firstly, both ayurvedic *vaidyas* and unani *hakims* relied heavily on pulse checking as a method to identify diseases. Another similarity between ayurveda and unani medical systems was the grounding in humoral theory. Both systems recognized that bodily 'humours' could cause physiological disorder, and that the natural environment is a prime determinant of health. There are also similarities between ayurvedic and unani classical texts. *The Madan-ul-Shifa*, considered the classical unani text, contains a preface and discussion about the science of medicine and the fundamentals of medicine (Jaggi 1981: 115). It has three chapters: the first deals with preliminary treatment, various stages of the treatment, impact of different seasons of the year, various kinds of surgical operation, etc.; the second chapter deals with conception and human anatomy; and the third with symptoms and treatment of different diseases (Ibid). The ayurvedic texts *Caraka* and *Susruta Samhita* have similar, corresponding topics and classifications of chapters. Apart from philosophical and textual similarities, both the ayurveda and unani systems heavily rely on plant, mineral and animal-based drug preparations.

It is contested indeed whether the introduction of unani medicine caused any decline of ayurveda. Critics have commented that unani medicine got patronage from the state and the royal court, and that this had a negative impact on the advancement of ayurvedic practitioners. Many ayurvedic practitioners were not employed in the imperial court, whereas unani practitioners were employed. However, another view regards the introduction of unani medical practices as positive for ayurveda, as both the systems benefited through mutual learning and sharing. Muslim scholars translated the anthologies of ayurvedic text into the Persian and Arabic languages, and adopted drugs and other therapies from ayurvedic practice from the thirteenth century on (Leslie 1976: 356).

The Europeans introduced Western medicine and Christian missionaries were active in promoting this system among the Indian masses. In recent Indian history, British colonial rule marked the entry of Western science and technology, which caused a decline of existing social institutions. The medical field was not excepted in these changes, and British administrative policy promoted the Western system of medicine. During the East India Company regime, different Europeans began to introduce Western allopathic medicine to the population. Many Company officials had consulted ayurvedic practitioners, in addition to European doctors, who also served as consultants to members of the Indian elite (Jeffery 1988: 50–51). During the British colonial rule, some Indians were given training in European medicine, as part of an expansion in medical services for the army (Ibid). At the same time, the Court of Directors in London encouraged its employees to investigate the value of local Indian ayurvedic and unani medicines and medical texts (Ibid: 51). As continuation of such effort a scheme was approved to open a Native Medical School in 1822 in Kolkata, and 20 students were enrolled in this program (Jaggi 1979: 10). This school taught both indigenous and Western medicine. It was the first attempt to develop an integrated medical education in India. As ayurvedic texts were written in Sanskrit and unani texts in Urdu, Sanskrit medical classes were conducted at the Kolkata Sanskrit College and Urdu classes in the Kolkata Madrassa (Ibid).

In 1833, Governor General Lord William Bentinck appointed a committee to inquire into the condition of medical training and the effectiveness of the functioning of the Native Medical School. The committee investigated and found the Native Medical School education defective, and recommended the immediate abolition of the Institution. The committee further suggested the formation of a Medical College for Indians in which the various branches of Western medical sciences already introduced in Europe should be taught in the English language (Ibid). That was the end of the first attempt at synthesis of Indian and Western systems of medicine in India. The next attempt to revive and legitimize ayurveda came at the later part of the British colonial rule through the introduction of integrated medical education, where students had to study both ayurveda and Western medicine for a medical degree program. The consequence of this was that "by the end of the nineteenth century ayurvedic practitioners widely recognized that in order to combat the increasingly widespread mimicry of European bodily practice it would be necessary to cope certain forms of European institutional practice" (Leslie 1976; Langford 2002: 7). Other scholars, too, noted the professionalization of indigenous medicine in modern India, where ayurveda in particular followed the Western medicine path as a result of the introduction of Western medicine during the colonial rule (Leslie 1976).

After decolonization, India became independent and emerged as a nation state in 1947. Efforts were made to revive ayurveda with state backing. These included adopting policies and changing strategies to provide better health care services and integrating ayurveda into mainstream health. Various committees were formed to make recommendation for the best use of ayurveda such as the Pundit Committee, the Dave Committee, etc. According to the recommendation of the Pundit Committee's Report, the Central Research Institute in Indigenous Systems of Medicine was created at Jamnagar in 1952 (Ministry of Health Report 1958: 6). The Dave Committee basically considered the question of the regulation of the practice of indigenous systems of medicine. The Dave Committee also produced a model syllabus for the integrated course. Finally in 1972, the Government of India, by an Act of Parliament, established the Central Council of Indian Medicine (CCIM) for regulating education and registration in ayurveda (Kurup 2002). The state health ministry formed a directory of Indian Systems of Medicine and Homoeopathy (ISM&H) during the 1970s, which has been renamed as the Department of Ayurveda, Yoga and Naturopathy, Unani, Siddha and Homoeopathy (AYUSH) in

2003. This department oversee the education and practice of ayurevda in contemporary India. Currently there are 510 ayurvedic institutions offering degree program with annually 44,050 enrolments in all over India (AYUSH 2011: 2).

1.4 China–India: Some Basic Demographic and Health Indicators

See Table 1.1.

Table 1.1 China–India demographic and health comparison

Category	Area of comparison	Area of comparison	China	India
1. Demography and health state	Population	Total population	1,360,720,000 in 2013[a]	1,210,193,000 (1st March 2011)[b], AYUSH (2012: 189)
		Male population	697.28 million (51.2%) in 2013[c]	623,724,000 (1st March 2011)[b], AYUSH (2012: 189)
		Female population	663.44 million (48.8%) in 2013[a]	586,469,000 (1st March 2011)[b], AYUSH (2012: 189)
	Life expectancy	Male	69.6 Years (2009)[d]	65.8 Years (2006–11), AYUSH (2012: 191)
		Female	73.3 Years (2009)[e]	68.1 Years (2006–11), AYUSH (2012: 191)
	Crude birth rate	Average	12.08 per thousand in 2013[a]	22.1 per thousand in 2010, AYUSH (2012: 192)
		Rural area		23.7 per thousand in 2010, AYUSH (2012: 192)
		Urban area		18.0 per thousand in 2010, AYUSH (2012: 192)
	Crude death rate	Average	7.16 per thousand in 2013[e]	7.2 per thousand in 2010, AYUSH (2012: 192)
		Rural area		7.7 per thousand in 2010, AYUSH (2012: 192)

(continued)

Table 1.1 (continued)

Category	Area of comparison	Area of comparison	China	India
		Urban area		5.8 per thousand in 2010, AYUSH (2012: 192)
	Natural growth rate	Average	4.92 per thousand in 2013[e]	14.9 per thousand (2010), AYUSH (2012: 193)
	Infant mortality rate	Total	15.20 per thousand life birth in 2013[f]	47 per thousand in 2010, AYUSH (2012: 193)
	Total fertility rate	Female	1.55 per woman (2014) estimated[g]	2.6 per women (2009), AYUSH (2012: 194)
2. Socio demographic profile	Sex ratio of population	Sex ratio at birth	117.14 in 2011[h]	940 females per thousand males in 2011, AYUSH (2012: 190)
	Urbanization	Urban population	731.11 million (53.73%) in 2013[c]	377.1 million (31.2%) in 2011, AYUSH (2012: 190)
		Rural population	629.61 million (46.27%) in 2013[e]	833.46 million (69.8%) in 2011[i]
	Literacy rate age 15 and over can read and write	Average	95.1% in 2010[j]	74.04% in 2011, AYUSH (2012: 191)
		Male	97.5% in 2010[e]	82.14% in 2011, AYUSH (2012: 191)
		Female	92.7% in 2010[e]	65.46% in 2011, AYUSH (2012: 191)
3. Public health facilities	Annual budget for health	Total	RMB 260.253 billion in 2013[k]	INR 373.300 billion in 2013–14[l]
		Budget for alternative medicine	RMB 0.858694600 billion in 2013[k]	INR10 billion in 2013–14[e]
		% of budget for alternative medicine	0.330% in 2013	3.73% in 2013–14

[a]National Bureau of Statistics of China (2012). Statistical communiqué of the People's Republic of China on the 2013 national economic and social development. P. 1. Retrieved from the http://www.stats.gov.cn/english/PressRelease/201402/t20140224_515103.html
Accessed on 30 March 2014

[b]AYUSH in India (2012). *Annual Report*. New Delhi: Department of AYUSH, Ministry of Health and Family Welfare, Government of India

[c]National Bureau of Statistics of China (2014). Statistical communiqué of the People's Republic of China on the 2013 national economic and social development. P. 1. Retrieved from the http://www.stats.gov.cn/english/PressRelease/201402/t20140224_515103.html
Accessed on 30 March 2014
[d]Health statistics by the end of 2009. National Health and Family Planning Commission of the People's Republic of China. Retrieved from the http://www.moh.gov.cn/publicfiles/business/htmlfiles/zwgkzt/ptjnj/year2010/index2010.html
Accessed on 30 March 2014
[e]Ibid
[f]CIA World Fact Book: Infant Mortality Rate. Retrieved from the http://en.wikipedia.org/wiki/List_of_countries_by_infant_mortality_rate
Accessed on 30 March 2014
[g]CIA World Fact Book: Total Fertility Rate (Children born/woman). Retrieved from the https://www.cia.gov/library/publications/the-world-factbook/fields/2127.html
Accessed on 30 March 2014
[h]National Bureau of Statistics of China (2012). Statistical communiqué of the People's Republic of China on the 2011 national economic and social development. P. 18
[i]Ministry of health and family welfare, Government of India. Census 2011, Key Indicators. Retrieved from the http://mohfw.nic.in/showfile.php?lid=2019
Accessed on 30 March 2014
[j]CIA World fact book. Retrieved from the http://en.wikipedia.org/wiki/List_of_countries_by_literacy_rate and accessed on 30 March 2014
[k]Ministry of Finance of the People's Republic of China Web page. Retrieved from the http://yss.mof.gov.cn/ and accessed on March 22, 2014
[l]Retrieved from http://health.india.com/news/union-budget-2013-14-health-gets-rs-37330-crore/
Accessed on November 2013

1.5 Conceptual Framework of This Book

1.5.1 Western Hegemony

Modernization and professionalization of indigenous medicine in China and India was influenced by the Western enlightenment and capitalist development. This started in China during late nineteenth century with the hand of *Qing* dynasty and promoted after the 1911 revolution and formation of Republic of China. The 1949 revolution and formation of the People's Republic of China regime also promoted Western medicine in China. In India, this modernization and Westernization has done much earlier with the British colonial hand. Although Western medicine is a relatively new phenomenon as compared to other systems of medicines in China and India it achieved dominant position with the hand of industrial capitalism, firstly in the West and gradually all over the world, and served the interest of capitalist class (Baer et al. 1997: 12). Western medicine was first brought to China by the Jesuit scholars of Peking for the use of the emperor and diffused only slightly outside the imperial palace. However, the penetration of Western medicine into China took place at the Christian missions, chiefly Anglo-Saxon. Gradually schools for Western medical education were opened in Peking then in Canton in 1870 and Tien-Tsin in 1881. In 1949, the year Republican rule collapsed, the number of practitioners formally trained in Western medicine reached to 38,875 (Xie 2002: 119). The trend continued during the Mao to the post-Mao era.

Similarly, Western medicine was brought to India by the European expansion and later imposed under the shadow of colonial administration. The London Missionary Society in southern India started medical relief during 1830s with a belief that "It could open a wide and effectual door into the hearts and minds of the natives, if only because medical aid was one of the very few forms of help which the Hindu is at liberty to receive" (Arnold 1993: 244). The missionarization of Indian peoples was an important feature of European expansion. Before the colonial invasion, ayurveda and other forms of Indian medicine were in the mainstream. However, the colonial outlook stigmatised ayurveda as 'traditional' and oppose to scientific Western medicine. At the same time the dominant status of Western medicine is "legitimized by the modern state and laws" that give Western medicine more protection (Baer et al. 1997: 29).

From a neo-Marxist perspective, Antonio Gramsci's idea of ideological hegemony is an important conceptual tool for this book. Gramsci posited that political leadership could be based upon consent rather than coercion and that such consent might be secured through the diffusion of the worldview of the ruling class (Gramsci 1978). This Gramscian thought corresponds to the nature of contemporary education and practice of indigenous medicine in China and India. The pattern and structure of today's Chinese medicine and ayurvedic undergraduate and postgraduate education follow a Western framework, which was put in place in India by the British colonial administration and in China by the Maoist nationalist administration. Traditionally, both the Chinese medicine and ayurvedic practitioners learned their medical skill through an apprenticeship system. However, the British colonial rule brought ayurvedic education under a Western institutional framework. After the independence of India from the British colonial rule in 1947 and the formation of People's Republic of China in 1949 indigenous medical systems adopted an integrated curriculum and incorporated a significant number of courses from the Western medicine.

Gramscian analysis of hegemony is particularly relevant here, as he noted that any dominant social group or core social group imposes its dominance for the purpose of taking over power and holding it (Gramsci 1978). A continuous struggle before and after the revolution is a pre-requisite to prolong the dominance (Ibid). Hegemony refers to a social, political, economic or cultural condition rooted in the equation of subordination and dominance. In the colonial context, "hegemony refers to the conventional modes of arranging compliance to constituted authority, and this authority's search for a langue which makes such compliances assured and habitual" (Kaviraj 1994: 26). Hegemony functions as a tool for creating legitimacy for the colonial apparatus of control to integrate a colonized society with colonial arrangement. From this perspective, hegemony basically suggests "the ways in which colonial ideology served by the ruling class by helping to make their rule appear natural and legitimate" (Engels and Dagmar 1994: 3).

The emergence of Western medicine in India implies both the hegemonic and coercive means. The medical class trained in Western medicine was formed among native Indians by the end of the nineteenth century, and Western medicine was privileged by colonial administration through administrative regulations. Many commentators agreed that the dominance of Western medicine in prestigious and well-paid areas was due to state patronage, while ayurveda declined because of administrative reluctance and negligence (Bala 1991: 17–18). The hegemonic power of Western medicine reflected in post-colonial India and the growth rate of Western medical colleges were much greater than that of ayurveda even after Indian independence.

Except Hong Kong and Macao, mainland China did not have a long history of going under European colonial rule. Although Western medicine was already introduced in China during late Qing dynasty the foremost promotion was done with the hand of nationalist rulers. After the 1911 revolution and formation of the Republic of China, many Chinese scholars and political elites felt the urgent need to firmly establish and assert its national identity. Apart from the political reform and technological initiatives, revitalization of medicine and health care came to the forefront (Xie 2002: 118). Overwhelming faith in the potential of Western science to solve China's problems led them to embrace Western medicine and ignore indigenous medical practices. The ruling elites considered the existence of indigenous medicine as potential barrier for China's modernization according to the Western line. Indigenous Chinese medicine practitioners were "blasted as ignorant and irrational" and the systems of Chinese medicine were treated as superstitious (Yip 1995: 27). In 1929, the Central Government passed a bill to ban Chinese medicine in order to clear the way for developing medical and health care service according that based on Western medicine (Xie 2002: 118). The situation reverses although problematically after the 1949 revolution and formation of the People's Republic of China. Instead of abandoning Chinese medicine the new ruling elites decided to revive Chinese medicine according to the Western line and with the help of Western science and technology. Integrating Chinese medicine and indigenous practices with Western modalities and incorporation of Western medical technologies in the practice of Chinese medicine was a key strategy under this effort.

1.5.2 Decline and Revival from Nationalist Inspiration

A second issue of this book is the revival of indigenous medicine in China during the Mao era and in India after the dismantling of colonial rule from nationalist inspiration and the ambiguity and challenges caused by nationalist claims of medical practices. Benedict Anderson stressed that "nationalism has enabled post-colonial societies to invent a self image through which they could act to liberate themselves from imperialist oppression" (Anderson 1983: 15). For Jonathan Spencer, "nationalism is the political doctrine" that claims "the idea of a group of people with a shared culture, often a shared language, sometimes a shared religion, and usually but not always a shared history"; which give them the right of political legitimacy to rule themselves (Spencer 1998: 391). In the above quotations there is a common feature that the principle of nationalism involves 'a sense of belongings' or feelings of consciousness that people use to develop their own group identity.

Before explain further on how nationalistic claim of indigenous medicine in modern China and India causes an ambiguous cause of revival let me spell out first the possible causes of decline Chinese medicine during the twentieth century and ayurveda during the British colonial rule in India. The first possible cause for the decline of Chinese medicine in Twentieth century could be the process of development. As I stated before that medical systems in both China and India were developed as knowledge and experience based science which is relatively dissimilar to Western experimental science. Until twentieth century China did not try to introduce "experiment-based innovation process" into Chinese medicine, instead heavily relied on "experience-based technological invention" (Lin 1995: 269–292). Experience based Chinese medicine was capable to provide a smaller size of population. While population has risen rapidly in China over the Centuries experience-based medical practice was unable to fulfill the need to large scale consumers. Experience based medical practice was also heavily relied on individualistic diagnosis and treatment method. In another word, Chinese medicine practitioners used imply individualistic diagnostic method and write individual prescription instead of standardized diagnostic method and prescription which Western medical science does. When demand for medical practitioner has risen dramatically because of the increase of population rapidly, experience based medical practice simple fail to meet the demand. While new technologies have come about through the trails and errors and Western medicine adopted all these new technologies it much successful to meet the demand of rapidly increase population in China. Another possible cause is the rise of epidemic disease such as small pox and incapability of Chinese medicine practitioners to safe thousands of life from Smallpox. Historical evidences suggest that small pox did not exist in China until the traders transported it to China from Egypt through India when they used Silk road (McCracken and Phillips 2012: 61). Classical Chinese medical text Huang Di New Jing also did not mentioned about Small Pox. When small pox appears in China the practitioners Chinese medicine found themselves helpless. The experiment of Edward Jonner in 1796 proved that vaccination with cowpox gives immunity to smallpox virus and contributed a critical break through against the virus which eventually leads to a miracle achievement in Western medicine to eradicate smallpox.

The nature of the socio-political institutions in pre-modern China was another major cause for her inability to introduce experiment based science in Chinese medicine (Lin 1995: 269–292). Until early twentieth century China was ruled by various dynasties and the totalitarian control by the state was not favorable to competition and scientific development. Civil service was deemed the most rewarding and honorable work because of the dominance of bureaucracy and priority for the most talented students to develop a career in civil service rather than become a scientist. The Chinese state also did not invest adequate resource and incentive for scientific experiment. As a result, scientist in pre-modern China were unable to rise as a dominant group in the society which causes the inability of developing Chinese medicine as experimental science.

Although some of the above mentioned reasons for the decline of Chinese medicine are also applicable to ayurveda in India, the different socio-political system contributed the major setback for development of ayurved as experimental science. From Mid-eighteen to mid-twentieth century India was under the European colonial rule first century by the East India Company and the second century by the British Raj. During the East India Company regime, different Europeans began to introduce Western medicine to the Indian population and many Company officials had consulted ayurvedic practitioners, in addition to European doctors, who also served as consultants to members of the Indian elite (Jeffery 1988: 50–51). However, this tolerance by the Company administration did not last long and Kolkata Medical College was founded on 1st February 1835 to offer Western medical education, and several colleges and schools were opened by the second half of the nineteenth century for teaching Western medicine in the English language (Jaggi 1979: 11). As a result of this, there emerged a new class of urban elites among the native Indians with a Western outlook (Dutta 2003: 72). They were trained in Western medical colleges founded by the colonial administration, and some of them were even exposed to British or European medical education (Islam 2008: 86). A second step was to promote Western medicine in India and subjugate ayurveda was, with the adoption of new legislation and regulation. In the 1910s, the Medical Registration Act was passed and enforced for compulsory registration of the practitioners of Western medicine, which disappointed the practitioners of ayurvedic medical systems (Jaggi 1979: 13). The positions of *vaidyas* were threatened by this law, which limited their right to become registered practitioner (Liebeskind 1996). Also, the Medical Degree Act restricted the use of the title 'Doctor' to those trained in Western medicine (Liebeskind 1996).

The introduction of Western medicine in India by the colonial administration came as a colonizing process and ayurveda was intentionally subjugated which contributed another cause for the decline of ayurveda. Western medical intervention in India as a 'colonizing process' and "the history of colonial medicine serves to illustrate the more general nature of colonial power and knowledge and to illuminate its hegemonic as well as its coercive processes" (Arnold 1993: 8). The introduction of Western medicine in India was a part of imperialism and the monopolization of Western medicine in Indian health care system was part of colonial rule. The dominance of Western medicine in prestigious and well-paid areas of practice during the colonial rule was due to state patronage. As a result of colonial hegemony over medicine, British policy favored the flourishing of the Western system of medicine, and that this proved inimical to ayurveda (Gupta 1976: 369).

In India, nationalism was born as an anti-colonial resistance. India is culturally and linguistically a diversified country where people from different states speak different languages in their everyday lives. The Indian central government recognizes several languages as official languages, although English and Hindi have been widely used in recent official documents. European linguistic nationalism did not develop in India as it did in Europe although the central Indian government is trying to promote Hindi all over the country. Since independence, Indian nationalism has been dominated by political interests, and religion had been used as a key trope to mobilise people under nationalistic inspiration by some political parties, who have tried to promote Hindu nationalism, although other parties have been prone to keep a secular Indian national identity.

Chandra brought an economic perspective to analyse Indian nationalism. In his view, the nineteenth century marked the entry of the Indian economy into world capitalism under the process of modernization and gradually transformed India into a "classic colony" (Chandra 1979: 4). As a result, "colonialism in India was as modern a historical phenomenon as industrial capitalism in Britain" (Ibid). However, colonial modernization and capitalist intervention influenced not only the Indian economy but also other social arenas such as politics, culture, administration etc., which Chandra called a "colonial cultural revolution" (Ibid: 7). The feelings of exploitation by the colonizers gradually developed into a sense of resistance in both political and economic arenas by native Indians, and this was called nationalism.

One of the pre-eminent features of Indian nationalism is its elitist character, as it was imposed from the top of the society. While India was a stratified society in terms of caste, class, religion, locality and ethnicity, not all the segments of the society participated or had similar access to participation in the nationalist project. The lack of an all-Indian political consciousness among people from different locals and provinces who hardly knew each other, spoke different languages and lead different lifestyles in terms of dietary practices, rituals, etc., was the key weakness under the common nationalistic framework (Seal 1973). The situation did not change even after independence and the nationalist movement since India's inception to 1947 has been a bourgeois democratic movement (Chandra 1979: 135). A potential danger of this bourgeois nationalism in India is that the political or social elites use nationalism to maintain their own power. Nationalism appeared in post-colonial India as similar to colonialism because of its elitist character.

In a post-colonial Indian society, it is expected that a citizen must participate in a modern lifestyle, work in industries or modern institutions, and engage in contemporary politics, but also hold the identity of his/her own nation; as Mondol puts it, "one should be modernized but never westernized" (Mondol 2003: 48). The medical field in India, especially the practice of indigenous medicines, encountered a similar paradox from the very beginning of its connection with the nationalist movement. While indigenous medical knowledge was linked with the cultural glory of the Indian past, the move to revive indigenous medical systems, ayurveda in particular, can be seen as a part of the rising national consciousness (Brass 1972; Bala 1991: 17). Although this trend started at the later part of the British colonial rule, it became prominent particularly after the decolonisation. The political lobby who believe on orthodox Hinduism and has dream to establish India as a Hindu nationalist country were active in colouring ayurveda as a part of Hindu nationalist consciences.

The rise of nationalism in China characteristically varies from India because of different political circumstance in two countries during the pre-nationalist era. In

India, nationalist moment arose as anti-colonial resistance and dismentalise the colonial rule was one of the prime objectives under Indian nationalist movement. In China, nationalist leaders fought against their own imperial ruler who have established a dynastic rule over the centuries. Chinese nationalism was inspired by the Western modernization and treated dynastic regime as barrier for enlightenment and progress. During the Republican era of the 1920s, attaining Western science, medicine, and technology was viewed to be crucial for the development of the modern state and science became an integral part to state formation and nation building (Chen 2005: 111). However, the republican nationalist leaders rejected Chinese medicine as part of rejecting Confucius values and introduced Western medical science as replacement (Wang 1995: 38). It was only during the socialist era when Chinese medicine became linked with nationalism by the new political elites. As the goals of Chinese socialist modernization relied heavily upon discourses of scientific rationality and civilization developed in the West science used to articulate national agendas and define the boundaries of Chinese medicine during the entire Maoist era (Chen 2005: 107–08).

Putting scientific values first and unifying the Chinese nation under the umbrella of scientific values continued as national goal under the Maoist socialist state through 1950s and 1960s (Ibid: 111). Scientists were regarded as intellectual elite that needed guidance and medical system and institutions were founded as a state institution on scientific principles (Ibid). This trend continued even in the post-Mao market reform era and Western medical science and technology has increasingly been utilized in the regulation and standardization of Chinese medicine (Chen 2005: 107). Almost any Chinese medical textbook in post-Mao China contains the phrase such as "Our nation has both an ancient and time-honoured ancestral medical tradition and a rich and varied modern medicine" (Brownell 2005: 144). For example, the editor of Chinese text *Bencao Gangmu* (condensed compendium of material medica) published by Foreign Language Press in Beijing wrote in the first line of his preface that "Traditional Chinese Medicine (TCM) contains a body of knowledge that the Chinese nation has accumulated through practical experimentation and theoretical research in promoting health and treating diseases over a period of thousands of years" (Li 2012: 27). Such nationalist claims of Chinese medicine intertwine the expectation in a post-colonial Indian society "one should be modernized but never westernized" (Mondol 2003: 48).

There are obvious challenges about nationalistic claim over a particular medical system. Many scholars believe that the trans-national era of medicine has been created or caused by the dissatisfaction or paradoxical claims of nationalism. Alter raised a few interesting questions regarding the state, which are concerned with the modernization of indigenous medicine in China and India and the role of trans-national hegemony to limit the nationalist articulation of indigenous medicine (Alter 2005: 6). There are several problems of the nationalistic claims about indigenous medicine. Firstly, different nation states claim the origin of the same medicine as their own. An example is Chinese acupuncture, which has been extensively practiced in Chinese communities for several thousand years (Needham et al. 2000; Alter 2005: 26). However, Dr. Ashima Chatterjee, a former MP in the

Rajyasabha of the Government of India, proclaimed in a speech on July 2, 1982, that "acupuncture was not invented in China but was, rather, an Indian innovation" (Alter 2005: 26). During another government-sponsored conference held on August 10, 1984, the president of the Indian Acupuncture Association, Dr. P.K. Singh, provided data and analysis showing that acupuncture had originated in India (Alter 2005: 26).

A second problem related to nationhood is the emergence of different nations in the same region during the post-colonial era. British India is a good example, as several nationalisms materialized after the colonial regime such as India and Pakistan. It is thus possible to argue that the development of ayurveda took place across all these countries. Thus each of these nations can claim ayurveda as their own. This can also be relevant to Chinese medicine which is practiced among the Chinese communities in neighbouring countries. Final discrepancy of nationalistic claim is related to the overlapping ideas and concepts among different medical systems. According to Alter, "the idea and knowledge of ayurveda" was "transported through an exchange of ideas that is probably more extensive than the borders of any one of the South Asian states or all of them put together" (Alter 2005: 2). In addition, there is conceptual overlap between key concepts in the various medical systems of Asia, such as *yin/yang* in Chinese and *prakrti/purusa* in ayurveda (Alter 2005: 2). There are enormous conceptual and methodological similarities between Chinese herbal medicine and ayurveda which I have discussed detail in Chap. 2 of this book.

1.5.3 Global Commodification

The final topic of this book is the process of globalization and commodification of Chinese herbal medicine and ayurveda. The trans-national and global character of medicine is one of the pre-eminent features developed over the last few decades. Indigenous medicine, which is usually claimed to be part of a cultural system within a particular geographical and political tradition or nation, is a good example. The economic reform in China which called as "open door policy" started in 1978 while India announced economic reform thirteen years later in 1991. Both the countries followed marketization as the orientation for economic reform and abolished economic restraints. Since then both the countries adopted an economic liberalization approach and positively encouraged the development of private enterprises. They also opened their markets to the outside world and emphasized the importance of economic globalization and integration into the world economy (Kaiyan 2013: 5–6). As part of this journey, many trans-national and national drug manufactures have invested in indigenous medical field promoted aggressive marketing campaigns for their health products and services. Many drug manufacturers have promoted indigenous medicine as a healthy alternative to Western drugs by emphasising the herbal and natural contents. Aggressive marketing for 'beauty, impotence, and health' products and 'massage, wellness, and spa related services' under the banner of indigenous medicine are indicators of commodifying indigenous medicine in China and India.

The term 'commodification' has been used in a variety of different ways in the social sciences. Commodification of indigenous medicine refers the process under which people consume indigenous medicine as much as other consumption product or necessities. Nichter and Nichter (1996: 269) define health commodification as "the tendency to treat health as a state which one can obtain through the consumption of commodities, namely, medicine". Bode explored how indigenous medicines have been transformed into modern health products for middle class consumers over the last few decades and how trans-national reworking of indigenous medicine in the West has transformed the practices of indigenous medicine within and outside of the country under the banner of globalization (Bode 2002; Hollen 2005: 91). Consumerism is one of the key features of modern capitalist society, in which various social services have been transformed into commodities. Massive industrialization and urbanization have created a new consumer class in contemporary China and India who has purchasing power of new consumer products. One of the pioneer tools to reach the consumer in modern society is advertising, and various electronic and print media have been used to propagate the advertisement of consumer products. Although traditionally health is considered social service in many welfare and socialist states, consumer culture has reversed the 'service content' of health to the extent that it has become a commodity; thus, health is viewed as a commodity, and people became the consumers of health care.

In the globalization of Chinese medicine and ayurveda, the media play an important role. Repeated advertisement on sliming, beauty, and diet supplement for women; and impotence, revitalization and energy boosting products for men in both the print and electronic media under the banner of indigenous medicine is a common phenomena in both the Chinese and Indian media spheres. Apart from health and beauty products, there is also the promotion of a natural lifestyle and natural treatment, spa treatment and beauty treatment.

Another issue that concerns the global commodification of Chinese medicine and ayurveda is the promotion of health tourism under the brand name indigenous medicine. Wellness is one of the prominent attributes of human health, as recognized in the World Health Organization's (WHO) definition: "Health is a state of complete physical, mental and social well-being and not merely the absence of disease or infirmity" (WHO 1978). The wellness approach has initiated a process of globalization which can be seen and used as an opportunity for the innovation and modernization of leisure and health resorts, spas, and tourism destinations (Nahrstedt 2004: 181). Both the Chinese medicine and ayurveda recognized as promoting the wellness aspect of health and containing the seeds of the concepts of health and wellness. Over the last few decades some resorts in China and India and abroad have been offering comprehensive wellness packages within Chinese medicine and ayurvedic health tourism for both domestic and overseas clients. The development of tourist resort or village circle clubs such as Zhuhai Ocean Spring Resort in China or Vedic Village in India where I conducted study could be seen as influence of globalization and commodification of Chinese medicine and ayurveda.

Wellness involves physical activity combined with relaxation of the mind and intellectual stimulus—basically a kind of fitness of body, mind, and spirit (Schobersberger et al. 2004: 199–200). There are two major aspects of wellness; the physical aspect and the spiritual aspect. The physical aspect emphasizes exercise or fitness, dietary practice, behavioural motivation, and environmental surroundings—what is called 'lifestyle change', or rectification. The spiritual element of wellness consists of purification and revitalization of mind and soul. Apart from physical fitness and spiritual purification, good nutrition, beauty, relaxation, mental activity, social harmony, and environmental sensitivity are also important element to achieve a high level of wellness (Nahrstedt 2004: 185).

Wellness and health tourism became complementary during the era of globalization, as most of the wellness activities persist under the health tourism scheme. Health tourism involves a wide variety of interrelated domains and product niches, including medical tourism, wellness tourism, spa tourism, reproductive and fertility tourism, complementary medicine tourism, etc. (Islam 2014: 53). Laws define health tourism "as leisure taken away from home, where one of the objectives is to improve one's state of health" (Laws 1996: 199). Health tourism can be relate to various physical or psychological subcategories, such as medical check-ups, beauty treatments, specialized surgery, slimness, improve fitness, diet, etc. (Laws 1996: 199). One of the noteworthy features of the development of wellness and spa tourism in China and India to provide indigenous health care services is the dramatic entry of women as consumer. The proponents of the Euro-American New Age have transformed early ayurvedic ideas about women's health into an essential segment of the modern wellness industry, and medicine is transformed into wellness (Selby 2005: 120). This trend has, however, extended in China and India within the last decade targeting middle class consumers who have sufficient disposable income to consume such products. Beauty and women become prime consumer targets for the recent development of wellness and spa tourism, and middle class professionals are the clients buying alternative health service packages provided by the wellness centres. Nahrstedt points out that 'fitness' was originally oriented toward young men, while wellness was first accepted by young women (Nahrstedt 2004: 185). Both cases recognize a dramatic entry of women into the consumption of indigenous medical products, which is contrary to classical practice: there is very little evidence of women's access to Chinese medicine and ayurveda as either practitioners or consumers in the past.

1.6 Methodology

This book is based on three different research projects conducted in China and India. The first project titled "Repackaging ayurveda in post-colonial India: Revivalism and global commodification" was a Ph.D. study project sponsored by the University of Hong Kong and carried on from 2003 to 2008 in India. A second project titled "Globalization and wellness health tourism in China: Trend, prospect and challenges" sponsored by the College Research Grant (CRG) of the United International College, Beijing Normal University-Hong Kong Baptist University and carried on from 2010–12 in the city of Zhuhai, People's Republic of China. The last project titled "The business of Chinese medicine today: commodification and paradigm" was also sponsored by the similar grant provided by the same institution and carried on from 2011–14 in various cities of China. The detail description of the research projects including background, research methods, and data analysis techniques were discussed in the following section:

The project carried on in India used qualitative study approach. In addition to empirical data collected through fieldwork, locally available documents such as various advertisement from local media, flyers from various health products, etc. have been screened for any related information. Some quantitative data has also been explored and utilized. Secondary sources including government statistics, annual reports of various companies, classical text books, leaflets, etc. were also consulted and incorporated in this book. The field work was conducted in Kolkata, the capital of West-Bengal, located in the eastern part of India. Kolkata is one of the oldest and most historically important cities founded during the early stage of British colonial rule, in the eighteenth century. It was also the capital of the British Raj until the early twentieth century.

The major reason for choosing Kolkata is my language advantage. It is a city habited predominantly by the Bangla-speaking ethno-linguistic group to which I belong. Apart from visiting individual respondents' houses in different locations, I conducted observation in Raja Bazar Dabur Ayurvedic Medicine Shop[5]; J.B. Roy State Ayurvedic College and Hospital in Raja Dinendra Street; Gray Street, which is popular for the locality of ayurvedic *kabirajes*[6]; Tarok Chaterjee Lane; Central Research Institute (Ayurveda) in Salt Lake; Vedic Village in Rajer Hat; Bhawanipore Ayurvedic Databya Ausadhalaya in Ashutosh Mukherjee Road; and Baidyanath Ayurvedic store in Bondel Road. Different forms and conditions of ayurvedic practice co-exist in Kolkata. Most needy people visit the public hospital, and I chose the Central Research Institute (Ayurveda). Middle class patients usually go to private practitioners or *kabirajes*. Apart from the health tourists from overseas affluent Indian patients and client who have disposable income visit Vedic Village, a recently-built ayurvedic tourist resort and spa in Rajer hat. Ayurvedic drug stores are scattered in various locations of the city. I chose Dabur Ayurvedic Medicine-a privately owned drug store used the name of Dabur India which is one of the largest ayurvedic companies in India. The fieldwork was completed in two phases during August–September 2004 and July–September 2005. The principal investigator also visited Eastern part of India in summer 2010 and winter 2014 respectively and continued to gather update information and some of these data have been used in

---

[5]Dabur Ayurvedic Medicine Shop is not a retailer operated by Dabur India Limited. It is a privately-own shop exhibiting the sign 'Dabur Ayurvedic Medicine".

[6]Kabiraj is the title of traditional ayurvedic practitioner who has a long family tradition of practicing ayurveda.

this book. Recent WebPages and statistical reports of the governmental and non-governmental organization deals with ayurveda have been visited, consulted and utilized in this book.

The major data collection techniques for primary data gathering employed in this research are: survey, individual interview with semi-structured questionnaire, and observation. Secondary data from electronic and print media and ayurvedic classical texts and photographs were also collected. I got verbal consent from interview respondents for use of individual photos. To understand the institutional foundations of ayurveda, the Central Research Institute (Ayurveda), J.B. Roy State Ayurvedic College and Hospital, Dabur Ayurvedic Medicine Shop and Vedic Village were selected for the following reasons: the Central Research Institute is the only public funded research institute in West Bengal doing clinical research on ayurveda and having a hospital unit. A relatively underprivileged community seek medical help from this institute because of government subsidy and the low cost of treatments. J.B. Roy State Ayurvedic College and Hospital is the only public funded college for undergraduate ayurvedic education in West Bengal. Dabur is one of the biggest drug manufacturers in India, and Dabur Ayurvedic Medicine Shop sell ayurvedic drugs mostly, but not exclusively, from Dabur India Limited. Vedic Village is a resort where middle class Indian and overseas clients take part in ayurvedic wellness programs. Since Kolkata has a stratified society, the selection of the above four institutions provided a complete scenario of ayurvedic practice in Kolkata, for all social classes. It also allowed for the investigation of the modernization of ayurveda in terms of education and research and the global commodification under the health tourism program in the Vedic Village. Baidyanath Ayurvedic Shop and Bhawanipore Ayurvedic Databya Ausadhalaya, a charity organization providing ayurvedic treatment, were also selected to provide greater understanding of the reality in ayurveda and its commodification process. Leaflets, flyers, therapeutic indexes, annul reports, and record books of patient admission were also collected. Data from different sources, including the government, were gathered to supplement the primary data. Some surveys among patients and customers were done with a pre-prepared questionnaire at the Dabur Ayurvedic Medicine Shop, Baidyanath Ayurvedic Shop, Bhawanipore Ayurvedic Databya Ausadhalaya and Tarok Chaterjee Lane. Five different questionnaires were utilized, with many common questions. Thematic content analysis of the classical ayurvedic texts *Caraka Samhita*, *Susruta Samhita and Ashtanga hrdayam* were done to gain deeper understanding of the ongoing practice of ayurveda.

Five categories of respondents were selected for interview: patients (40), ayurvedic practitioners (20), ayurvedic undergraduate students (20), ayurvedic Kabirajes (10), and 4 overseas patients and clients from the Vedic Village, for a total of 94 interview respondents. Out of the 40 patients, 20 were from public ayurvedic hospital and came from relatively low socio-economic groups; 20 from private practitioners' chambers came from relatively affluent socio-economic backgrounds. An equal number of male and female patients were chosen for this research.

During the first phase of fieldwork, in August–September 2004, all the respondents were selected by purposive sampling. Many patients and physicians were asked randomly for interviews, and only those willing were interviewed. The sample size during this phase was 20 patients from public hospital and 15 physicians from different institutions. During the second phase of fieldwork, from July–September 2005, a survey among 55 patients who visited private ayurvedic practitioners (including physicians and *kabirajes*) was conducted. 20 respondents out of the 55 were intensively interviewed, with a balance of males and females. All survey respondents were asked to sit for intensive interviews. However, some did not agree due to time constraints, and 20 among the willing patients were selected randomly. Prior interview appointments were made and most of the interviews were conducted at the patients' houses or preferred places such as offices etc. A few interviews were also carried out in the waiting rooms of physicians' chambers, especially among those patients who came from outside Kolkata.

Ten categories of question were asked to the practitioners, students and *kabirajes*. Questions related to their duration of practice, training background, reasons for choosing ayurveda as profession, specialization, common problems they encounter, visiting fee and the pattern of common disease patients visit to them, were the first category. Second category of question related to comparison with Western medicine. These includes: knowledge on Western medicine, perception about Western style training program in ayurveda, their social status compare to Western practitioners. Next category of questions focused their perception about the impact of the British colonial rule on ayurveda. Health policy, system and integration related questions were in the fourth category. These include; the role of government after independence, perception about the integration of ayurveda into the mainstream health system, current health policy related to ayurveda, etc. Religion, caste, politics and nationalism related question were next category. The final three categories of questions on gender, commodification, drug manufacturer, and consumerism related. A sample blank questionnaire for the practitioners has been attached in the appendix section (Appendix A).

All the *kabirajes* and students were interviewed during the second phase of fieldwork. *Kabirajes* of at least 2 generations were selected according to their family traditions and reputations. A survey was also carried in the Dabur Ayurvedic Medicine Shop on the consumption patterns of the consumers and the best-selling products for about 7 working days among 205 customers (134 from the first phase and 71 from the second phase of field work). Table 1.2 shows the socio-demographic profiles of the respondents those interviewed.

Eight elderly *kabirajes* had had formal institutional training in addition to their apprenticeship backgrounds; they had all come from traditional ayurvedic families, and this had grounded their apprenticeships in their family backgrounds. Two had studied in *tolls,* and had only completed the apprenticeship system; both of these were around 90 years old. Two had the Ayurved State Faculty (ASF) diploma, which was a 3-year ayurvedic programme after secondary education. Four had the Member of Ayurved State Faculty (MASF) degree, which was a five-year integrated degree programme. For this programme, students studied ayurveda for 3

Table 1.2 Socio-demographic profile of the interview respondents from India

Category of respondents					
Category	Ayurvedic practitioner	Kabirajes		Undergrad students	Patients
Number	20	10		20	40
Total	90				
Religious affiliation (for the practitioners and students)					
Category	Hinduism	Islam		Buddhism	Sikhism and others
Number	45	3		1	1
Total	50				
Age (for the practitioners excluding students)					
Category	Below 20	21–40	41–60	61–80	Above 80
Number	Nil	7	13	8	2
Total	30				
Education (for the practitioners)					
Category	Undergraduate (student) (BAMS[a])	Graduate (BAMS)	Graduate (ASF[b], MASF[c]/ Ayurved Acharja[d]	Post graduate (BAMS, MD)	Other form of education (toll[e] or only apprenticeship)
Number	20	20	8	10	2
Total	50				

[a]Refers of Bachelor of Ayurvedic Medicine and Surgery which is a five and half year undergraduate program including one year internship
[b]Refers to Ayurvedic State Faculty which is a three years graduation program
[c]Refers to member of Ayurvedic State Faculty which is a five years graduation program equivalent to today's BAMS program
[d]In some states of India used to offer this title for ayurvedic graduates which is equivalent to MASF degree
[e]A school for receiving ayurvedic training under a particular kabiraj's supervision. These schools were abolished after the formation of the Central Council of Indian Medicine in 1970s

years, followed by 2 years of allopathic training. The MASF course later became equivalent to the Bachelor of Ayurvedic Medicine and Surgery (BAMS) course. Of those surveyed, one had the MASF, MD and Ph.D. degree, while one had the Ayurved Acharja degree which is equivalent to the MASF. Ayurvedic graduate degree was titled differently in various states of India before the introduction of the BAMS course—for instance, MASF in West Bengal, Ayurved Acharja in Bihar. Only BAMS course is being offered in India today as undergraduate degree programme (Table 1.3).

Table 1.3 Educational attainment of ayurvedic graduates (those interviewed)

Degree of the Ayurvedic Physicians			
BAMS	BAMS, MD	BAMS, MD, Ph.D.	
20	10[a]	2	
Specialization			
Kayachikitsha (internal medicine)	*Drobbogun* (pharmacology)	Medical plants	*Krimirog*
5	3	1	1
Practice of profession			
Work at govt. institutions and don't attend private patients	Work at govt. institutions and attend private patients	Work at private institutions and attend private patients	Total
5	6	9	20

[a]Out of the 20 physicians having BAMS degree, 10 pursued further postgraduate course leading to the Degree of Doctor of Medicine (MD) and 2 physicians completed both the MD and Ph.D. course

Content analysis was another research tool applied in this study to generate data. This included content analysis of classical ayurvedic texts, popular magazines and television advertisements. Three classical ayurvedic texts were selected for analysis: *Caraka* and *Susruta Samhita*, which are the most popular classical texts used in the eastern part of India, and *Astanga Hrdayam,* which is extensively used in Southern India. Relevant chapters of the above texts have been analysed in various sections of this book to support the arguments. Concerning magazines, three of the most popular magazines published in Kolkata in Bangla language were chosen, and only *Puga* issues (Puga is the biggest religious festival for the Hindu community) for 1411 (2004) Bangla year were analysed. These magazines are *Anand Bazar*, *Anand Mela* and *Desh Patrika.* Only ayurvedic/natural and herbal products advertisements published in these magazines were selected, and their contents were analysed. Apart from this, advertisements of WWS Company manufactured ayurvedic products and Tele shop providing facilities ayurvedic products/diet supplements broadcast on the Bangla television channel were chosen for content analysis because of the fact that it spent large amount of time for advertisement. I relied on manual coding for qualitative analysis, with respondents representing various categories and sample size being moderate. I used the SPSS program for quantitative analysis. Content analysis of the media was also carried out.

The project titled "Globalization and wellness health tourism in China: Trend, prospect and challenges" included two questionnaires survey among three types of respondents including 100 tourists/visitors (including people from Hong Kong citizens of Chinese ancestry and foreigners living in Hong Kong), 50 clients who received various form of massage services and 50 service providers who provide massage and related services in China. The survey among tourists/visitors was conducted in Jiuzhou port immigration checkpoint, Zhuhai City, Guangdong Province, in June–July 2011 and April 2013. Zhuhai was selected for two reasons: firstly, this is a coastal city of China's southern Guangdong Province and has many beaches with crystal clear sea water. Both the private and public sectors have interest in developing Zhuhai as a tourist hub. Zhuhai is also one of the special economic zones of Southern China. And secondly, the research team was based in Zhuhai during carrying out this project. The respondents were selected by simple random sampling in the Zhuhai Jiuzhou port immigration check point. The major questions asked during the survey were: Are you familiar with wellness health tourism? Do you consider yourself as a wellness health tourist? Have you ever received any wellness related services or purchased any medical/health or wellness related products in China? What are the major reasons to purchase such product or services? How do you evaluate the quality of the product and services you received? Do you have any suggestion improving the quality? Have you encountered any problem or difficulties during receiving services? How much money you usually spent for each session and how do you feel about the cost? Have you ever taken any wellness health tour outside your country? If yes, how do you compare the service between China and that destination? Do you have any ideas about the professional background of your service provider? What is the source of your information about the service center from where you have received service? Do you consider China as an ideal place for wellness health related service or the service you have received? A sample blank questionnaire for the tourist/visitor those surveyed has been attached in the appendix section (Appendix B). Apart from the survey, observations were made during 2011 in two establishments: Ocean Spring Resort and the Dragon Union Foot Massage Center[7] in Zhuhai. These places are famous for offering health rejuvenation services such as foot massage, body massage, Chinese medicine massage, hot spring, spa products, etc., under the label of Chinese medicine. The research team tried to interview the client and service providers at the resort and center, but the management of the resort and center did not allow them to do so. They also tried to collect some statistics but were not successful because of the unwillingness of the management. They thus relied on content analysis and collected information available from the web page of the resort, and from free printed material and flyers available in the resort and center during the visit. Table 1.4 provides a comprehensive socio-demographic profile of the respondents those surveyed.

The second questionnaire survey was conducted among two types of respondents: 50 clients who received various massage related services and 50 service providers. The surveys were carried on in Tangjiawan market area of Tangjiawan Township of Zhuhai city, Guangdong province, the People's Republic of China.

[7]In the year 2014 Dragon Union Foot Massage Center was renovated and replaced by a shopping mall.

Table 1.4 Socio-demographic profiles of the tourist/visitor respondents those surveyed under the Globalization and wellness health tourism project in China

Category						Total
Nationality	HK	USA	Singapore	Other countries including, Korea, Germany, England, South Africa, Mongolia, Spain, Australia, Poland, Belgium, Iceland, Malaysia, India, Russia and Thailand		
	56 (56%)	15 (15%)	13 (13%)	16 (16%)		100
Age	Below 30	30–49	50–69	70 or above		Total
	8 (8%)	41 (41%)	38 (38%)	13 (13%)		100
Sex	Male	Female				Total
	63 (63%)	37 (37%)				100
Occupation	Manager/CEO/Director/Entrepreneur	Students and English teachers	Office workers	Engineers, designers, technicians, retirees, housewives, lawyers, etc.	Others	Total
	32 (32%)	24 (24%)	14 (14%)	16 (16%)	14 (14%)	100
Purpose of visiting China	Business	Travel, holiday, sight seeing	Jobs or study	Visit relatives or ancestors' graveyard	Others including attending a Chinese medicine practitioner	Total
	42 (42%)	27 (27%)	24 (24%)	4 (4%)	3 (3%)	100
Duration of stay during current visit	Less than a month	Less than a year but more than a month	More than a year			Total

(continued)

Table 1.4 (continued)

	82 (82%)	16 (16%)	2 (2%)			100
If consider himself/herself as wellness health tourist	Yes	No	Don't have clear idea about wellness health tourism			Total
	40 (40%)	54 (54%)	6 (6%)			100
Health status	No health problem	Minor health problem	Have health problem			Total
	82 (82%)	18 (18%)	Nil			100

There were 18 massage and related service providing establishment found in Tangjiawan market—an area of approximately 1 km^2: 4 massage centers, 9 salons, 4 beauty parlours and 1 spa. These include Tangjiawan Ying-Wu Hair Salon,[8] XinLi Lu Hair Salon, JuLong FaYi, Shang Yi Hair Salon, YanZi Foot Massage, Jie Mei Bao Jian Zhongzin, Dragon Union Foot Massage Center, Dragon Union Hair Salon, etc. The massage service centers provide a range of services such as body massage (*quán shēn àn mó*); various forms of Chinese and herbal medicine foot treatment (*zú bù àn mó*), including Chinese medicine foot treatment, Tibetan medicine foot treatment, foot treatment for kidney health, hot spring foot massage, foot massage for beriberi, cupping, etc. Salons also offer a broad spectrum of services including hair wash with head and shoulders massage, Thai hair wash + ginger juice + face wash, Thai hair wash + water therapy + face wash, Thai hair wash + ice therapy, face therapy (to take away blackheads, and to moisturize and apply whitening mask), fire treatment, haircuts, and non-professional head and shoulder massage and massage for whole body. Beauty parlors provide services such as face therapy, massage for back, arm, hand, and shoulder, and face massage. The survey was conducted among the respondents from the above establishments. Of those clients and service providers surveyed in Tangjiawan market, all the service providers were migrant workers with relatively low education whereas the majority of the clients came from Guangdong Province and had higher educational backgrounds than the service providers. The majority of the service providers came from the neighboring provinces, such as Hunan, Jiangxi, and Guangxi Zhuang Autonomous Region, and this exemplifies the relatively higher economic development of Guangdong Province. Table 1.5 shows detail socio-demographic profiles of the respondents those surveyed.

A pre-coded questioner with few open ended questions were asked the clients. These questions include: What type of service you are taking? How often you come here? Why do you choose here? How do you evaluate this service? How much money do you normally spend for this service each time? What do you think about the price? How much you spend for every month for this type of service? Would you please describe your experience after the service? Are you satisfied with the quality of service here? What is your suggestion to improve the quality of service? Do you have any idea about the professional training/ background of your service provider? Is the professional training for the service provider important for you and why? What are the problems you encountered during taking services? What should be done to promote this sector in China? A sample blank questionnaire for the clients those surveyed has been attached in the appendix section (Appendix C).

Similar questionnaire was used to survey the service providers and the major questions were asked are: What type of service you provide? What type of professional training you have to do this job? (Please describe your skill) Do you think professional training/skill is important? How do you evaluate this service (for

[8]Many hair salons in Tangjiawan area also provides massage services with unskilled service providers.

Table 1.5 Socio-demographic profiles of the client and service provider respondents those surveyed under the Globalization and wellness health tourism project in China

Background indicator		Clients (total number 50)	Service providers (total number 50)
Education	College/University	50%	6%
	Middle school[a] or lower	24%	70%
	Other forms or levels of formal education	26%	24%
Residence or home town	Zhuhai City	18%	Nil
	Other cities, impoverished towns or countryside of Guangdong Province	50%	34%
	Neighboring provinces	32%	66%
Monthly income	RMB 3000 or below	46%	66%
	RMB 5000 or above	10%	6%
	Income levels between RMB3000 and RMB5000	Unknown	28%
Age	30 or below 30 years	44%	78%
	Above 30 years of age	56%	22%
Sex	Male	56%	22%
	Female	44%	78%
Marital status	Married	66%	38%
	Single	32%	62%

[a]Nine years of middle school education is compulsory in the People's Republic of China although not everyone attends

relaxation and rejuvenation, stress reduction, etc.)? Why did you choose this profession? For how long you are working in this profession? Do you enjoy this profession? Will you continue to work in this profession? Have you signed a contract with the company? How many clients you have to serve a day? What type of difficulty you usually encounter during providing service? Do you find any differences between male clients and female clients during providing services? Does this job bring you any occupational risk/diseases? (If yes, does your company pay for treatment? Do you consider the service you provide having health benefit? (If yes, how?) Do you use any Chinese medicine/herb/Chinese medicine therapy? (If yes, please describe the therapy) Where did you learn about this therapy and for how long? What improvement of this industry could make to provide better services for the clients? What are the other things you expect to provide better service but not available here? Do you think this sector should be promoted in China? Are you familiar with the government policy/regulations about promoting wellness/spa/health tourism in China? What the government/related authority need to do to promote the sector? A sample blank questionnaire for the service providers those surveyed has been attached in the appendix section (Appendix D)

The third and last research project titled "The business of Chinese medicine today: Commodification and paradigm" was based on fieldwork conducted in various locations of South, Central and North China including the cities of Zhuhai,

Shenzhen, Foshan and Guangzhou in Guangdong province, Zhenzhou in Henan province, Shenyang in Liaoning province, and Beijing. The major techniques of data collection were face-to-face interview with open ended questionnaire, survey with questionnaire, observation, informal discussion and content analysis. The study began in June 2011 with a survey among 50 undergraduate and graduate students from Henan University of Chinese medicine in Zhengzhou city. Questionnaires were distributed among students in a free study classroom and asked them to fill in. These students were in various stages of their study ranging from undergraduate to graduate level. Any student who is interested to fill the questionnaire could participate in the study and their selection was random. A briefing about the research projects and its aim and objectives were provided before distributing the questionnaire. The questionnaire was written in both the Chinese and English language but all the students answered in Chinese language.

A two stage translation from Chinese to English was conducted by two different translators in order to ensure the accuracy of the translation. The major questions asked the students during survey were: Why did you choose to study CM? Have you ever tried to get admission in a Western medical college? (If yes, how many times?). What was your first priority of study either CM or WM? Do you think your social status is lower than a student/professional trained in Western medicine? (If yes, why?). Are you/will you involve in cross practice (prescribe drugs from Western system)? How do you compare CM with WM? How do you compare the traditional/apprentice CM education and contemporary education system? Do you have any family background on CM? What are the major limitations you encounter about contemporary CM education? How do you see the development of CM health products/commodity? Do you think various drug manufacturers are misleading CM? (Please explain). Do you think CM has lost its authenticity because of the development of CM health products? (Please explain). Do you think CM will be replaced by WM one day because of the integrated education system? How do you see the integrated medical practice? How do you see the relation between CM, Chinese nationality, culture, etc.? Do you consider CM as complete medical system or cultural practice? Do you think drug standardization is a major concern for the quality control of CM? In your opinion, what should be done do promote CM? A sample blank questionnaire for the Chinese medicine students those surveyed has been attached in the appendix section (Appendix E). Another fieldtrip was conducted in June–July 2012 at Guangzhou University of Chinese medicine. Two different sessions of informal discussion was conducted with 5 undergraduate and 5 graduate students with a particular line of information about their education and practice.

The last phase of fieldwork was conducted from June to September 2014 in the city of Zhuhai, Shenzhen, Foshan, Beijing and Shenyang. A total 20 Chinese medicine practitioners were interviewed face-to-face with an open ended questionnaire. Two out of twenty practitioners have long family apprenticeship from Grandfather to Date apart from their professional training. However, there was one practitioner who did not go through professional training from modern Chinese medicine college but relied only on family apprenticeship. He is above 80 years old.

Table 1.6 Socio-demographic profile of the Chinese medicine practitioners those interviewed

Location			
Province/Municipality	City	Hospitals	Number of practitioners interviewed
Guangdong	Zhuhai	Zhuhai Liuhe Hospital	1
		Zhuhai Chinese medicine Hospital	1
	Shenzhen	Shenzhen Futian Chinese medicine Hospital	6
	Foshan	Foshan Hospital of Traditional Chinese Medicine	1
Beijing Municipality	Beijing		2
Liaoning	Shenyang	Chinese medicine Department of Shenyang Hunnan District Hospital	6
		Chinese medicine Clinic Department of Shenyang Chinese medicine Hospital	3
Total			20
Age			
20–40	41–60	61–80	Above 80
11	6	1	2
Total			20
Sex			
Male	Female	Total	
12	8	20	
Family background			
Came from apprentice system/continue family line	Family has other member(s) as CM practitioner	Family has other member(s) as WM practitioner	Nobody from the family is medical practitioner
2	4[a]	2	12
Total			20

[a]Two practitioners have both the Chinese and Western medicine practitioners in their family under this category

Detail background information of the interviewed practitioners could be found in Table 1.6.

Sixteen questions were asked to all the practitioners. These includes: the reasons to become Chinese medicine practitioner, duration of practice and if they have any family background on Chinese medicine practice; their detail training and professional background; if they have ever tried to get admission in a Western medical college and their priority of study either Chinese medicine, Western Medicine or Integrated Medicine; If they think their social status is lower than a practitioner of Western medicine; if they are involved in cross practice (prescribe drugs or use diagnostic methods from Western medicine); how do they compare apprentice education with contemporary education? How do they see the development of health products and diet supplements under the brand name of Chinese medicine? If they consider the manufacturing of patent drugs by the pharmaceutical company mislead Chinese medicine? If they hope that Chinese medicine will gradually replace by the Western medicine because of integrated education model? How do they perceive the relationship between Chinese medicine and Chinese politics? Do they consider Chinese medicine as a complete medical system or cultural practice? How do they view the drug standardization and quality control? How do they compare classical drug formulation with modern patent drug? And what are the challenges they encounter during practice Chinese medicine and what should be done to overcome these challenges? A sample blank questionnaire for the Chinese medicine practitioners those surveyed has been attached in the appendix section (Appendix E).

All the interviews were conducted in Chinese because of the interviewees' preference. Interviews were recorded by the audio recording. The audio records went through two stages of transcription and translation from Chinese to English by two different translators. Respondents were selected through employ a purposive sampling method and contacted with the help of private network of the research team. The research team tried to interview practitioners from several Chinese medicine hospitals through an official protocol but failed.

Apart from the survey and interview, this book also uses online data available in the web page of Beijing University of Chinese Medicine, Guangzhou University of Chinese medicine, and Beijing Tong Ren Tang, one of the leading manufacturers of Chinese herbal medicine. Classical Chinese Medical texts such as *Huang Di Nei Jing* and *Bencao Gangmu* were also analysed.

1.7 Outline of Chapters

This book consists of seven chapters. Chapter 1 deals with the conceptual framework and methodology used in three different research projects those contributed this book. Chapter 2 focuses on the theoretical, methodological, and historical similarities and differences among Western medicine, Chinese medicine and ayurveda. This chapter also examine and analyses the content of the classical texts in Chinese medicine such as *Huang Di Nei Jing* and *Bencao Gangmu* and ayurvedic texts including *Caraka Samhita* and *Susruta Samhita*. Preservation of health and prevention of diseases are the key topics discussed in the above texts. Chapter 2 analyses the secret and methods of preserving health as suggested in the text. The similarities among various methods presented in the Chinese and Indian medical texts in the following aspects: food and temperate diet; sleep and non-celibacy; and seasonal regimen are the particular focus of this chapter.

Chapter 3 emphasizes the education and training in Chinese medicine and ayurveda from historical time to date. This chapter particularly emphasizes the development of formal education in Chinese medicine and professionalization according to the Western line during Mao era. In India, this chapter emphasizes the colonial and post-colonial state intervention in ayurveda, especially looking at the dispute between colonial subjugation and post-colonial revival. This chapter further analyzes the integration of Chinese medicine and ayurveda in mainstream health service delivery and argues that the professionalization of Chinese medicine and ayurveda according to Western line reproduces Western hegemony and legacy. The situations from Mao to post-Mao era in China and after the decolonization India have been examined.

The commodification of Chinese herbal medicine and ayurvedic health products especially for middle class consumers is a new trend developed over the last few decades. The content of medicine has been shifted from 'medical account' to 'natural product' because of globalization. Many biggest national and trans-national drug manufacturers have appreciated this trend and invested aggressively to fuel this. Chapter 4 examines the ambiguity of commodifying indigenous medicine in China and India. Through using some large pharmaceutical companies as example such as Beijing Tong Ren Tang in China and Dabur India Limited in India this chapter shows how indigenous medicine has been shifted from a home/family invented medicine to a global health commodity for profit maximization. Today large share of these pharmaceutical companies are not generated by the indigenous drugs but through selling various health, beauty and cosmetic products. In order to create a market niche, these drug manufacturers are instrumental in exploiting the natural content of indigenous medicines. This chapter argues that Chinese herbal medicine and ayurveda has been transformed from indigenous medical systems to a global health commodity for mass consumption by the hand of these drug manufacturers. At the same time, many modern graduates of Chinese medicine and ayurveda are paying less attention on fundamental principle of their medical systems and following the market trend.

The entry of women as indigenous health product and cosmetics consumer is another trend developed over the last one-two decades because of the development of a new market niche. Female body has been transformed to a natural body where female health has symbolised with beautiful body by the global market forces. Similarly, there is a steady growth of production and marketing impotence product for male which equates male body as masculine body and men sexuality has been symbolized as power of masculinity. Chapter 5 examines how Chinese herbal medicine and ayurveda has been used as brand name to sell sex and beauty products which is contextually paradoxical to their representation in the medical texts. While men's impotence discussed in Chinese medical text *Huang Di Nei Jing* as deficiency of kidney *Qi* and virilisation therapy discussed in the ayurvedic text *Susruta Samhita* requires following a routine and lifestyle change to enhance sexual energy, modern drug manufacturers are not following such requirements in promoting impotence products. The pharmaceutical companies this seeks to redefine masculinity with reference to sexual power. At the same time, this section also explores how women's bodies were represented in Chinese and Indian medical texts as primarily for reproduction, and how this female reproductive body has been transformed into a beautiful female body in the contemporary Chinese and Indian market. The large pharmaceutical companies are thus instrumental in redefining the female body in order to establish a market niche for various cosmetic and beauty products.

Chapter 6 examines how Chinese medicine and ayurveda have been used as a brand name to cater various product and services to new consumer and tourists. It explores the development of the notion of indigenous medicine and lifestyle related service and products in response to contemporary demand. A couple of resort and establishment such as Ocean Spring Resort and Dragon Union Foot Massage Center located in the Southern coastal city of Zhuhai in China were investigated and observed. In India, a case study on the Vedic Village located at the Eastern city of Kolkata was examined. This chapter further explores the development of wellness and spa tourism across China and India, which has targeted the middle class consumers having adequate disposable income to engage such consumption. It analyses how the natural content of healthy life as discussed in indigenous medical texts has repackaged by tourist resort and wellness centers for health rejuvenation and relaxation.

Chapter 2
History, Theory, and Method from the Classical Texts

2.1 Introduction

It is a common question from various corners if there is similarity and differences between Chinese medicine[1] and ayurveda[2] and how these similarities and differences correspond to Western bio-medicine. Based on readings of Chinese and Indian classical texts, conversation and interview with the traditional and modern practitioners I have divided these similarity and differences in three broad categories: historical; theoretical; and methodological. First part of this chapter spells out how the classical texts of Chinese medicine including *Huang Di Nei Jing* and *Bencao Gangmu*, and the classical texts of ayurveda including *Caraka Samhita*, *Susruta Samhita* and *Astanga Hrdayam* grounded the foundation of these similarity and differences. Prevention of disease and preservation of health are major goals in both the Chinese medicine and ayurveda. Although Western bio-medicine in recent decades is increasingly focusing on prevention it is still dominated by curative care. Next part of this chapter examines how prevention has been presented in Chinese medicine and ayurvedic text and what are the methods prescribed by these texts to preserve health. Practitioners played a key role in the origin and development of Chinese medicine and ayurveda. As stated before that medical practice in various Asian civilizations were historically preserved by particular families who transferred the knowledge and skill to next generations within the family. Final part of this chapter discusses the ideal quality and characters a practitioner should have.

---

[1]In this book Chinese medicine refers to herbal medicine although there are other systems of indigenous medicine practiced in China.
[2]In this book Indian medicine refers to ayurveda although there are other systems of medicine practied in India and called as Indian medicine.

M.N. Islam, *Chinese and Indian Medicine Today*,
DOI 10.1007/978-981-10-3962-1_2

2.2 History

Historical similarities and differences among Western bio-medicine, Chinese medicine and ayurveda could be analyzed from two aspects: Firstly, the relation between medicine and divinity; and secondly, the development of drug and prescription to treat diseases. These two aspects have been discussed detail in the following section.

2.2.1 God and Divinity in Medicine

Both the Chinese medicine and ayurveda has developed as a 'knowledge based science'[3] and relatively dissimilar to a laboratory based Western medical science by origin and history. The acknowledgment and recognition of meta physical world is one of the key features of Chinese medicine and ayurveda while Western bio-medicine arguably claims as to be secular[4] in nature. Many examples could be given from the Chinese and ayurvedic texts to illustrate the similarities on the presence of godly characters and supernatural events in Chinese medicine and ayurveda. One of the eight branches of ayurveda is *Bhutabidya* (psychiatry and demonology). The *Bhutabidya* deals with the mental and spiritual peace of the patients. When someone loses his/her mental and spiritual balance—because of the influence of demons, giants, deities, gods; or, divine, celestial or natural spirits; or cannibalism; etc.—the *Bhutabidya* prescribes possible tactics to restore mental and spiritual health; and sacrifices (e.g., of. animals, etc.) for the sake of the planet and nature (*Susruta* 1999, sutro sthana, Chap. 1, and paragraph 4–11).

In the ayurvedic texts, there are several gods regarded as the inventor of medicine. In the *Rgveda*, Lord Rudro was also addressed in connection with medical topics (Mukhopadhyaya 1922–29: 173). He is described as "the depository of all sciences" and "the possessor of healing medicines" (Ibid). Also, Lord Siva is considered to be the first proponent of the science of medicine in the *Puranas* and is quoted in many places as an authority on medical subjects (Ibid). Both the *Caraka* and *Susruta Samhita* texts recognize ayurveda as having a divine origin, and many godly characters have been regarded as divine physicians. The origin of ayurveda mentioned at the commencement of the *Caraka Samhita* text is an indication of the presence of godly characters in ayurveda. Mythologically, ayurveda in India

---

[3]This term I first adopted from a Professor of J B Roy Ayurvedic College and Hospital in India in 2004 during my interview with him. He is a representative of 13th generation ayurvedic family and had learned ayurveda not only from modern ayurvedic institutions but also from family and apprentice tradition. I am sure he retired a decade back from his job but I prefer not to disclose his name.

[4]There are scholarly debate about this argument which I discussed detail in my article "Medical secularism vs. religious secularism: new era of ayurveda in India", ***Indian Journal of Social Work***, Volume 75, Issue 2, pp. 575–616. Mumbai: Tata Institute of Social Sciences.

originated in the heaven from Lord Brahma, a divine character who passed on this knowledge to Dakshaprajapati and then to the Ashwinikumaras (*Caraka 2003,* sutro sthana, Chap. 1, paragraph 1). When diseases approached in heaven, Maharshi Bharadwai approached Indra and acquired the knowledge of ayurveda. Subsequently, Maharshi Atreya learnt ayurveda from Bharadwai and taught it to Agnivesh and other shishos (followers). Agnivesh authored the Agnivesh Tantra, or *Caraka Samhita.* (Ibid, paragraph 1–3).

Chinese medical classic *Huang Di Nei Jing* also came to us as a conversation between legendary emperor Huang Di and his physician/minister Qi Bo. *Huang Di Nei Jing* is the combine outcome of two books namely: *Suwen* (Basic Questions or The Plain Questions), and *Lingshu Jing* (The Divine or Spiritual Pivots) (Zhu 2009: 2) which represent various spiritual elements and divinity in the realm of medicine and health practice. A wide array of specialists, including shamans who uses prayer incantations, diviners, and exorcists during the pre-Han period provided health guidelines and healing to the members of royal families as well as commoners (Cook 2013: 5). The illness of the ruler of the Eastern Zhou state of Jin and his diagnosis and treatment by the multiple diviners, shamans, and medical specialists clearly illustrate the acknowledgement of the existence of metaphysical world or supernatural sprits in Chinese medical thought (Ibid: 18). The existence of religious healing to treat the illness caused by the super natural forces continues to coexist today with modern Chinese medicine practice, especially the remotest villages (DuBois 2013: 277).

Another Chinese medicine text *Bencao Gangmu* also recorded the divine power or miraculous power of different herbs, plants, and medicinal components those are used to heal various complex diseases. For example, the text denotes in the description of *Huangqi* herbs that "it is a herb used in ancient time for divination purposes" (Li 2012: 27). Similarly *Renshen* is considered as miraculous herb. Renshen is also called as *Shencao* and *Shen* means magic or miraculous and *cao* means herb. The text denotes a myth in the description of *Renshen* (Li 2012: 49). The mythological story said that, "in Shangdang during the time of emperor Wen of the Sui Dynasty, there was a family which heard a kind of calling from the backyard of the house at night but nothing could be found there. About half a kilometre away, people finds herb with an extraordinary shape. A pit five chi deep was dug around the herb, and a root in the shape of a man with four complete extremities was found. Then there was no more calling at night" (Li 2012: 49). Many mythological stories similar to this and divine function of herb and plants could be found all over the above text.

2.2.2 *Development of Drug and Prescriptions*

Most of the drug formula and therapeutic methods applied in Chinese herbal medicine and ayurveda were developed by the practitioners and preserve it as family secret. This secret knowledge has been transmitted from generation to generation within the same family or lineage. Practitioner from a particular family was skillful to treat a particular form of disease. Some of the famous medical texts in China and India were also written by a particular physician. For example, *Caraka Samhita* text was written by *Caraka* and *Susruta Samhita* text by *Susruta* who was a physician and surgeon in ancient India. *Bencao Gangmu* (Compendium of materia-medica) in China was also written by Li Shizhen (1518–1593 A.D.), a famous physician during the Ming dynasty and belonged to a family with a generations-long tradition of medical learning and practice (Hammond 2013: 151). The medicines described in the *Caraka* and the *Susruta Samhita* contains a broad array of animal, vegetable and mineral substances which is very similar to the drugs and formulas prescribed in the *Bencao Gangmu*. There are 1892 medicines, and 11,096 prescriptions could be found in Li Shizhen compiled *Bencao Gangmu* which took him to spend 30 years to finish (Li 2012).

2.3 Theories

Apart from historical similarities and differences among the Western bio-medicine, Chinese medicine and ayurveda there are also uniqueness and dispute in theory and philosophical development of the above three systems. While the development of Western medicine could be seen as part of European modernity and enlightenment Chinese medicine and ayurveda have relatively older history. The rise of modern clinical micro-biology and bio-chemistry enormously help the development and validation of many theories developed in Western medicine. The theory of microorganism which laid the foundation for Western bio-medicine was validated in the late 19th century and became the corner stone of Western medicine and clinical microbiology. It also leads to many important innovations such as antibiotics and modern hygiene practices. Since the focus of Western bio-medicine is disease which is largely caused by microorganism, a removal of microorganism became prime objective of Western medicine. The invention of antibiotic and its' use as drug to remove micro-organism became a fundamental theoretical principle of Western bio-medicine during the nineteenth century.

On the contrarily, the principle of medical systems in China and India is largely based on a balance theory which held that the human body is filled with various substances or humors such as bile, air/wind, phlegm, blood, etc. If these substances are in balance a person is healthy. All diseases and infirmities are resulted from an excess or deficit of one of these substances. For example, various form of Chinese medicine follow a theory of balance between yin and yang. There are four major theoretical concepts used in Chinese medicine. These are: *dao*, the fundamental way of the Universe that determines all existence; *qi*, the cosmic vital force or energy that pervades life and determines the functioning of the human body and mind; *yin-yang*, the two complementary aspects of *dao* that alternate in their interaction to create the rhythms of nature and the body; and the five phases (wood, fire, earth, metal and water), the basis of an extensive correspondence system at the root of diagnosis and treatment (Kohn 2005: 1–8). Once people born, they start to an interchange of the two dimensions of *qi*-prenatal *qi* and postnatal *qi*. Soon they begin to lose their postnatal *qi* as they interact with the world through shallow breathing, improper nutrition, emotional outbursts, and intellectual tensions. Once people have lost a certain amount of postnatal *qi*, they get sick. The goal of healing is to replenishing of *qi* with medical means such as massages, diets, herbs, lifestyle change, etc. (Ibid). The theory of *yin* and *yang* holds that the universe consists of two opposing but mutually dependent forces that complement and supplement each other and maintain a constant balance. To achieve a good health a balance between the forces of *yin* and *yang* in the human body should be maintained (Ibid). *Yin* and *yang* are subdivided into five phases and correspond with five organic substances of the *dao* such as: minor *yang* linked to wood, major *yang* with fire, *yin/yang* with earth, minor *yin* with metal and major yin linked to water (Kohn 2005: 22). In their natural rhythm, the five organic substance of the *dao* have two functions: Firstly, these create a harmonious cycle through continues production. For example, water comes about through rainfall and makes things grow, so that there is lush vegetation and wood arises. Wood dries and becomes fuel for fire and fire burns and creates ashes which eventually become earth after long time consolidation. Earth over long periods of consolidation grows metals in its depth and metals in the depths of mountains attract clouds and stimulate rainfall, thus closing the cycle. The second function of the five organic substances of the *dao* is to serve as a system of checks and balances which ensure mutual control among them such as: water can extinguish fire and fire can melt metal. Followed by the cycle metal cuts wood and wood contains earth. Further earth dams water and water again extinguishes fire and begins the natural cycle (Ibid: 23).

Similarly, according to ayurveda, the human being is a creation of *panchamabhuta* (five cosmic elements: space, air, fire, water and earth) and *atta* (soul) (*Susruta*, sutro sthana, Chap. 1, paragraph 18). The *panchamabhuta* are considered the basic building blocks of nature, responsible for all physical existence. Another powerful conceptual tool in ayurveda is that of the three *dosha* (humour) including *vata-pitta-kapha* (air/wind-bile-phlegm). The five cosmic elements or *panchamabhuta* and seasonal elements have different impacts on the enlargement, reduction, and recovery of *vata-pitta-kapha* (three humours) because of their changing nature according to time and seasons and are very essential for health (*Susruta* 1999; sutro sthana, Chap. 1, paragraph 24). According to ayurveda each human being is born with a unique combination of the three *doshas* (humours), and that this natural balance is what is responsible for the physical, mental and emotional differences among people (Joshi 1997: 9). *Ritucharya* (seasonal practices) have an important role on human health and all the changes in climatic conditions impact on health. When a seasonal change brings a shift in wind conditions, air temperature, humidity and/or rainfall, it will impact the balance of the *doshas* within human bodies (Ibid: 9).

According to the *Caraka Samhita* text, all the physiological diseases are originated and caused by the alteration of *vata-pitta-kapha* (air/wind-bile-phlegm) or the functional capacity of *doshas* (humour) (*Caraka* 2003, sutro sthana, Chap. 1). As a result, if the equilibrium of the *doshas* is maintained, the disease cannot take place in the body. The *Caraka Samhita* also recognizes that physiological disorders should be cured by taking *zuktighotito oushad* (logical medicine) and engaging in *daibo karmo* (spiritual activities); and all mental disorders should be cured through applying *gana* (knowledge), *biggan* (science), *dharjo* (patience), *sriti* (memory), etc. (*Caraka* 2003, sutro sthana, Chap. 1, paragraph 3). The *Susruta Samhita* text recognizes that the body and the mind are the two complementary constituents of a living being and the sources of disease: some diseases emerge from the body, others from the mind, and a few are both from the body and mind (*Susruta* 1999, sutro sthana, Chap. 1, paragraph 20). It is thus clear that a pool of theoretical similarities could be found between Chinese herbal medicine and ayurveda in relation to their textual representation.

2.4 Methods

The methodological similarities and differences among Western-biomedicine, Chinese medicine and ayurveda largely refers to treatment method and prescription imply in various system. Western bio-medicine and Chinese herbal medicine and ayurveda, perhaps, differ most fundamentally in their approaches to healing and diagnostic methods they imply. Western bio-medicine has historically relied heavily upon surgery and chemical and synthetic drugs produced by pharmaceutical factories to heal. On the other hand, both the Chinese medicine and ayurvedic treatments relied on plant, herb, mineral and animal based drug preparations and on dietary practices, with the later in particular placing more onus on the individual patient for healing. Thus, Western bio-medicine represents a faster route of healing for those who could afford it, delivering quicker results through surgery and medication, but arguably had a negative impact on lifestyles and diet (Islam 2012: 5–6). The diagnostic methods applied in Western bio-medicine also require sophisticated modern technology and clinical laboratory facilities whereas diagnostic methods used in the practice of Chinese medicine and ayurveda are less technological. For example, commonly used four major form of diagnosis: watching, smelling, asking, and pulse checking in Chinese medicine basically requires individual practitioner's experience, concentration and knowledge rather than sophisticated technology. Ayurvedic diagnostic methods are divided into two broad types: the examination of the patient and the diagnosis of disease. The patient is not considered only as a case of disease but also as an individual human being with all his/her attributes, such as lifecycle, family history, genetic substance, lifestyle, body building mechanism, quality of tissue, age, sex, dietary habit, mental condition, digestive power, etc. (Kurup 2002).

While most of the treatments in Western bio-medicine operate at the symptomatic level, treatments under Chinese medicine and ayurveda work at much deeper causative levels. In Western medicine disease is an unique phenomena which can happen randomly and relatively neutral to person, place and time. The principle of Chinese medicine and ayurveda state that nothing exists in isolation, so that everything people interact with, including diet, family, work, relationships, etc. has an effect on health. For example, there are two major principle of treatments followed in ayurveda: firstly; cause-effect relation which believes that nothing can happen without a cause and a particular causative factor is responsible for the development of particular effect; and secondly; self regression which believes that when a state of disease appears the components which caused the disease shall by themselves undergo a phase of regression i.e., there is a natural tendency of the body to revert back to normalcy. The role of a physician is to develop the body's defense and make the individual body immune system stronger, so that the cause of disease goes away on its own and that it does not return back. The physician ensure this process through employing certain medical means or procedures such as prescribing drugs or using other procedure suggested in the ayurvedic texts including purification, dietary change, behavioral motivation, correction or lifestyle change, etc. (*Susruta* 1999, sutro sthana, Chap. 1, paragraph 21). The *Susruta Samhita* categorizes the causes of disease into four types. *Agunto* (sudden) diseases are caused by external strikes (an arrow for instance). Physical diseases are related to dietary habits and are caused by inappropriate food habits: because of inappropriate dietary habits, bile, blood, air and phlegm in the body mislead, causing physical diseases. Mental diseases are generally caused by anger and hate, but also by jealousy, fear, sadness, greed, sex, poverty, excitement, sorrow, etc. Finally, normal diseases are caused by hunger, thirst, lack of sleep, etc. (*Susruta* 1999, sutro sthana, Chap. 1, paragraph 20).

Chinese medicine perceives the cause of disease as imbalance of *yin* and *yang* which could be in two broad categories: destruction of equilibrium between the various parts of the body; and the destruction of equilibrium between the body and environmental conditions. The factors those cause the disturbance in the balance of the body are: exogenous pathogenic factors which includes atmospheric changes such as wind, cold, summer heat, dampness, dryness and fire. When these climatic conditions are excessive, individual human lost his/her ability to adopt. There are also endogenous pathogenic factors or emotional factors such as joy, anger, worry, anxiety, sorrow, terror and fight which can also cause the imbalance of *yin* and *yang*. Apart from exogenous and endogenous factors there are other factors acknowledged by Chinese medicine such as trauma, improper diet, exhaustion, and over-indulgence in sex. These factors can also cause the imbalance of the body and eventually cause disease. If the vital energy or *qi* is sufficient pathogens cannot invade the body (Dong and Zhang 2002: 23). The balance among mind, soul and the body are the key factors to maintain health and prevent disease in both the Chinese medicine and ayurveda. For example, the *Caraka Samhita* text denotes that human pain, pleasure, activity, knowledge—everything depends on the balance of mind, soul, and body (*Caraka* 2003, sutro sthana, Chap. 1, paragraph 1–4).

The standardization of medical diagnosis, treatment and drug prescription has become one of the key features in the practice of Western bio-medicine in modern era which is relatively dissimilar to Chinese medicine and ayurveda. Since Western bio-medicine has become mainstream health care services available in all the modern states, the standardization of diagnosis and treatment of disease has become one of the unique features. For example, for a general medical checkup of human body Western bio-medicine requires several clinical, laboratory and radiological tests as standard procedure of diagnosis including blood test, urine test, X-ray, Ultrasound, Electrocardiogram (ECG), etc. Western medical practitioners also need to follow a standard treatment for certain categories or group of diseases. On the other hand, Chinese medicine and ayurveda, at least historically, do not require following any standardized treatment method and drug prescription. Both the medical systems believe that every human is unique. Their disease symptom may be same but the causes of the symptom may be different. Since both the Chinese medicine and ayurveda treat at causative level and try to root out the cause of the disease instead of destroy the symptom, they imply different treatment methods for similar symptom depending on various factors related to individual patient. Both the systems further believe that the beginning of diseases may be identical but their ends are different. Chinese medical text *Huang Di Nei Jing* denotes that two general treatment modalities employ in a variety of ways depending on various conditions of the patient and degree of the diseases namely: straight treatment and paradoxical treatment (*Huang Di Nei Jing*, the plain questions, seventy-fourth article, 2009: 267). In a straight treatment a disease is treated straight such as cold is treated with heat while paradoxical treatment methods treat a disease paradoxically such as treat heat with heat and cold with cold. The degree of straightness or paradoxical is determined by the disease's degree. Generally the slight or elementary stage of disease could be treated straight and severe stage is treated paradoxically (Ibid). However, the text also suggested that in exceptional circumstances individual doctor may imply straight first and then paradoxically or paradoxically first and then straight method to treat the disease (Ibid). The root of a disease must be treated and the cause of a disease must be sought. Once the *qi* is harmonized the disease can be terminated, the text further added.

A similar but not the same classification of treatment method could also be found in ayurvedic text *Astanga Hrdayam*. The text in its' fourteen chapters of *sutro sthana* mentioned two type of treatment methods described by the lord *Atreya* and other sages: *Santarpana* (nourishing) and *apartarpana* (depleting). *Santarpana* is also called *brmhana* (expanding) and *apartarpana* is called *langhana* (thinning, slimming). *Brmhana* is for expanding the body or make the body bigger than usual shape while *langhana* is for making the body light or thin. The text suggested that earthy and watery elements should be included in *brmhana* therapy whereas fire, wind and sky related elements should be included in *langhana* therapy as a general rules (Vagbhatas, 2009: sutro sthana, paragraph 2–4). *Langhana* therapy which makes the body light or thin are two kinds: *sodhana* (purification) and *samana* (palliative). *Sodhana* or purification therapy generally expels the *dosas* (air/wind-bile-phlegm) related disease or disorder out of the body forcibly through following five methods depending on the individual conditions. These are: decoction enema, emesis, purgation for the body, purgation for the head, and bloodletting (Ibid, paragraph 6–7). *Samana* or palliative treatment does not expel the increased *dosas* out of the body, nor causes the increase of the normal *dosas* but make the abnormal *dosas* normal.

Seven methods are suggested during implying *samana* or palliative therapy; digestive carminatives, hunger producing/stomachic, withstanding hunger/avoidance of food, withstanding thirst/avoidance of drinking water, physical exercise, exposure to sunlight, and exposure to breeze/air/wind (Ibid, paragraph 6–7).

Astanga Hrdayam text also discussed the physical conditions of person those needs expanding and thinning therapy, preparation procedure of these therapies and the seasonal routines people need to following during taking therapies. Those people who are emaciated by various diseases; already used many medicines or therapies; drunk large quantity of wine; body is tired because of over indulgence of sex with women or over grief; carrying heavy loads; body became very thin because of long distance walk or injury to chest/lungs; who's body is dry because of the loss of moisture; having weak body; having *vata* predominant constitution; pregnant woman; mother passing her post-natal stage; children or elderly should use *brmhana* or expanding therapy. *Brmhana* therapy should be prepared by the use of meat, milk-sugar-rice, sugar, ghee, honey, and enema prepared by sweet substances and fats. *Brmhana* therapy also requires good sleep, sleep in a comfortable bed, oil-massage, bath, comfort and happiness of the mind to make it more effective. However, peoples who do not have the previous conditions could also use *brmhana* therapy during the summer season to keep their health (Ibid, paragraph 9–10). A *langhana* or thinning therapy is require for those peoples who are suffering from diabetes; fever; disorders of poor digestive activity; stiffness of the thighs; leprosy and other skin diseases; recently cured from snake poisoning; abscess; diseases of spleen, head, throat, and eyes; who are obese (accumulation of fat). However, *langhana* therapy should also be used for people suffering from other type of diseases during the dewy season (Ibid, paragraph 11).

Huang Di Nei Jing suggested two types of formula during prescribing herbal drugs: Odd prescriptions which refers a singular recipe with little herbs and special function; and even prescription refers multiple recipe with many herbs and wide functions (*Huang Di Nei Jing*, the plain question, seventy-fourth article, 2009: 279). The text also denotes the hierarchy among herbs in terms of their efficacy and effectiveness and classifies as three categories: monarch or chief herb/s, minister herb to assist the monarch herb/s, and envoy herb to respond the minister herb/s (*Huang Di Nei Jing*, the plain question, seventy-fourth article, 2009: 280). In an odd prescription, a recipe with a monarch and two minister herbs or two monarchs and three minister herbs are usually used whereas in an even prescription two monarchs and four minister herbs or two monarchs and six minister herbs are used. Various rules of prescribing formula could also be found in the text. For example, the text added that an odd prescription would be made to a proximate disease and an even prescription would be made to a distant disease. An odd prescription should not be made to promote sweating and an even prescription would be avoided to discharge downward. Herbs with heavy smells and flavors should be used in an urgent case whereas herbs with thin smells and flavors should be used in a moderate case. A large recipe usually should have little kinds of herbs and a small recipe should have many kinds of herbs. The text further mentioned about the method of double recipe where it suggests that if a disease cannot be defeated by an odd recipe adopt an even recipe and if an even recipe cannot defeat a disease, contrary-assistances herbs could be used (Ibid). Apart from historical, theoretical and methodological similarities between Chinese medicine and ayurveda both the systems put especial emphasis on preservation of health and prevention of diseases. The above mentioned text books from Chinese medicine and ayurveda contains several chapters on how to maintain health and stay away from illness through following some health preservation rules and methods. These rules and methods of preserving health as presented in classical texts have been discussed detail in the following section.

2.5 Rules of Preserving Health and Prevention of Disease in Chinese Medicine and Ayurveda

With the rise of health movement in 1980s the slogan "prevention is better than cure" has become popular worldwide and new consciousness about body-beauty-health has grown among urban residents. Mass campaigning on physical exercise, outdoor activities, sports, and the promotion of gym culture became an important part of this new health consciousness. Although this development was brought into the market by the Western medicine practitioner and promoted by the modern states under the framework of Western medical care, the seed of the idea could be found in Chinese medicine and ayurvedic texts. The failure of Western medicine to provide curative care for mass people due to lack of accessibility, affordability and the adverse effect many governments seeks alternative care. Preventive medicine has become relatively cheaper and easier options for them. This is, however, did not make any significant change in the curative focus of Western medicine but helps incorporating some of the preventive approaches from Asian medical thoughts. Under a curative focus, disease gets absolute focus instead of the person. Mainstream Western medical practice is still dominated by curing disease and surgical intervention. Most of the contemporary development in Western medicine focuses on medical technological innovation, surgical instruments, and drug development to cure disease or infirmities.

Medical traditions in Asia from its very inception focus on prevention of disease and maintain the health of a healthy person. One of the major similarities between Chinese herbal medicine and ayurveda is their preventive focus. Chinese medicine is essentially a prevention-oriented medicine and its preventive philosophy is expressed at two level: prevention against the occurrence of disease; and prevention against its further development if disease has already occurred. The *su wen* (The plain questions) part of the *Huang Di Nei Jing* text has several articles explained the importance and procedure of health preservation and disease prevention (*Huang Di Nei Jing:* 2009, the plain questions, first article). The text emphasizes four secrets of preserving health: follow a daily routine; took temperate diet; keep the essential *qi* perfect; and minimize the desire and maximize the funs of health care (Ibid).

Following the rules of the seasons is another prerequisite to preserve health according to *Huang Di Nei Jing* which has mentioned four seasons in a yearlong seasonal cycle: spring; summer; autumn; and winter (Ibid, The plain questions, second article). Similarly it is mentioned in the *Susruta Samhita* text that ayurveda has two purposes: firstly, to cure patients; and secondly, to maintain the health of healthy persons (*Susruta*, sutro sthana, Chap. 1, paragraph 20). According to ayurvedic text *Astanga Hrdayam*, there are three constant supports of human body: *Ahara* (food or dietary practice), *Nidra* (sleep), and *abrahmacarya* (non-celibacy) such as sexual activity (Vagbhatas: 2009, sutro sthana, Chap. 7, paragraph 52). The above texts also discuss the preservation of health and prevention of disease through following a daily regimen and the regimen of different seasons (Ibid, chaps. 3 and 4). In the following sections I will make a comparative discussion on the major aspects of preserving health and prevent diseases mentioned in both Chinese medical and ayurvedic texts. I have chosen three major areas suggested by the above texts as to preserve health and prevent disease: (1) A routine of food and dietary practice which is key to maintain a strong digestive and metabolic system; (2) A routine of sleep and non-celibacy which is considered one of the major secret to preserve health; and (3) A routine of seasonal regimen to maintain a balance between human body-mind and external environment.

2.5.1 A Routine of Food and Dietary Practice

One of the foundational constituents in both the Chinese herbal medicine and ayurveda to maintaining health is temperate diet. The concept of *patto-opotto* (diet vs. no-diet) anticipated in the *Susruta Samhita* is a core constituent of ayurveda. The *Onnopanbidhi* (Dietary rules and regulation) chapter in the text, places special importance on food and dietary habits and explains the quality and components of different cuisines for dietary regulation. The *Susruta Samhita* presents a conversation between Susruta and Lord Dhanontori in which Susruta salutes Dhanontori and asked: "*My Lord! You have said that dietary intake is the secret of power for all living creatures. The growth of body and its strength depends on food intake. Recovery from disease or illness and the calm of the sense organs is also ensured by cuisine. The root cause of any ill health is inappropriate food intake. If a physician is unaware of the dietary habits of the patient he is not able to diagnose diseases and restore health for the patients*" (*Susruta* 1999, sutro sthana, Chap. 46, paragraph 2).

Susruta Samhita text has classified foods into various categories and described the quality, ingredients, organic and caloric components, metabolic functions, relations of particular foods with nature and the locations where they grow, functions in the body, times of intake, and the potential dangers of inappropriate intake (i.e., wrong times, seasons, proportion, etc.). **Rice** is the first category, and is divided into various sub-categories depending on location of production (i.e. wet land, muddy land, dry land, etc.), as the quality of the rice and its function in the human body depends on the type of location in which it grows. There are eighteen types of instruction available in the *Susruta* concerning the best use of rice as food for human body and health. **Green** crops, lentils, red pulses, beans, enamel, vetches, gram, sesame, mole cowry, barley, etc., make up the next group of foods in the *Susruta Samhita* text. **Assorted meats** including beef, mutton, ram, deer, peacock, dove, lion, tiger, different sea animals, snakes, buffalo, duck, chicken, crocodile, and several fishes, including both sea fish and fresh water fish are in the third group of food. **A variety of fruits** constitute another group. **Vegetables** are in another category. **Radishes**, tubers and salted food are the next group. **Desserts** are the final group (*Susruta*, sutro sthana, Chap. 46, paragraph 1–553).

Apart from foods and their ability to influence the human metabolic system *Susruta Samhita* also suggested the following rules and regulations for regular dietary practice: the kitchen should be wide, clean and purified, and surrounded with obedient people; cooked foods should be preserved in a neat and clean area of the kitchen by honest and obedient persons; a black iron pot should contain ghee/fat category of foodstuffs, meat should come in a silver pot, while straw and grains types of food should be preserved in stone pots; eye-catching foods, cold water and milk-based food should be on copper plates, and various drinks including alcohol should be stored in earthen or clay vessels; fruits, *laddu*, etc., should be presented on the right side of the hungry person; meats, drinks, milk, desserts (*peao*), custards on the left side of the hungry person; he hungry person should eat an appetizer (*modhur*) first, the main course and salted foods (*onno and lobon*) in the middle and dessert (*ros*) at the end (*Susruta* 1999, sutro sthana, Chap. 46, paragraph 504–07).

Susruta Samhita also discussed the ideal conditions and surroundings for food intake and provided following suggestions: food should be consumed after sitting in a comfortable place; and the body should be kept in a vertical position and unnecessary sluggishness or rush should be avoided during food intake" (Ibid, paragraph 511). The text further recommended the appropriate time of the day for eating in various seasons and suggested that: those foods that function against disease should be taken in the morning if the night is longer than the day in a particular season; food should be taken in the afternoon if day is longer than night in another season; meals should be taken at least once between day and night if day and night are of equal duration in a particular season—Autumn, Spring, etc. (Ibid, paragraph 511–513). *Susruta Samhita* text recommended the avoidance of uncooked, unripe or spoiled (*bashi, pacha*) food, as well as insufficient or over intake and reminded the consequence failure to follow such suggestion. For example, the text noted that: uncooked food increases disease which may even lead to death; spoiled food causes loss of appetite; over intake brings on lazy feelings; and inadequate diet causes loss of energy. Enough rest after dietary intake and sitting like a king until tired comes is also suggested by the text. The text further mentions the rules to follow for positive digestion and give following suggestions: walk 100 steps after a moderate rest of taking meal; lying down on a bed on the left side after finish walking. The text also suggests smelling perfume or listening to music after dietary intake, which has a positive effect on digestion. However, the text also warned that "noisily laughing, smelling perfume or listen to music during eating may cause vomiting" (Ibid, paragraph 517–27). There are two major sources of human food mentioned in the above text and both the sources have medicinal values: plant-based sources and animal-based sources. Plants are of various types such as: *banaspoti* (those plants that produce only fruits but do not produce any flowers); *brikho* (those trees that produce both flowers and fruits); and *oshodhi* (those plants that die after their fruits have ripened). Animal based food sources are also categorised into four genus: *jaraus* (animal and human); *andos* (birds, snakes, and other reptiles); *shabdos* (ants and other insects); and *udvijo* (those animals that eat plants and grass) (*Susruta* 1999; sutro sthana, Chap. 1, Paragraph 22–23).

Caraka Samhita ayurvedic text also puts special importance on food and beverage. The text mentions the following conversation among sages about the origin of human diseases and its relation to individual dietary habits at its beginning: *"Kasipoti Bamok (a sage) asked Lord Atray about the causes of human growth and disease. Lord Atray replied that good beverages are the reason for human growth, while over intake of foods increases disease"* (*Caraka* 2003, sutro sthana, Chap. 24, paragraph 3). The text discussed quantitative dietetics which is concern about the amount of food an individual should intake each meal or within a day. The text denotes that a person should eat in proper quantity which depends upon the power of digestion and metabolism. The definition of proper quantity of food provides by the text states that "*the amount of food which, without disturbing the equilibrium of the body, gets digested as well as metabolized in proper time, is to be regarded as the proper quantity*" (*Caraka* 2003, sutra sthana, Chap. 5, paragraph 3–4). For example, if food taken in the evening and does not disturb equilibrium of *dosas* (*humors*) as well as *dhatus* and gets digested and metabolized by the morning then that would be the standard measurement of food to be taken by the individual (Ibid, paragraph 4). This standard measurement will certainly vary from individual to individual and no standard measurement should be prescribed for all individuals simple because the power of digestion even of a single individual varies from time to time, the text added. However, quantity of food also has relation with the quality and the text has made the following suggestions an individual need to follow during in-taking food: if the food article is heavy, only three fourth or half of the stomach capacity is to be filled up; after having taken food, one should never take such heavy articles like pastries, rice, boiled and flattened rice; even when hungry one should take these articles only in proper quantity; one should not regularly take heavy articles such as dried meat, dry vegetables, lotus rhizomes, and lotus stalk; one should never take the meat of a diseased animal; one should not regularly take articles such as boiled butter milk, pork, beef, meat of buffalo, fish, and curd; one should regularly take the food articles such as *sastika* (a kind of rice harvested in sixty days), *sali* (another variety of paddy), rock salt (only for preparation of food articles), rain water, ghee, meat of animals dwelling in arid climate and honey (Ibid, paragraph 5–13). Taking in appropriate quantity of food certainly helps the individual in bringing strength, complexion, happiness and longevity without disturbing the equilibrium of the *dhatus* and *dosas* of the body, the text further added (Ibid, paragraph 8).

Caraka Samhita text categorized food into the following ten broad categories: (1) Grains with husk (*Sukadhanya*), (2) Pulses (*Samidhanya*), (3) Meats (*Mamsa*), (4) Vegetables (*Saka*), (5) Fruits (*Phala*), (6) Greens (*Harita*), (7) Alcoholic drinks (*Madya*), (8) Water (*Jala*), (9) Milk and milk/dairy products (*Gorasa/Dugdho*), (10) Sugarcane products (*Iksu*) (Valiathan 2003: 110). Each category includes a large number of food, their composition, metabolic function, and health benefits. Only milk and milk/dairy products category of food has been presented in Table 2.1 as an illustration[5]:

Not only quantitative dietetics ayurvedic texts also discussed about qualitative dietetics. One of the major topics discussed under qualitative dietetics is incompatible food. *Astanga Hrdayam* text denies incompatible food as those foods causes aggravation (increase) of the *dosas* (humors) and cannot be digested or metabolize properly and do not expel them out of the body through evacuation. Taking or consuming incompatible foods have been considered as similar to consume poison or artificial poisoning which can cause disease or death (Vagbhatas 2009: sutra sthana, paragraph 29). There are many foods and materials incompatible and it is not possible to write the list of all incompatible food materials in this chapter. The text has mentioned several food items as incompatible which could be found in the following list:

Meat of animals from marshy region is incompatible with seven particular items: black gram, honey, milk, food prepared from germinated grains, radish and molasses.

> Among the meats from marshy region fish, chilichim fish (a special variety of fish which has red spot line on the body and red eye, and quite often travel on the dry land) in particular is very incompatible and dangerous with milk. (Ibid: paragraph 30)

Sour or acidic substances are generally incompatible with milk and all the fruits which contain sour/acidic compound are incompatible with milk including mango, jackfruit, coconut, hog-plum, jamboline, plantain-flower, palm, pomegranate, *kot-bel*, tamarind, etc. (Ibid: paragraph 31).
Drinking of milk should be avoided after consuming green leafy vegetables.
Meat of boar should not be consumed along with the meat of porcupine.
Meat of spotted deer and cock should not be partaken with curds and yoghurt.
Uncooked meat should not be taken with the soup of radish.
Buffalo meat should not be consumed with kusum vegetable.
Roasted meat of white headed vulture bird should be avoided.
Milk pudding and beer should be avoided.

---

[5]This illustration has been prepared by the author and based on the book The Legacy of Caraka written by M S Valiathan and Published by Oriental Longman Private Limited in 2003. For the detail description and analysis please consult any authentic version of the original Caraka Samhita text.

Table 2.1 Classification of food according to *Caraka Samhita* text

Category of milk and milk/dairy products	Qualities	Effects in the body	Health benefit/medicinal values
(*Gorasa/Dugdho*) Cow's milk	Sweet, cold, soft, lubricant, viscous, smooth, slippery, heavy, slow and pleasant	Good for everyday live Beneficiary for weak person Increase fat and strength	Help to recover from weakness, tiredness from hard work, memory loss, breath, thrust, hunger, minor fever and urinary disorder
Buffalo's milk	Heavier and colder than cow's milk Rich in fat		Good for sleeplessness person Good for those with powerful digestion
Camel's milk	Rough, hot, mildly saltish, light		Useful for treating constipation, worms, abdominal disorders, piles and swelling
Mare's and ass's milk	Hot, saltish, rough, light		Builds strength, relieves vita, recover from the disorders of extremities
Sheep's milk	Hot		Causes hiccups, shortness of breath
Goat's milk	Astringent, sweet, cold, light	Goats drink little water and do exercise Goats eat bitter leafs	Constipating, beneficial for internal bleeding, diarrhea, wasting, cough and fever
Elephant's milk	Heavy and build strength		Stabilizes body
Human milk	Lubricant		Vitalizing, builds strength, revives life energy, used as local application in nose and eye for treating bleeding and pain, respectively
Curd	Lubricant and hot	To be discarded in autumn, summer, and spring	Improves appetite, builds strength, indicative of good fortune, aphrodisiac, beneficial in nasal diseases, diarrhea, fevers, loss of appetite, difficult urination and emaciation
Yogurt	Hot and heavy, acidic, increase appetite	Avoid to ear yogurt at night and during summer, autumn and spring Do not eat yogurt without mixing with	Increase fat and produce sperm, increase feces, help to recover from winter fever and loss of appetite

(continued)

Table 2.1 (continued)

Category of milk and milk/dairy products	Qualities	Effects in the body	Health benefit/medicinal values
		sugar, ghee, honey or juice of *amloky* fruit Do not eat bad quality of yogurt Violation of these rules may cause fever, hamper in bile, epilepsy, or memory loss	
Butter milk			Useful in the treatment of piles, abdominal disorders, urinary obstruction, swelling, poor appetite, and poisoning
Fresh butter			Improves appetite, induces constipation, improve abdominal disorders, piles, and facial paralysis
Ghee (Cow's)	Cold and sweet	Best for all fats	Improves intelligence and semen Useful in treating poisoning, insanity, fever, and phthisis Old cow ghee can help to recover from intoxication, seizures, phthisis, pain in the ear and head, and pain in the female genitalia
Milk varieties and preparations	Heavy	Appropriate for those with excellent digestion	Saturating, promotes bulk, and effective if poor sleep

Mixture of equal quantities of honey, ghee, muscle-fat, oil and water in their combination of any two, three or all of them together is incompatible with each other.
Mixture of honey and ghee though in unequal proportion consumed followed with rain water as an after-drink is incompatible.
Honey and seeds of *puskara* are incompatible.
Wine prepared from honey, wine prepared from dates, wine prepared from sugar, drinks made from milk all together are incompatible.
Haridra and mustard oil are incompatible.
Upodaka leaves processed with paste of tila are incompatible and cause diarrhea.

Meat of *balaka* (demoiselle crane) bird along with *varuni* (supernatant fluid of wine) and *kulmasa* (green gram and other pulses cooked over steam) are incompatible.
Meat of *balaka* bird fried in fat of boar soon takes away the life and should be avoided.
Meat of black partridge, peacock, iguana lizard, common quail, grey partridge, cooked over by the fire of wood and processed with or fried in castor oil are incompatible.
Meat of *haridra* bird smeared with ash and sand (as a method of cooking) and consumed along with honey can kills the person quickly and should be avoided.
Milk should not be taken with salt.
Butter should not be taken with leafy vegetable.
Old food materials should not be consumed with new materials.
Ripped materials should be avoided consuming with green materials (fruits).
Very hot substance should not be taken with very cold substance.
Sweet milk rice, wine and hospose (a diet cooked with rice-lentil and other spices) should not be taken together.
Honey, ghee and water should not drink together in equal quantity
(Ibid: paragraph 38–45).[6]

However, there are some general rules to determine the incompatibility of foods: those diseases caused by taking incompatible food items should be cured through taking those medicines having opposite quality. For example, those troubles arising from consuming of incompatible foods could be treated either with purification therapies (emesis, purgation, etc.) or palliative therapies, opposite of their nature. Or people should intake the opposite quality food items, so that incompatible/poison foods which have already taken cannot cause any harm of the body (Ibid: paragraph 46–47). The text also noted that consuming incompatible foods do not produce disease or cause herms for certain people and conditions such as: those who are habituated to do exercise or other physical activities; those who used to take fatty food items; who have strong digestive power; those who are in his/her young/adult age; those who are strong; those who are accustomed to consume incompatible food; and if consumed in a very little quantity (Ibid: paragraph 48).

Apart from ayurvedic texts Chinese text *Huang Di Nei Jing* also put great emphasis on food as a recipe in the prescription of formula which helps recovering from disease. The text denotes that when greatly poisonous herbs are used to treat a disease, the treatment should be stopped when the disease is recovered sixty percent and rest of the recovery would come from proper food intake such as grains, meat, fruits and vegetables. Similarly when commonly poisonous herbs are used in a particular formula prescription, the treatment should be stopped when the disease is recovered seventy percept, and in the case of using slightly poisonous herbs, the treatment should be stopped when the disease is recovered eighty percent flowed by using non-poisonous herbs, ninety percent (*Huang Di Nei Jing* 2009, the plain

[6]Some of the items do not have equal English term and has been excluded.

questions, seventieth article). For example, in the making up of a prescription, *Gancao* root is taken as the monarch herb since it neutralizes the toxins of 72 stone and chemical drugs and 1200 herbal and wood drugs. It is also effective for harmonizing drugs in the same prescription and called as imperial instructor (Li 2012: 5). In all the prescriptions there is a role for food and dietary practices to play restore the health completely.

Another Chinese Medical text *Bencao Gangmu* which is the master peace in the practice of herbal medicine comprises 52 volumes, describing 1892 drugs, and with 1109 illustration. These drugs are categories under 16 categories and some of the categories are food or food therapy which people intakes during everyday meal. The above mentioned 16 categories are: water, fire, earth, metals and stones, herbs, cereals, vegetables, fruits and wood-an evolution from minor to major, utensils, animals with scales, shells, fowls, animals, and human (Li 2012: 33). Many of these herbs are used preparing soup for everyday meal, waters for drink, vegetable, fruits, fish and animal's meat for everyday diet and nutrition. The text recorded 12 drugs in the categories of sesame, wheat and rice; 18 drugs in the category of millet; 14 drugs in the category of beans; and 29 drugs in the category of brewed and prepared items in its volume 22–25. All these items are used as food in everyday meals. From volume 26–28, *Bencao Gangmu* prescribed 32 categories of drugs as pungent, 11 drugs in the category of melons and 15 category of fungi. 11 drugs have also been described in the category of the five fruits, 31 drugs in the category of exotic fruits, 13 drugs in the category of spices, 9 drugs in the category of melons and berries, 6 drugs in the category of aquatic fruits in volume 29–33. Volume 5 of the text also recorded drugs comprises from water and there are 13 drugs under the category "waters from heaven" and 30 drugs under the category "waters from earth" (Ibid: 35). From volumes 43–44 the text recorded 31 drugs in the category of fish and 28 drugs in the category of fish without scales and from volumes 50-51 the text recorded 28 drugs in the category of domestic animals, 38 drugs in the category of wild animals, 12 drugs in the category of mice, and 8 drugs in the category of other animals (Ibid: 36). All these records symbolizes the importance of using medicine as food in the practice of Chinese herbal medicine.

2.5.2 A Routine of Sleep and Non-celibacy to Preserve Health

A second major factors discussed in ayurvedic texts to preserve health is following a rules to sleeping and non-celibacy/sexual activities. Chinese text discussed sleeping under the seasonal regimen which I will discuss in the next section. Sleep and non-celibacy affects human body and mind. *Astanga Hrdayam* text from ayurveda denotes that human happiness and unhappiness, nourishment (good physique) and emaciation, strength and debility (weakness), sexual prowess and impotence, knowledge and ignorance, life and its absence (death)—all are depends on sleep. Sleep indulged at improper time, in excess or not at all destroys happiness (health) and life (Vagbhatas 2009, sutra sthana, Chap. vii, paragraph 56). There are three dimensions of sleep the text mentioned: keeping awake at nights (avoiding sleep) which is dry (causes dryness inside the body); sleeping during daytime which is unctuous (causes moistness inside the body); and taking a nap through sitting comfortably (during day) is neither dry nor unctuous (increase of moisture). Although day sleep is good for health the text suggests night as the best time for sleep (Ibid: paragraph 57). The text further provides the following suggestions about day sleep and ask everybody to follow:

> Everybody has to take a day sleep during the summer seasons because of the three reasons: *vata* (air/wind) of the *dosas* undergoes mild increase during the summer because of the heat; dryness is more because of the harsh summer hit and withdrawal of moisture by the sun); and nights are shorter. Day sleep is usually cooling or refreshing and it can bring the peace/balance in *vata* (air/wind) and destroy the harshness. Since night is smaller during summer, the duration of night cannot fulfill the need of sleep and day sleep can fulfills this short come.
>
> Day sleep in other seasons causes the aggravation of *kapha* (phlegm) and *pitta* (bile). It is good for those peoples who are exhausted by (too much of) speaking; riding; walking or traveling; drinking wine; sexual intercourses; carrying heavy load; tired with physical exercises or activities; tired by anger, grief, and fear; suffering from bronchitis, hiccup, and diarrhea; aged; children; debilitated; emaciated; having injury to the chest; pain in the abdomen; thirsty; indigestion; assaulted and intoxicated.
>
> People who are habituated day sleep also need to go through day sleep all the seasons. It is good for them because day sleep maintains the normalcy of the tissues and the *kapha* (phlegm) nourishes the body (Ibid: paragraph 58–60).
>
> Day sleep is forbidden for those people who are having pore of fat and *kapha* (phlegm), takes fatty materials daily, and addicted to eating.
>
> Those people suffering from diseases of poison and of the throat should sleep less at night (Ibid: paragraph 61).

The text further discussed about the problem of unexpected/sudden/immature sleep and excessive sleep and advocates various methods to avoid such conditions. Unexpected sleep can cause fever, addiction, sluggishness in the body, disease in the vein, vomiting, obstruction in urinary, and evacuation process. In order to overcome those diseases caused by unexpected sleep, people should use strong emetics, nasal drops and fasting (or thinning therapy). The text further suggested following remedy to overcome excessive sleep: taking part in sexual intercourse, grief, fear and anger. By these methods, the *kapha* gets decreased leading to loss of sleep (Ibid: paragraph 62–64).

At the same time loss of sleep could leads to squeezing pain in the body parts, heaviness of the head, too much of yawning, lassitude, exhaustion, giddiness, indigestion, stupor, and diseases of *vata* origin, the text further added. Since both the immature sleep and loss of sleep causes harms for health the text suggested sleeping two quarter or three quarter of the night according to someone's habit. The text also discussed about the proper time of sleep at night and suggests that one should sleep at the proper time at nights daily as much as desirable. Proper time has to be determined according to individual's habit and there is no absolute measurement. If someone is habituated sleeping on a particular time of night that would be the proper time for him/her. In case someone has kept awake at night beyond the time he/she habituates to (not accustomed to) for unavoidable reason, he/she should sleep for half of that period, the next morning without taking any food, the text added (Ibid: paragraph 65–66). Those suffering from little sleep or no sleep should indulge in the drink of milk, wine, meat soup and curds as food. They should also take oil massage and mild squeezing of the body, bath, anointing the head, ears and eyes with nourishing oils, comforting embrace by the arms of the wife, harboring the feeling of satisfaction (of having done good deeds), restoring to things which are comforting to the mind as much as desired. All these actions could bring peace in mind and happiness and lead to good sleep. If someone follow the regimen of celibacy and not crazy about sexual intercourse and contented with happiness he/she could falls asleep on habituated time (Ibid: paragraph 67–69).

Regarding non-celibacy or sexual activities *Astanga Hrdayam* text perceived a gender biased view and gives absolute right to men over sexual intercourse. Women's role in sexual activities as presented in ayurvedic texts is secondary and only relevant to satisfy men's desire.[7] The text suggested that in order to perform better sex and maintain good health a man should avoid sexual intercourse with the following group of women: if she is not lying with her face upward; during her menstrual period; if not liked and her activities are displeasing; if her vagina (genitals) is dirty and troublesome; a very obese or emaciated woman; a pregnant or post-natal stage woman; a woman other than wife; nun; and other vagina of animals like the goat, buffalo, etc. (Vagbhatas 2009: sutra sthana, paragraph 69–72). The text also provided a list of places, time and circumstances when a man should avoid sexual intercourse. This list includes: abode of the teacher; abode of the gods and kings in the monasteries; burial ground; places of torture and of sacrifice; meeting of four roads; days of special significance such as new moon, full moon, eclipses, festivals, mourning days, etc.; organs which are non-sexual such as the mouth, knees, anus, etc.; avoid beating (causing injury) the head and region of the heart (during sexual intercourse) (Ibid). Man should not indulge in copulation after a heavy meal, without keen intention, during hunger and thirst, when his body is in uncomfortable postures, with very young girl or aged woman, when troubled by other urges such as urine, feces, etc., and during sickness (Ibid). Failure to follow such rules can result giddiness, exhaustion, weakness of the thighs, loss of strength, depletion of tissues, loss of acuity of senses and premature death, the text warned.

The text further provides a seasonal routine for sexual activities and suggest that man can have sex daily as much as he likes after making use of aphrodisiacs and obtaining strength during *hemanta* and *sisira* (snowy and cold seasons), once in three days during *vasanta* and *sarat* (spring and autumn) seasons and once a

---

[7]I have discussed this issue detail in one of my article "The promotion of masculinity and femininity through ayurveda in modernIndia (2013)", ***Indian Journal of Gender Studies***, Volume 20, Issue 3, pp. 415–434. New Delhi: Sage Publication (Co-author Kuah-Pearce, K E).

fortnight during *varsa* and *grishma* (monsoon and summer) seasons. After copulation a man should indulge himself in bath, applying scented paste, exposure to cool breeze, drinking of syrup prepared from sugarcane, cold water, milk, meat juice, soup, *sura* (fermented liquor prepared from grains), and then go to sleep. Following these rules a man can gain vigor of the body returns quickly to its abode again, the text added. Man can also gain good memory, intelligence, long life, health, nourishment, acuity of sense organs, reputation, strength, and slow ageing if he follows these disciplines in the sexual intercourse (Ibid: paragraph 73–76). A third factor to preserve health and prevent diseases is to follow a seasonal routines which has been suggested by both the Chinese and ayurvedic texts. In the following section I will discuss how seasonal regimen has been presented in the above texts.

2.5.3 A Routine of Seasonal Regimen to Maintain Health

Su Wen part of Chinese classic *Huang Di Nei Jing* discussed seasonal regimens at least in three different chapters: Chap. 2 on *Si Qi Tiao Shen Da Lun* (On preserving health in accordance with the four seasons); Chap. 5 on *Yin Yang Ying Xiang Da Lun* (The corresponding relation between the Yin and Yang of human and all things and that of the four seasons); and Chap. 64 on *Si Shi Ci Ni Cong Lun* (The regular and adverse treatments of Acupuncture in the four seasons). These chapters analyze the secrets of living long life, classification of seasons and seasonal cycles, role of different seasons correspond to human health, appearance and characters of different seasons, a set of ideal behaviors human needs to perform to preserve health or seasonal rules and finally the negative effects of disobedience to seasonal rules. In Chinese text seasonal cycle consists to four seasons and begins with spring and end by winter. The remaining two seasons are summer and autumn. Season corresponds to *qi* (vital energy) and the nourishment or deficit of *qi* happens in differently in different seasons. These waves of *qi* correspond to human body and mind and a following the seasonal rules can help to maintain the balance between *qi* and body-mind which eventually preserve health.

The first article of *Su Wen* also discussed how to achieve longevity and why live a long life and the procedure to preserve health. This article analyses a range of issues: starts from human's fertility and reproductive ability in various ages; appropriate age for conceiving baby and the pick time for reproduction; various types of human lived in ancient time and their individual methods of preserving health, etc. The article starts with a conversation between legendary emperor Huang Di and his minister/doctor Qi Bo where the emperor asked his doctor: "why the ancient people lived over hundred years but nowadays only fifty"? The doctor replied that:

> *"ancient people follows the daily routine, took temperate diet, know how to keep the essential qi perfect, and minimize the desire and maximize the funs of health care. However, nowadays people work against the routine, full of desires, take intemperate diet such as wine, over indulgence of sex and hanker after a moment of pleasure" (Huang Di Nei Jing*, the plain questions, first article, 2009: 284).

The above conversation clearly illustrates the importance and methods of health preservation and prevention and the secrets of living long life through following three methods: minimize desire, follow daily routine, and taking temperate/ moderate diet. The second article from *Su Wen* focused on the health preservation methods according to four seasons. Topics under this articles includes the rules of various seasons, climate changes, and the effect of disobeying the law of natures. Table 2.2 has been prepared by the author on how to preserve health and live a long life according to the knowledge from the text *Huang Di Nei Jing*:

The text further provided the rules of health preservation and suggests the following techniques to preserve health: keep indifferent, tranquil, and cool to all desires; harmonize the genuine *qi*; and defend the spirit inside. The text denotes that if people had calm and care-free minds with little desires; hearts are restful without fears; bodies are overworked without fatigue; genuine *qi* is harmonious and smooth; what they desire could be acquired; and what they anticipated could be obtained; people will feel what they eat are delicious, what they wear are comfortable, and their customs gleeful, the superiors and inferiors were satisfied with their status, their favorites and desires could not disturb their vision, peoples are not bothered by things, people are submissive to the norms of health preservation" (Ibid: 286). In its second article the text discussed how human and nature are mutually corresponding and how human could preserve health according to the regularity of the following four seasons: spring is for generation; summer is for growth; autumn is for harvest; and winter is for storage (*Huang Di Nei Jing*, the plain questions, second article, 2009: 291). This article further discussed how the *qi* of the four seasons correspond with the *qi* of *yang* and *yin* and the *qi* of the four *zhang* organs (liver, heart, lung and kidney) of the human body. It denotes that *yin* and *yang* of the four seasons are

Table 2.2 Rules of preserving health according to *Huang Di Nei Jing* text

Time (ancient vs. nowadays)	Secret of living long life	Result
Ancient people	Followed the canons of the yin and yang	Their body forms co-existed with the spirits Could enjoy natural ages Only died after they were a hundred
	Practices physical exercise appropriately	
	Temperate diets	
	Led regular lives	
	Did not work against the routine	
Nowadays	Take wine as beverage	Feeble in fifties
	Lead an abnormal life as a routine	
	Make sex when being drunken	
	Essence is exhausted by desires	
	Genuine *qi* has driven away by favorite things and do not know how to keep the essential *qi* full	
	Not good at regularizing spirit	
	Hanker after a moment's pleasure against the funs of health care	

the root of all things and *yang* should be nourished during spring and summer seasons and yin should be nourished during the autumn and winter seasons to preserve human health. Obedience to the changes of the four seasons can help to prevent disease and prolong life, the article concluded (Ibid: 295).

Table 2.3 has been prepared by the author based on the discussion about seasonal regimen and health preservation according to *Huang Di Nei Jing*:

Huang Di Nei Jing text further denotes that variation of climates affect the flourishing, declining, life and death of all living things and human has to take care of health with obedience to climate changes. If human is obedience to climate changes vital *qi* could be preserved and longevity could be achieved. Otherwise, human will contract diseases and perish, the text added (Ibid: 294). The article divides the condition of the heaven into two categories: normal condition and abnormal condition, and notes the characteristics. During the normal condition of the heaven, heavenly *qi* is clear and bright and conceals virtues and runs endlessly. At the same time the following conditions could be found during the abnormal condition of the heaven:

> *gloomy and the sun and moon are not bright; evils may poison the space between the heaven and earth; heavenly yang qi is blockaded and the earthly yin qi is weak; the clouds and fogs do not brighten; all living things lose their energy and most famous trees die; the harmful evils greatly devastate the nature; the wind and rain are not moderate; trees and paddy field cannot flourish; the bandit wind comes frequently; the torrential rains usually fall down; and the four seasons cannot preserve their normal variations* (Ibid).

The article warns that if human are disobedience to the rules of health preservation during the abnormal condition of the heaven, they will die in the midst of their normal life-span.

In India all the three ayurvedic major texts *Caraka Samhita*, *Susruta Samhita* and *Astanga Hrdayam* describes *ritucarya* (seasonal regimen) as important determinant to maintain health and classifies the year into six seasons: Winter, Spring, Summer, Rainy, Autumn, Dewy and each season contains two months duration. Ayurvedic texts discussed the classification of seasons, characteristics of different seasons, what people should eat and drink in various seasons and what not to eat and drink, the ideal behavior and actions human should perform in different seasons and the actions they should avoid. According to these texts the earth is controlled by the movement of sun, moon, and wind. These three gods (they are considered as god in the texts) correspond to human *dosas* (humor) which affect the state of health. The *Astanga Hrdayam* text particularly emphasizes the condition of the natural environment in different seasons with reference to air, water and the location of sun and moon. It advises the duties of individual human to maintain balance between health and seasons (Vagbhatas 2009, *surto sthana*, Chap. 3). The text denotes that moon covers the earth, sun suck the earth and wind take care of the species of the earth with the asylum of the sun and moon. Seasons and three bodily components such as digested food, *dosa*, and strength are governed by the sun, moon and wind. Seasons contribute a seasonal cycle which is continuously moving. Seasonal cycle starts from a moment and end to a decade. Moment is the smallest

Table 2.3 Seasonal regimen and health preservation according to *Huang Di Nei Jing* text

Season	Duration (months)	Called as	Appearance or characteristic	Human ideal behavior	Behavior correspondences to	Effect of disobedience
Spring	3	Generation (new creation such as new leaf on the tree) and staleness elimination	Lively *qi* of the heaven and earth is growing Everything is flourishing	Go to bed later and get up early Stroll slowly in the garden Loosen the hair and relax the body Let thoughts act vigorously Make things alive and not dead Give things to others and not deprive others of things Reward others rather than punish	Spring *qi* Ways of nourishing generation	Liver will be impaired A cold disease will occur in the summer A bad basis for summer growth
Summer	3	Exuberance and beauty	Heavenly *qi* and earthly *qi* cross Everything blooms and bears fruits	Go to bed late and get up early Not be abhorrent ofsun-shine Turn away mind from anger Let spirit become vigorous Let the yang *qi* discharge to the outside	Summer *qi* Ways of nourishing growth	Heart will be damaged Malaria will occur in the autumn A bad basis for autumn harvest
Autumn	3	Stability	Heavenly *qi* is swift and harsh Colors of the earth are	Sleep early and get up early with the cocks	Autumn *qi* Ways of nourishing harvest	Lung will be hurt Diarrhea containing undigested foods will occur in winter A bad basis for winter storage

(continued)

Table 2.3 (continued)

Season	Duration (months)	Called as	Appearance or characteristic	Human ideal behavior	Behavior correspondences to	Effect of disobedience
			solemn and clear	Make the mind calm and to moderate the torment of the harsh autumn *qi* Astringe the spirit to make the autumn *qi* safe Ensure not to expose mind so as to make the lung *qi* clear		
Winter	3	Blockage and storage	Water is frozen and the earth is cracked Yang *qi* of nature is stored without disturbance	Sleep early and get up late when the sun shines; Make mind seemingly hidden Evade cold and approach warmth Do not sweat excessively to render *yang qi* frequently depleted	Winter *qi* Ways of nourishing storage	Kidneys will be spoiled Atrophy and *qi* reversal diseases will occur in the spring A bad basis for spring generation (*Huang Di Nei Jing*, The Plain Questions, second article, 2009: 291)

time unit of the seasonal cycle lasted a duration equivalent to pronouncing a letter such as "A". Fort-night (according to the appearance of the moon) which is in two kinds: dark and bright is the second largest time unit under seasonal cycle followed by month which lasts two fort-nights, seasons which lasts 2 months; *Ayaon* contains 6 months, year contains 12 months, and *Zhug* (decade) contains 5 years. From a moment to decade is called seasonal cycle which is continuously moving according to the circle. The text further noted that season is similar to god and is self-sufficient. Seasons are divided into two broad categories: *Dokhenayon* (Southern solstice) and *Uttornayon* (Northern solstice) according to the movement of the sun. Rainy, Autumn and Dewy seasons are classified as southern solstice and during these seasons the sun releases the strength of the people and the moon become stronger; the sun loses its strength; salt, food, and honey produce more; the earth becomes cooled by the clouds, rain and cold wind; and all living species become stronger. The sun also moves on south direction during these three seasons. Winter, Spring and Summer seasons are considered as northern solstice and the sun and wind become stronger and dry during these seasons and take away all the cooling qualities of the earth. The bitter humor in the nature increases and all living species become weaker. The sun also moves on north direction during these three seasons. The text further suggested that the strength of human is generally maximum in cold seasons i.e. winter and dewy; poor in rainy and summer seasons; and medium (moderate) in remaining seasons. All the six seasons make different impact on human body, mind and *dosas* (humors), the text added (Vagbhatas 2009, *sutro sthana,* Chap. 3, paragraphs 1–7). Table 2.4 has been prepared by the author and based on his understanding of the seasonal regimen discussed in the above text:

2.6 Medical Practitioners in Chinese Medicine and Ayurveda

Practitioner in both the Chinese medicine and ayurvedic practice play an important role not just to treat the patient and cure the diseases but also to prevent disease and maintain health of the community. Ancient tradition demanded that a physician should be truly a friend, philosopher and guide, in both the spiritual and material life of the sick person who approaches him for the cure to his/her disease (Gopinath 2001: 62–63). Since medical tradition in China and India provide a complete lifestyle they also discussed about moral and ethical issues, goal of moral and spiritual life and the means and suggested modes to fulfil those goals. For example, ayurveda emphasizes the ideals of human life and the importance of health. There are four basic life goals or prime values for each individual. These are: *dharma* (ideals), *artha* (money or material accumulation), *kam* (pleasure, excitement, sex), and *mokthi* (liberation) (Ninivaggi 2001: 37). All these four life goals indicate that moral and ideological values were highly regarded in ayurveda. The *Susruta Samhita* describes the terms and conditions for selecting a student to become a *vaidya* (title of the ayurvedic physician). According to the *Susruta Samhita* text:

Table 2.4 Seasonal regimen according to *Astanga Hrdayam* text

Name of the season	Characteristics	What to and not to eat	What to and not to do
Regimen during Dewy and Winter	People are strong Fire in the alimentary tract and digestive activity becomes powerful because it gets obstructed from spreading out by the cold atmosphere Night is longer and people feel hungry in the morning People become energetic and accumulate more heat but cannot sweat The cold wind retards the release of body heat and enhance the digestive fire Even heavy foods becomes digestible If adequate food is not available, the digestive fire consumes body *rasas* (liquid) and cause *vata* (air) disturbances	Oily, sour and slated products of the meat of creatures living in water, marshy land and burrowed holes are appropriate Eat the following food or food items: soft and smooth meat, sugarcane sweet or dates sweet, wine, vinegar, beans, pulse, enamel, various delicious foods prepared from milk and sugarcane and oily food **Avoidance** Cold drinks, insufficient intake of food, pungent, bitter, and astringent foods	Must do evacuation in the morning and follow the routine of daily regimen Massage oil gentle on the head first and then on the body Take bath after the exercise with ayurvedic soap and remove the oil from the body Use ayurvedic mild perfume after taking a bath Use mild warm water for sanitation and bath Use warm cloths and sleep under warm blanket Cover the body with enough warm cloths Seats and beds should be covered with thick cloth or quilt made of wool, silk, hide and leather Enjoy or consume sun heat or fire heat logically and according to the need Always use shoe Stay indoors and in the ground floor of the house Keep the house warm by fire Women who have well developed thighs, breasts and buttocks should use fragrant fumes, and keep their body warm **Avoidance** Do limited exercise and arm fight and foot fight with other peoples who also do exercise before the oil remove When snow falls and winter deepens, exposure to frosty winds should be avoided
Regimen during Spring	*Kapha* (Phlegm) which has undergone increase in cold seasons becomes liquefied by the heat of the sun in spring The rising heat of the sun perturbs body fat and cause various disorder This is the season to savor youth and beauty, and the woods	Eat foods which are easily digestible and dry (Moisture-free, fat-free) Diet with barley and wheat as staple and mix with honey Eat meat of rabbit, deer, quail and partridge and those animals live in desert like land Drink the juice of mango-fruits mixed with fragrant substances Drink wine with same age friends for increase the sense of wellbeing	Disease should be controlled quickly by resorting to strong emesis, nasal medication and other therapies such as evacuative procedures like emesis Physical activities such as limited exercise is permitted Do dry massage and mild trampling Take bath and gargles with warm water Anoint the body with the paste of *karpura, candana,* and *aguru* (some herbs and

(continued)

Table 2.4 (continued)

Name of the season	Characteristics	What to and not to eat	What to and not to do
		Drink should be served by the beloved (women) which has been made more pleasant by the sweet scent of their body and the grace of their lily-like eyes. The drink, thereby producing satisfaction to the mind and heart Unspoiled beverages such as fermented infusion, fermented decoction, fermented sugarcane juice, fermented grape juice, hones water, or water boiled with extract of trees such as asana, *candana*, etc. should be taken **Avoidance** Foods which are hard to digest and cold should be avoided Avoid diet which is heavy, sour, oily, and sweet Wine should not be taken or if every necessary, take in very little quantity Or diluted with more quantity of water Taking large doses wine can cause debility, burning sensation and delusion	plant powders written in ayurvedic texts) Use of *kumkum* (collyrium) and medicated smoke Application of *sandal* and *agaru* (some herbs and plant powders written in ayurvedic texts) paste on the body Spend time in quite, cool and peaceful garden surrounded with lake in all sides Do sexual intercourse in a place where having little sun heat because of the dense trees, where cuckoo (bird) is signing, and various flowers trees always provide smell Spend some day time in the flowers garden with friends and exchange sweet words, pleasant games, storytelling, and be happy **Avoidance** Avoid day sleep
Regimen during Summer	The sun rays become powerful day after day and appears to be destructive for all things *Kapha* (Phlegm) decreases day by day and *vata (air)* increases consequently	Foods which are sweet, light (easy to digest), fatty, cold and liquid should be taken Drink cornflower mixed with cold water and sugar after taking bath in cold water Boiled white rice with *kunda* (pumpkin) flower should be eaten along with the meat of animals from desert like land **Drinks/liquid** Meat juice which is not very thick and mixed with pepper powder and sugar Syrup which is sweet, sour and salty Khandava which is prepared with many herb, plant or fruit substances and having all the tastes Syrup prepared with fruits such as coconut, mango, etc. Buffalo milk mixed with sugar and cooled by moon and stars **Procedure to drink**	**Day time (day regimen)** Daytime should be spent in forests which have all trees reaching the sky (very tall) such as *sala*, *tala* (Palmyra tree grow in the Indian subcontinent), etc. which obstruct the hot rays of the sun In houses around which bunches of flowers and grapes are hanging from their creepers Sheets of cloth spreading sweet scented water has to be used to fan the air Bunches of tender leaves and fruits of mango should be hang on all around the indoor house Sleep on soft bed prepared with petals of flowers. Spend the remaining part of the day inside the house cooled by water fountains Get rid of the heat of the sun **At night (night regimen)**

(continued)

Table 2.4 (continued)

Name of the season	Characteristics	What to and not to eat	What to and not to do
		Cool the drinks and added with powder of *patra* (a herb written in ayurvedic text and grows in Indian subcontinent) Kept inside a fresh mud pot Fermented drinks should be drunk in mugs of mud or shell Water kept in mud pot along with flowers of *pata karpura* (an ayurvedic herb) should be used for drinking **Avoidance** Salt, pungent and sour food	Sleep on the terrace having good moon light (this will help relieved exhaustions due to heat of the day) Anointing the body with paste of *candana* (A herb grows in Indian subcontinent) Wearing garlands Wearing of very light and thin dress Fanning with fans made of leaves of *tala* (Indian palm) or large leaves of lily Sprinkling cool water softly **Mental peace** Listening the sought from birds like parrot or mynah bird Talking with children or beautiful women pleasantly Watching the nearby move of beautiful women wearing bangles of soft lotus, and blossoms of lotus in their hair **Avoidance** Physical exercises Exposure to sunlight Sexual activities
Rainy season	The digestive activity which becomes weak and debilitated by the summer heat during summer further decrease during the rainy season *Doshs* (humors) get aggravated because of the thick clouds, full of water, cold wind, water getting dirty because of rain Many diseases occurs	Old grains for food, meat-juice processed with spices etc. Meat of animal from desert-like lands Soup of pulses Wine prepared from grapes and fermented decoctions, which are old or mash Whey, thin water of curds processed with more souvarcala and powder of pancakola Rays water or water from deep wells, well boiled should be use for drinking Eat predominantly sour, salty and fatty food with honey on those days when there is no sunlight. These foods are easily digestible on that condition A hungry person should take bitter, sweet and astringent tastes foods, and easily digestible foods such as rice, green gram, sugar *amlaka* (a fruit grows in Indian	Avoid moving on foot but move by vehicles Use perfumes Expose clothes to fragrant-fumes Dwell in upper stories of the house Avoid heat, cold and snow Avoid exposure to snow or mist Avoid sleeping at day time and the eastern breeze

(continued)

Table 2.4 (continued)

Name of the season	Characteristics	What to and not to eat	What to and not to do
		subcontinent), patola, honey, and meat of animals from desert like lands Drink that water which gets heated by the hot rays of the sun during day and gets cooled by the cool rays of the moon during night, for many days continuously **Avoidance** Indulgence in alkaline substances Satiation with hearty meal Use of dadhi (one kind of card) and muscle-fat	
Autumn season	Persons who have become accustomed to the cold of *varsa* (rainy season) suddenly get exposed to the warm rays of the sun The *pitta* (bile) which undergoes increase in the bodies during *varsa* (rainy season) increase further during autumn Water gets heated by hot rays of the sun during day and gets cooled by the cool rays of moon at night Earth is detoxicated, plare uncontaminated and neither moisture nor dry	People should take foods which are of bitter, sweet, astringent tastes, and easily digestible (rice, green-gram, sugar, *amalaka*, honey and meat of animals of desert like lands) **Avoidance** Moisture or fat food Those food difficult to digest Big pieces of animal meat	Evening should be spent on the terraces of houses which are white (by painting) Anointing the body with paste of *candana, user, and corpora* (some ayurvedic powders) Weargarlands of pearls and shinning dress Enjoy moonlight and relaxes yourself Expose to snow (mist) **Avoidance** Indulgence in alkaline substances Satiation with hearty meal use of curds, oil Eastern breeze (Vagbhatas 2009, *Sutro stahna,* Chap. 3, Paragraph 8–63)

> "A *guru* (master) must select a junior physician or *shisho* (student) from *Brahman, Khatrio or Vaisho* castes. The student should have good family background; be young in age, and strong, polite, intelligent, and meritorious; and have a powerful memory. His tongue, cheeks and teeth should be narrow. His mouth, eyes and nose should be *sharol* (straight). He must have strength to bear hard work" (*Susruta*, sutro sthana, Chap. 2, paragraph 2).

After selecting a student a *guru* (master) should ask the student to recite a *montro* (hymn) in the presence of fire. The *montro* spells out that:

> "The student should avoid *kam* (excitement), greed, anger, arrogance, jealousy, cruel words, lies, etc. He should cut his nails and hair regularly and stay clean and purified, wear decent dress and be fond of truth (*shatobroto*). He should be a follower of Brahman, and courteous. He should not visit any place without the permission of his master. He should follow his master in how to sleep, sit, eat and study. Disobedience of these rules may cause damage for the student's professional career and make him unsuccessful in achieving the fame of a famous *vaidya*" (*Susruta*, sutro sthana, Chap. 2, paragraph 4).

Simultaneously, a master should be vigilant, to ensure that the student obeys all the rules and regulations in order to avoid misunderstandings that might result in conflicts and tensions between the disciple and himself (*Susruta*; sutro sthana, Chap. 1, paragraph 4). Many humanistic and moral suggestions are also provided by the *Susruta Samhita*. For instance, "a physician should treat the poor, the teacher and the refugee the same as a member of his own family, and treat them with his own medicine" (*Susruta*; sutro sthana, Chap. 1, paragraph 5). The *Caraka Samhita* also acknowledges that a *vaidya* should have four major qualities. Firstly, he should have sound knowledge of the subject matter. Secondly, he should observe the treatment of many patients and be acquainted with expertise by watching the treatment procedures of many famous physicians. Thirdly, he should gain sufficient skill in treatment methods and procedures. Finally, he should be self-purified and spiritual (*Caraka* 2003, sutro sthana, Chap. 9, paragraph 5).

As for the second theme, the *Caraka Samhita* compares the qualities of noble physicians with those of the Brahmins, the priests of Hinduism. In the text, a *vaidya* (physician) was given a position superior to that of a Brahmin. The *Caraka Samhita* text states that "an intelligent and logical chancellor will be adored as a preceptor by the human being who is called a Brahmin. The Brahmin is twice born, but the *vaidya* is thrice born; while the title *vaidya* is not acquainted by birth. If the Brahmin learns the Vedas and attains knowledge of medicine and medication he can be treated as a *vaidya*" (*Caraka* 2003, chikitsha sthana, Chap. 1, paragraph 1). The idealistic character of a *vaidya* is presented in the *Caraka Samhita*, where "a real physician should be knowledgeable about scripture, medication, the treatment philosophy, and the economics of health" (*Caraka* 2003, sutro sthana, Chap. 9, paragraph 5). Not only skill in medicine and medication, but also self-purification and knowledge of scriptures and other social qualities are key determinants for the success of a *vaidya*, the *Caraka* emphasises.

The final theme in the *Caraka* is the careful recognition of the superiority of the Brahmin as an ayurvedic practitioner, and states that ayurveda should be studied by the Brahmin, Kshatriya and Vaisya castes—the Brahmin would study ayurveda for scholarship, the Kshatriya for self-defence and the Vaisya for prosperity, and to maintain their own Dharma (ideal), Ortha (wealth) and Kama (sex) (*Caraka*, sutro sthana, Chap. 30, paragraph 2). The text further furnishes that "a knowledgeable and ideal person can achieve Dharma if he takes good care of his parents, siblings, friends and seniors during their sickness and gives advice according to ayurveda" (*Caraka* 2003, sutro sthana, Chap. 30, paragraph 2).

Huang Di Nei Jing text also discussed the quality, characteristics and methods of health preservation followed by person knowledgeable about health preservation. The text strongly suggested to follow the lifestyle and suggestion of those person. According to the text there are four category of human considered as master of health preservation, know the secret of health, and follow the rules of seasons and *yin* and *yang* to preserve health: genuine human, supreme human, sages, and

Table 2.5 Methods of health preservation according to *Huang Di Nei Jing* text

Types of human	Methods of health preservation
Genuine human	Mastered the rules of the heaven, earth, *yin* and *yang* Mastered about inhaled and exhaled the essential *qi* of nature Independently defended the spirits inside Kept the skin and muscles vigorous all the time Their life has no end
Supreme human	Lived during the middle ancient time Adapted themselves to changes of the *yin*, *yang*, and four seasons Staying above the secular world Accumulated the essences and protected the spirits Prolonged their life and strengthened their bodies
Sages	Lived in harmony with the heaven and earth Submitted to the rules of the eight winds (wind from the east, south, west, north, northeast, southeast, southwest, northwest) Adapted their hobbies and desires to the ordinary world Did not harbor any anger and resentment Their bodies were not fatigued by matters outside Their mind were not perturbed inside They kept tranquil, optimistic and self-contended Their life-span could be reached to hundred years
Sagacious human	Followed the rules of the heaven and earth Acted in accordance with the running of the sun and moon Ascertained the changes of the stars Submitted to the *yin* and *yang*, and differentiated the four seasons Their life-span was prolonged to the boundaries of its natural; limitation (Ibid)

sagacious human (*Huang Di Nei Jing*, the plain questions, first article, 2009: 289). Based on the author's understanding of the article the Table 2.5 has discussed the methods of health preservation followed by the above four categories human[8]:

2.7 Conclusion

The first objective of this chapter was to introduce the history, theory and method of Chinese medicine and ayurveda presented in the classical texts and find their similarity and differences. Historical similarity grounded in the process of development and practice. Both the Chinese herbal medicine and ayurveda has developed as knowledge based science and the practice continued through a family line where medical knowledge and skill stayed as family secret. At the same time historical difference lays on religious and supernatural connotation. Ayurveda has

[8]The term "human" is used by this author. Original book used the term "man".

divined origin and many godly characters present in the practice of medical skill and treat diseases. Thus, ayurveda arguable connected to Brahmanism and or Hinduism. While there are legendary characters exists in Chinese medicine such as emperor *Huang Di*, etc. there are not too many religious inspiration found in the development of Chinese herbal medicine. Use of humoural and or balance theory is a common feature in both the medical system which contributes the major theoretical similarity. Chinese herbal medicine supports the balance in *qi*, *yin/yang* and five phases (wood, fire, earth, metal and water) while ayurveda suggest the balance among three *dosas* (humours of human body), *vata-pitta-kapha* (air-bile-phlegm). There is also methodological similarity and difference between the two systems which has been discussed detail in earlier section of this chapter.

Another objective of this chapter was to analyse how various actions and activities are suggested to prevent disease and preserve health in the above texts. This helps to compare the contemporary practice of Chinese medicine and ayurveda with the textual presentation. Following a seasonal regimen, daily routine and food and dietary practice are the key process discussed in all the above texts to preserve health. Although there are four seasons mentioned in Chinese text and six seasons in ayurvedic text there is similarities about the rules and regulations need to be followed to prevent diseases.

Chapter 3
Professionalization According to Western Line: Education and Health Service Delivery

3.1 Introduction

Professionalization of indigenous medical education and practice in China and India according to the Western line took place in two different parts of twentieth century from a nationalist inspiration. In China, it was precisely done after the formation of the People's Republic of China in 1950s with the hand of the communist leadership. In India, it was launched during the British colonial rule in the early twentieth century. One of the key features of this professionalization is to introduce an integrated education curriculum and practice combining indigenous medicine with Western methods and modalities. Indigenous medical schools were founded according to Western line and offered programs with various duration. Those students enrolled in indigenous medical school needs to learn a number of courses taught in Western medicine apart from indigenous medicine courses. They were also allowed to practice Western medicine after graduation although there were some restrictions. After more than a half-century of integrated practice in China and India indigenous medicine still stays marginal position. Western medicine dominates in the mainstream health service delivery and accounted large share of the national health budget. In China total annual budget for health is RMB 260,253 billion in 2013[1] whereas budget for indigenous medicine is RMB 0.858694600 billion,[2] accounted only 0.330% of the national health budget. Similarly in India the annual budget for the ministry of health and family welfare is INR 373,300 billion in 2013–14[3] whereas budget for the ministry of AYUSH[4] is

[1]Ministry of Finance of the People's Republic of China Web page. Retrieved from the http://yss.mof.gov.cn/ Accessed in March 22, 2014.

[2]Ministry of Finance of the People's Republic of China Web page. Retrieved from the http://yss.mof.gov.cn/ Accessed in March 22, 2014.

[3]Retrieved from http://health.india.com/news/union-budget-2013-14-health-gets-rs-37330-crore/ Accessed on November 2013.

[4]AYUSH refers to Ayurveda, Yoga and Naturopathy, Unani, Siddha and Homoeopathy.

M.N. Islam, *Chinese and Indian Medicine Today*,
DOI 10.1007/978-981-10-3962-1_3

INR 10 billion,[5] accounted only 3.73% of the national health budget. The number of Western medicine college/Universities and registered practitioners are also larger than other systems of medicine in China and India. There are 1,782,057 registered doctors for Western medicine in 2012[6] in China whereas the number of registered Chinese medicine doctor is 356,779.[7] India also has a huge imbalance between the number of Western medicine doctors and AYUSH doctors which are 853,195[8] in 2012 and 785,185 in 2010 respectively (AYUSH 2011: 2).

Nonetheless, China and India have become frontline countries having a history of more than half century integrated medical practice. However, integration has also brought new challenges for the education and health services delivery. This chapter investigates the current trend of integration in education and practice and the challenges they face. This argues that the nationalist revival of indigenous medicine in China and India reproduces Western hegemony. The nationalist governments restructured traditions instead of reviving traditional education, training and apprenticeship. Modern-day practitioners of indigenous medicine in China and India perceive their training from the Western medical outlook.

First part of this chapter introduces a historical preview of indigenous medical education in China and India and explores the contrast between traditional education and contemporary education. In particular, it focuses on undergraduate and graduate education and explore how new educational arrangements reproduce Western hegemony. Key features and indicators of contemporary education and the challenges they are facing have been discussed in the second part of the chapter. Final part of this chapter deals with the contemporary practice and health service delivery provided by the modern graduates. This part also examines the perception of apprentice practitioners about indigenous medical practice and the dispute between modern graduates and them.

3.2 Evolution of Indigenous Medical Education in China and India

Unlike *Taiyishu*, family education and apprenticeship education were the main ways of education for Chinese medicine until recent decades (Wangzhong 1996). Medical knowledge and skill were kept as a family secret under family education

[5]Ibid.

[6]China Statistical Yearbook. (2013). *21–2 Employed Persons in Health Care Institutions*. Retrieved March 19, 2014 from http://www.stats.gov.cn/tjsj/ndsj/2013/html/Z2102e.htm.

[7]The basic situation for Chinese medicine doctors in China (2012). Retrieved March 19, 2014 from http://www.satcm.gov.cn/1999-2011/atog/2012/A07.htm.

[8]Medical Council of India (2011–12). *Annual Report (Amended) 2011–12, p. 6*. New Delhi: Medical Council of India.

Retrieved from http://www.mciindia.org/pdf/Annual%20Report.pdf Accessed on November 2013.

and transferred from one generation to another within the family or lineage. Family education starts from childhood where a junior member from the family sits in senior member's chamber and assists him to prepare drug or treatment. The basic mode of learning under this system is observation, assisting the senior and experiment with the senior practitioner. There is no fixed duration of study or education curriculam and generally it is a lifelong learning process. Apprenticeship education could be treated as part of family education with some differences. Generally under the apprenticeship education system, a senior practitioner has a small school where several students could enroll and learn medical training and expertise from him. Often these junior students live at their master's house as a junior member of the family and accompany him when he attained patients. The major mode of learning are: attending some basic lectures given by master, observation when he attends patient, assisting him and do experiement with him. There is also no fixed duration of learning and whether the student will leave the master or not depends on individual student's wish.

Students generally leave the master after few years and open policlinic. In family education, external members are generally excluded from gaining medical training and skill from the senior practitioner while apprentice education allows external member to learn. Family and apprentice education system in Chinese medicine dramatically declined after the foundation of Chinese medicine colleges according to the Western line in 1950s (Islam 2016: 59).

Founded during the Tang Dynasty (598–907 A.D.) to train imperial physicians, *Taiyishu* was one of the earliest institutions to professionalize Chinese medicine. It was also favoured by the Song dynasty and called as *Tai Yi Ju* (the Imperial Medical Ministry) and survived with slight modification until the Ming dynasty (1368–1644 A.D.) (Huard 1970: 367). Students could learn various medical specialities in *Taiyishu* such as internal medicine, material-medica, ophthalmology, forensic medicine, dietetics, sexual hygiene, paediatrics, gynaecology, and dermatology (Gaggi 1979: 14–15). In 1913, the All-China Society for Traditional Chinese Medicine was founded and a Central College of Chinese Medicine was established in 1930 (Charlie Changli Xue et al. 2006: 776). The professionalization of Chinese medicine according to Western line started after the foundation of the People's Republic of China in 1949. In 1950s, Mao Zedong the then founder of the People's Republic of China delcared that "Chinese medicine is a great treasure-house, and efforts should be made to explore and raise it to a higher level" (Xie 2002: 119). Followed by that declaration four colleges were established in four different parts of China in 1956 to teach Chinese medicine according to the Western line. These are: Beijing College of Traditional Chinese Medicine in North China; Guangzhou College of Traditional Chinese Medicine in South China; Shanghai College of Traditional Chinese Medicine in East China; and Chendu College of Traditional Chinese Medicine in West China. Most of the Chinese medicine colleges and Universities are currently offering undergraduate programs on Chinese Herbal Medicine, Integrated Chinese medicine, Acupuncture and Moxibustion, and

Tuina.[9] One of the common features of these programs is to combine Chinese medicine with Western modalities and introduce an integrated education curriculam. The Chinese constitution also promulgated in 1982 and declared that the state should develop both modern/Western medicine and indigenous Chinese medicine and the present constitution also emphasises the modernization of Chinese medicine (Xie 2002: 119). The key features of contemporary professionalized education in Chinese medicine are: having fixed duration of study and curriculum; students learn different subject from different master; needs a registration or license to practice after graduation; and adopted some methods and modalities from Western medical science (Islam 2016: 60). Currently, there are 32 specialist Chinese medicine Universities in China, with a total annual intake of approximately 16,000. In addition, 58 other tertiary institutions have Chinese medicine departments. Furthermore, 25 institutions provide Master degree programs; 14 provide Doctorate degree programs; and 15 offer postdoctoral training in Chinese medicine. In addition to tertiary institutions, 51 technical colleges across China also provide Chinese medicine education (Charlie Changli Xue et al. 2006: 776).

In ancient India, the Rishis and Munis (legendary early ayurvedic practitioners) who practiced and popularised ayurveda are represented as teaching their students under the shade of trees, near to forests or in open areas, surrounded by mountains, for two major reasons. Firstly, ayurveda was based on herbal-natural materials and these raw materials for preparing medicines were accessible in the mountains and forests. Secondly, ayurvedic healing involved religious and spiritual treatment. Living close to forests and mountains was considered an advantage for the spiritual concentration of practitioners and for gaining deep knowledge of medicinal plants and herbs. The compilers of the ayurvedic texts, *Caraka* and *Susruta*, were also used to lead a natural lifestyle.

Ayurveda became a subject of study in the Universities of Takshasila (2nd century B.C.) and Nalanda (7th century A.D.), and many well-known personalities from different countries such as Japan and China received training in these two universities. The University of Takshasila attracted medical students from far and near and all the specialities in medicine and surgery were highly developed even at that time (Ministry of Health 1958: 1). For instance, Javika, a famous ayurvedic physician in Buddhist legends, underwent professional training for seven years at the University of Takshasila (Bala 1991: 39).

Apart from family education apprenticeship education was the major form of training for ayurvedic practitioners in early days India which followed Brahminical religious lines. The student usually lived in the home of his *guru* (master) as a junior member of the family, and gradually they developed an intimate personal relationship with each other (Basham 1976). The young medical student became linked with his teacher by supernatural and eternal bonds. After being accepted by

[9]Beijing University of Chinese medicine offer courses such as Chinese medicine, specialization in research and experimental training (7-year combined program leading to Bachelor and Master in Medicine), Chinese medicine (5-year program leading to Bachelor of Medicine), Acupuncture-Moxibustion and Tuina (5-year program leading to Bachelor of Medicine), etc.

the *guru* to study ayurveda the young student was treated as 'thrice-born' (*tri-jonmo*), which distinguished him from the ordinary Brahmin, who was only twice-born (*djonmo*). The *guru* required the young student to be honest, to follow vegetarianism, and to obey him during his studentship. A student was entitled to use the title *vaidya* and was allowed to conduct normal medical practices after the successful completion of training. He could then leave his *guru's* house and establish his own professional territory (Ibid).

Apprenticeship system is called as *guru-mukhi-biadya* in the state of West-Bengal in India. In Bangla language (or Bengali), a *guru* is a knowledgeable person, *mukhi* means centric, and *biadya* means knowledge. Thus, *guru-mukhi-biadya* refers to learning knowledge from a particular knowledgeable person who acts as a master. The tradition of ayurvedic learning under the *guru-mukhi-biadya* system continued in Bengal until the establishment of the Central Council of Indian Medicine (CCIM) in the 1970s by the Indian parliament. After the foundation of CCIM, only those ayurvedic practitioners trained in modern ayurvedic institutions got the right to become registered ayurvedic practitioners. The newly-founded council declared it obligatory for an ayurvedic practitioner to become registered under the council in order to continue practicing, which limited the right of practitioners trained under the apprenticeship system. As the graduates trained under the apprenticeship system did not get the right to become registered practitioners, this system was eventually abolished, although the gradual decline of the apprenticeship system had begun in the mid-nineteenth century, when Western medical colleges were founded in India.

Under the apprenticeship system, the *guru* (master) had a *toll* (school) in his house where junior students got practical training in ayurveda. Like China, the students lived at the master's house as junior members of the family, or in the same community, so that they could stay in touch with their master. The *guru* used the title *kabiraj* and taught the students from ayurvedic texts written in Sanskrit. In the *toll* system, the *guru* or ayurvedic *kabiraj* trained his apprentices without demanding private tuition fees and that "the relationship between the *kabiraj* and student was that of a *guru* and disciple" (Gupta 1976: 368). Students were first instructed in Sanskrit grammar, literary texts, and logic, and gradually completed the preliminary course related to classical medical texts (Ibid). As it was hardly possible for a teacher to go through all the topics from the classical texts within a short period of time, students were made familiar with the basic knowledge of their *guru*, and later on they could read the other topics themselves (Ibid: 368–369). According to a general code of treatment, the *kabiraj* would investigate the patient's illness and general state of health and observe the appearance and behaviour of the patient. Finally the *kabiraj* would examine the pulse, eyes, abdomen, and tongue of the patient according to his traditional skill and expertise. The young students also observed their master's diagnosis and learn the treatment methods and modalities. Apart from theoretical training, students assisted the *kabiraj* when patients visited him, and they accompanied their master to homes to treat severely ill patients in order to gain clinical experiences (Ibid). The *kabiraj* or master also taught the students on the knowledge and preparation of herbal remedies and the use of herbs and plants for medicine.

Under the apprenticeship system, each of the *kabirajes* tended to specialize in one area of treatment, and some gained great fame in their areas of specialization. Most of these *kabirajes* established their own *toll* (school). The *toll* functions as an institution to promote the skill and fame of that *kabiraj* who founded and operated it. Those trained under these *kabirajes* would stand a good chance to attract patients to them (Islam 2008: 150). After graduation, most of these students would leave the *toll* and start their own practices.

Unlike formal education systems, apprenticeship training does not have a specific time period for completion of the training. In most cases, it depends on the individual student's capability to learn, and sometimes it might take many years of training before he is deemed to be proficient by his master. After years of practice and becoming known, the student would found his own *toll* and teach new students. However, students always regard the contribution of their *guru* as having contributed to their success, no matter how famous and popular they become in professional life.

In 1822 the colonial administration in India founded the School of Native Doctors in Kolkata on Western lines, where lectures were given on modern (allopathic) medical subjects side by side with ayurveda. The assumption here was that, while the native indigenous practitioners were already knowledgeable about ayurveda, they also needed to learn Western medicine. However, a committee was appointed by the British Governor General Lord William Bentinck to evaluate the program, which reported that the training program was defective and recommended its immediate abolition (Ministry of Health 1958). Hence, the School was abolished and an Western medical college was opened in Kolkata in the year 1835. After that, the training course in ayurvedic medicine was transferred to various Sanskrit colleges. At the beginning of the twentieth century, ayurveda was separated from the Sanskrit colleges and many independent new ayurvedic teaching institutions were established in various parts of British India. However, most of the newly-founded ayurvedic training institutions adopted integrated education curricula, where some courses from the Western medical sciences were taught side by side to ayurvedic courses (Ministry of Health 1958: 25). This trend continued even after decolonization. In 1970s The Central Council of Indian Medicine under the Ministry of Health was founded monitoring, standartized and supervised ayurvedic and other form of indigenous medicine. A pure ayurvedic curriculum was introduced in late 1970s under the title of Bachelor of Ayurvedic Medicine and Surgery (BAMS) and standardised as undergraduate course all over India. This program only contains ayurvedic courses for five and half year duration including one year internship in hospital. Until now this is the only government approved undergraduate program for ayurvedic education.

3.3 Contemporary Education in China and India

As stated before that contemporary education and practice in Chinese medicine is an outcome of the effort launged during the Mao era and follows Western line. Chinese medicine colleges/Universities and hospitals were founded in various cities which follows similar structure to Western medical care. These newly founded institutions offered education programs from pre-undergraduate to post-graduate level with various duration and subject areas. Currently there are 33 Universities offering Chinese medicine courses, enrolling 48,000 students every year. There are also 53 secondary schools with 50,800 students every year offering Chinese medicine courses (Dutta 2009:387). One of the common features of these college/Universities was to combine Chinese medicine with Western medicine and develop an integrated medical practice.

The following table shows the general pattern of education structure in Chinese medicine in contemporary China (Table 3.1).

There are couple of distinct features could be found under these new education structure. Firstly; adoption of large number of courses in the curriculam which are taught in Western medicine. For example, Beijing University of Chinese medicine under its'School of Pre-clinical Medicine offers programs on Chinese medicine specialization in Chinese and Western Integrated Medicine which leads to a Bachelor of Medicine and Master of Clinical Medicine degree. The duration of this program is seven years and includes subjects from both the Chinese medicine and Western Medicine. The list of Chinese medicine subjects under this program are: Basic Theories of Chinese medicine; Chinese Diagnosis; Chinese MateriaMedica; Chinese Medicinal Formula; *Huang Di Nei Jing*; *JinGui Yao Lue; Wen Bing Xue*; Chinese medicine Schools of Thought; Chinese Internal Medicine; TCM Surgery; TCM Pediatrics; TCM Gynecology; TCM Emergencies; TCM Ophthalmology; Acupuncture and Moxibustion. The program also includes subjects from Western medicine such as: Anatomy; Physiology; Pathology; Basic Pharmacology; Biochemistry; Diagnosis; Western Internal Medicine; Immunology; Surgery; Dermatology; Histology and Embryology; Molecular Biology.[10]

Another distinctive feature is that educational institution offers various courses with different specialities. Although the braoder objective of the new education structure was to produce more Chinese medicine practitioners to increse the supply of health care provider and fill the vacume positions, Chinese medicine institutions are offering specialities which are not directly related to practitioner. For example, Beijing University of Chinese medicine offers programs such as Pharmaceutical Engineering, specialization in biological pharmaceutics (4 years), Pharmaceutical

[10]Ibid, Retrieved from the following link: http://www.bucm.edu.cn/eapdomain/ViewNote?ptid=2&nid=32642&unchecked=true Accessed on December 26, 2014.

Table 3.1 General pattern of education structure in Chinese medicine in contemporary China

China			
Level of education	Program duration (years)	Available program	Programs title and comment
Below undergraduate	3	Diploma program/Vocational training	For example Chinese Nursing (3-year diploma program) offered by the Beijing University of Chinese medicine
Undergraduate	4–5	Chinese medicine Programs (Producing Chinese medicine practitioners) Chinese medicine (5 years) Acupuncture Programs (Producing practitioners) Acupuncture, Moxibustion and Tuina (5 years) Chinese Materia Medica Program (Producing non-practitioners) Chinese Materia Medica, specialization in analysis of Chinese materia medica (4 years) Pharmaceutical Engineering, specialization in biological pharmaceutics (4 years) Pharmaceutical Engineering, specialization in the pharmaceutics industry (4 years) Chinese Nursing Programs Nursing (4-years) Nursing, oriented toward international nursing (4-years)[a]	Program leading to Bachelor of Medicine Program leading to Bachelor of Medicine These programs are example and offered by the BeijingUniversity of Chinese medicine for the Chinese students Program leading to Bachelor of Nursing Program leading to Bachelor of Nursing
Second Bachelor	2–3 after first Bachelor		A 3 years second Bachelor degree is possible after 4 years first bachelor or a 2 years second Bachelor degree is possible after 5 years first Bachelor program

(continued)

Table 3.1 (continued)

China			
Level of education	Program duration (years)	Available program	Programs title and comment
Combining Bachelor and Masters	7 Years	Chinese medicine, specialization in research and experimental training Chinese medicine, specialization in Chinese and western integrated medicine Chinese medicine, specialization in clinical practice Chinese medicine, specialization in orthopedics and traumatology Chinese medicine, specialization in acupuncture-moxibustion and tuina Chinese medicine, specialization in acupuncture-moxibustion and Tuina and oriented toward international exchange Chinese medicine, specialization in acupuncture-moxibustion and Tuina and oriented toward rehabilitation	Combined Program leading to Bachelor and Master in Medicine Combined program leading to Bachelor of Medicine and Master in Clinical Medicine[b] Do Do Do Do Do
Masters	2–3 after Bachelor		A 3 years Master degree after 5 years Bachelor
Doctor	3 after Masters		A 3 years program after 7 years Combining Bachelor and Master or a 3 years program after 3 years Masters and 5 years Bachelor

[a]These programs are offered by the Beijing University of Chinese medicine. Retrieved from the following link: http://english.bucm.edu.cn/teaching_research/teaching/24270.htm Accessed on June 28, 2015

[b]These programs are currently offered by the Beijing University of Chinese medicine. Retrieved from the following link: http://www.bucm.edu.cn/portal/media-type/html/group/en/page/default.psml/js_pane/P-1270a6cdfd7-1000e Accessed on December 26, 2014

Engineering, specialization in the pharmaceutics industry (4 years), Nursing, oriented toward international nursing (4-years), etc.[11]

How do the students and graduates from modern Chinese medicine institutions perceive their education? Of those suyveyed, majority of the students from the modern college are in-favor of traditional apprentice education. Statistics reveals that 42% students rated apprenticeship or family education were better than contemporary education and 24% think both the educations have merits and demerits. Beside, those surveyed 35% of the Chinese medicine practitioners rated apprentice education as better than contemporary education and 20% noted both the systems have own advantages and disadvantages. The following advantages and disadvantages have been summarized from the students'and practioners'perception about apprentice or family education and modern education (Table 3.2).

Professionalization of ayurveda in India according to Western line was a nationalist attempt launched during the early twentieth century. The All-Indian Ayurved Mahamandal and the Indian National Congress on Ayurveda (1920–38) made one of the earliest attempts to revive ayurveda. Subsequently, the Indian National Congress adopted a resolution to further popularize ayurvedic schools, colleges and hospitals. As a result, ayurvedic schools and colleges were opened in various major cities in India such as Varanasi, Madras, Delhi, Bombay and Mysore, and in the state of Bengal following Western style of education. At a conference of health ministers of various states in 1946, the delegates strongly recommended offering diploma and degree courses and the introduction of ayurvedic post-graduate courses for the graduates of Western medicine (Ministry of Health 1958: 2). In the year 1946, the Chopra Committee directed that ayurvedic education be better coordinated and integrated with Western medical education, and this was another landmark in ayurvedic education. By 1958 there were 76 institutions in India teaching ayurveda, 49 of which had adopted integrated education. The universities of India were also considering making affiliation with ayurvedic teaching institutions around this time, and some of the ayurvedic educational institutions offering integrated course were already affiliated to universities (Ibid). Students taking a degree under the integrated ayurvedic education curriculum during 1950s were required to take 12 individual subjects in anatomy, physiology, fundamental principles of ayurveda (i.e., ayurvedic *sharir*) and their philosophical approach in relation to *darshanas* (ayurvedic philosophy), pharmacology and therapeutics, *dravya guna* (discussion of drugs), *Rasa Shastra* and *Baishajya Kalpana* (ayurvedic pharmacology and chemistry), pathology and bacteriology, modern medicine, surgery, midwifery and gynaecology, medical jurisprudence, *Rog nidana* and

---

[11]These information was based on the programs offered by Beijing University of Chinese medicine and Guangzhou University of Chinese medicine. Retrieved from the following link: http://www.bucm.edu.cn/portal/media-type/html/group/en/page/default.psml/js_pane/P-1270a6cdfd7-1000e Accessed on December 26, 2014.

Table 3.2 A comparison between apprentice/family education and modern education

Category	Advantages	Disadvantages
Family/apprentice education	More practical and real knowledge drives from practice; Imply one-to-one teaching method which is elite and can provide students a solid foundation; Can cultivate highly skilled students; Can cure many chronic diseases which are epidemic in the society; More opportunity of doing clinical practice; Chinese medicine is a science relate to experience; Students could be specialized on a particular area	Focused on a specific case and too strait and inflexible; Imply limited learning methods; Can work only in some small clinics but not in the big hospitals
Modern/ contemporary education	Students would have more aggressive visions; More students could be trained; Very systematic and students can learn modern anatomy; More flexible; Students can gain more general and theoretical knowledge on various areas of Chinese medicine such as internal medicine, gynecology, pediatrics, etc.; Students can also learn some diagnostic and treatment methods from Western medicine	Chinese medicine education is not suitable for the large class teaching (students cannot learn the essence of Chinese medicine from group education); Time limitation (learning Chinese medicine needs long time, but the rigid time focuses on certain definition); Theoretical education; Neither Chinese medicine nor Western medicine skills can be mastered by students; Duration of in-class learning is too long and do not have enough chance to learn from practice; Students have little chance to ask question because of large class size

chikitsa (disease identification and treatment), *Swastha Vritha* (i.e. preventive medicine) (Ibid).[12]

In 1970, Central Council of Indian Medicine Act came in force and Central Council of Indian Medicine was founded in New Delhi to overseas the education in ayurveda. Subsequently the integrated education curriculum was abolished and pure ayurvedic course was introduced all over India. This course is called Bachelor of Ayurvedic Medicine and Surgery (BAMS) for five and half year duration including

[12]For details of the recommended syllabus for undergraduate education please see the Government of India, Ministry of Health Report of the Committee to assess and evaluate the present status of Ayurvedic system of medicine 1958: 50.

one year internship. There are about 510 colleges/institutions/universities were registered under the Department of Ayurveda, Yoga and Naturopathy, Unani, Siddha and Homoeopathy (AYUSH) recently renamed as Ministry of AYUSH, Government of India in 2011 (AYUSH 2011: 2). These institutions have a yearly 26,790[13] admission capacity for undergraduate study and 2384 admission capacity for post-graduate study in 2010 (AYUSH 2011: 26). Apart from graduate education, there are also 14 institutions all over India that offer pharmacy-training courses in ayurveda (AYUSH 2003: 217–218). In 2010 there were 785,185 AYUSH registered practitioners (AYUSH 2011: 2). There were also 8898 licensed pharmacies under AYUSH in 2010 those are manufacturing ayurvedic and other indigenous drugs (AYUSH 2011: 2). Ayurvedic drug manufacturers are licensed and regulated under the Drugs & Cosmetics Act, 1940. The education structure of ayurveda in contemporary India has been summarized in the following Table 3.3.

In the current ayurvedic syllabus for undergraduate education, prescribed by the Central Council of Indian Medicine (2003–2004), students need to attend 18 courses for four and a half years training (excluding the one-year internship). These are as follows: for the First Professional Examination (one and a half years), History of Ayurveda, *Padartha Vijnana* (physics), Sanskrit, *Astanga Samgraha* (eight branches of ayurveda), *Sarira Racana Vijnana* (anatomy), *Kriya Sarira Vijnana* (physiology); for the Second Professional Examination (one and a half years), *Svastha Vrtta* (hygiene), *Dravya Guna-Vijnana* (discussion of drugs), *Rasasastra* and *Bhaisajya Kalpana* (ayurvedic pharmacology and chemistry), *Roga Vijnana* and *Vikrti Vijnana* (pathology), *Caraka Samhita*, *Agada Tantra* (toxicology) and *VyavaharAyurveda ka Vidhi Vaidyaka* (jurisprudence); and for the Third Professional Examination (one and a half years), *Prasuti Tantra* and *Striroga* (obstetrics and gynaecology), *Kaumarabhrtya* (paediatrics), *Kayacikitsa* (internal medicine), *Salya Tantra* (surgery), *Salakya Tantra*, and *Caraka Samhita*.[14] Clinical internship is the final phase of training, and a graduate is expected to conduct actual practice of medical and health care and acquire skills under supervision, so that he/she may becomes capable of functioning independently.

The formalization of the ayurvedic education system and its curriculum has brought mixed responses from the practitioners and students. Out of the 20 physicians and 20 students surveyed in 2004–2005, 65% of the physicians and 80% of the students respectively perceived the current ayurvedic curriculum and the introduction of the BAMS course favourably, while 30% of the physicians and 20% of the students feared the dilution of ayurvedic contents. Those who favoured the new education curriculum argued that the ayurvedic system needed to adapt to modern

[13]This number includes not only ayurveda but all other Indian systems of medicine including Yoga and naturopathy, Unani, Siddah, and Homeopathy.

[14]Central Council of Indian Medicine (2003–04) B.A.M.S. curriculum and text books, No.3:3–56 (2003–04) (Translator Vd. Pawankumar R. Godatwar). New Delhi: Central Council of Indian Medicine.

Table 3.3 Education structure of ayurveda in contemporary India

India			
Level of education	Program duration (years)	Available programs or subjects of study/specialty	Program titles and comments
Pre-Ayurved Course	1–2	1 year program was equivalent to Higher Secondary/PUC and 2 years program was equivalent to SSLC/Matriculation[a]	Continued until 1990 and no longer been in effect
Undergraduate	5.5 including 1 year internship	1 Area Bachelor of Ayurvedic Medicine and Surgery	(BAMS) Ayurvedacharya
Post-graduate (Could be only studied after the completion of five and half years BAMS)	3	22 Areas General Medicine (Ay); Ayurvedic specialty of Bio-cleansing Process; Gynecology and Obstetrics (Ay); Surgery (Ay); Ayurvedic Para-surgical Procedures; Ophthalmology (Ay); ENT and Head (Ay); Oral and Dental Management (Ay); Pediatrics (Ay); Psychiatry (Ay); Pathology (Ay); Toxicology (Ay); Pharmacology (Ay); Alchemy Pharmacy (Ay); Preventive Medicine (Ay); Ayurvedic Compendia; Ayurvedic Fundamental Principles; Anatomy (Ay); Physiology (Ay); Anesthesia Radiology[b]	MD (Ayurveda Vachaspati)/MS (Ayurveda Dhanwantari)[c] Students can study and get MD/MS degree on 22 different subjects
Post-graduate Diploma	2	16 Areas D[d]. Panchkarma;	Diploma in (any of the 16 areas) Ayurveda

(continued)

Table 3.3 (continued)

India			
Level of education	Program duration (years)	Available programs or subjects of study/specialty	Program titles and comments
(Post-graduate Diploma Program could be studied only after the completion of five and half years BAMS program)		D. Kshar Karma; D. Ras Shastra and Bhaishajya Kalpana; D. Dermatology (Ay); D. Nutrition (Ay); D. Public Health (Ay); D. Obstetrics and Gynecology (Ay); D. Pediatrics (Ay); D. Pharmacognosy (Ay); D. Psychiatry (Ay); D. Ophthalmology (Ay); D. Geriatrics (Ay); D. Anesthesiology (Ay); D. Radio-diagnosis (Ay); D. Orthopedics (Ay); D. Clinical Pathology (Ay)[e]	For example, Diploma in Dermatology (Ayurveda)
Ph.D. (Doctor of Philosophy) (Could be only pursued after the completion of five and half years BAMS program + 3 years MD/MS program)	3-4 (Generally and depends on individual college/ University and student)	Depends on students' area of interest, available resource, etc.	Ph.D. programs are offered by some reputed ayurvedic Universities/post graduate colleges and every institution has own policy, rules and requirements

[a]Central Council of Indian Medicine (2015), Indian Medicine Central Council (1989) (Minimum standards of education in Indian medicine) Regulations, 1986. Retrieved from the following link: http://ccimindia.org/cc_actregulations_1986.html Accessed on June 28, 2015
[b]Only English translation of the subjects has included in this table
[c]There two different titles depend on subject of study
[d]D. refers Diploma in
[e]Ministry of AYUSH (2015), Regular courses available in ayurveda. Retrived from the following link: http://indianmedicine.nic.in/ Accessed on June 28, 2015

demands and that the old apprenticeship was no longer appropriate in modern Indian society. Furthermore, they felt that the adoption of technology and scientific knowledge would enable the ayurvedic system to modernize and globalize. However, there continues to be dissatisfaction with the current ayurvedic curriculum. Of those surveyed, 90% of the *kabirajes* noted that there was room for improvement. Others commented on the market orientation of the ayurvedic practitioners, whose goal is to obtain good jobs and good salaries. One of the main problems mentioned by the students and practitioners is the outdated ayurvedic curriculum taught at the college. 45% of the students regarded the BAMS course curriculum as outdated. Some of the students' comments follow.

> Our syllabus should be modernized and we need a comprehensive and comparative syllabus with Western medical science. We are still studying *vata-pitta-kapha* (air, bile and phlegm) as the central principle of ayurveda, which has no practical value today while modern pathology has developed to the highest stage. We need to exclude those topics and adopt biochemistry from Western medical science. We are studying the number of veins or pulses in the human body. Obviously it had an importance during olden days but not today. Science has made significant progress and many aspects of olden ayurveda are inapplicable today and need further modernization or modification.

> We have a combined syllabus of ayurveda. As a result, students can't understand what to study and how to study or how much modern medical science and how much ayurveda needs to be studied? Since ayurveda does not have emergency medicine we have to study modern pharmacology, anatomy and physiology, pathology, etc. Simultaneously, we also have to know the ayurvedic pharmacology (*roshoshastro*). It becomes very difficult for a student to complete both the courses at a time—that was a major problem I encountered. We know a little of ayurveda and little Western medical science, and become masters of neither ayurveda nor Western medicine.

Another factor that has impacted on the choice of students to study ayurveda is the language barrier—as noted by 25% of the students surveyed. Ayurvedic materials were originally written in Sanskrit and most of the available publications and reading materials are in Hindi. The Bengali students found it difficult to read subjects in Hindi or Sanskrit. It was especially difficult when a teacher taught ayurveda in Bangla due to his/her poor oral skills and expertise in Hindi, while the prescribed readings for the students were in Hindi. There are many terms and narratives they found difficult to understand, and students found it difficult to understand the deep knowledge of ayurveda because of their poor or lack of language skills. They found topics, such as *Sharir Kira* (ayurvedic physiology), *Sharir Rochana* (ayurvedic anatomy), *Astango Shangraw* (eight branches of ayurveda), *Sanskrit*, *Padartho Biggan* (physics), etc., totally unfamiliar. Students found it difficult to bridge the gap between these indigenous forms of medical practice and those of the modern Western scientific medical system that they have been exposed to and are familiar with.

3.4 New Development

Professionalization of Chinese medicine and ayurveda according to Western line has produced new features over the decades. These features are distinctive and have become an integral part of the process of modernizing indigenous medicine. One of the features is called integrated medical practice combining indigenous medicine with the methods and modalities from Western medicine. In China, it is called "integrated medicine" or "medical practice" and in India it is described by the term "cross practice". Another distinctive features caused by professionalization is the tendency among students and practitioners to become a doctor and compete with the practitioners from Western medicine. Increasing scientification and judgement of indigenous medicine from the Western science and ignoring its own history, theory and method is an immediate outcome of this development. Graduates from the modern Chinese medicine and ayurvedic institutes intend to get a salaroid job in big hospital or clinic and act like a Western physician and use the title "Dr." instead of their traditional title *Daifu* or *Kabiraj* or *Vaid*. Gaining prestige and improving social status of the graduates is another feature brought by the professionalization. In the following section I have discussed these three features.

3.4.1 Integrated Medical Practice/Cross Practice

Prescribing Western drugs and using diagnostic methods from Western medicine have become one of the key features in the practice of Chinese medicine. Practitioners those gradauted from the modern institutions have to study courses from basic Western medical science such as anatomy, physiology, diagnosis, pathology, pharmacology, etc. They take advantages of their education curriculum. The Chinese government policy prohibits prescribing Western drugs for Chinese medicine and Integrated medicine gradautes if they work in a Western medicine hospital. Graduates from Integrated medicine can only practice Western medicine if they work in a Chinese medicine hospital. The Chinese law prohibits the graduates from Chinese medicine to prescribe Western drugs. This is, however, not followed. Those surveyed 86% students from the Henan University of Chinese medicine would prefer to prescribe Western drugs apart from Chinese drugs regardless their training background. At the same time, 90% of the practitioners those surveyed have noted that they prescribe drugs and use diagnostic methods commonly used in Western medicine. The only practitioner (5%) who does not prescribe Western drugs is an apprenticeship practitioner who did not go through the professional education. Major motivations behind this trend are: gaining knowledge on Western medicine during training because of the curriculum; Western medicine has powerful drug which can save peoples life in emergency situation; and Western diagnostic methods are objective and more accurate than Chinese method such as pulse checking, smelling, observing and listening.

Integrated medical practice in India is best known as "cross practice". Under the cross practice ayurvedic patented drugs were overwhelmingly used by the Western medicine physicians and vice versa. It is not uncommon for Western[15]-trained doctors to prescribe ayurvedic herbal drugs because of their known effectiveness and minimum side effects. Drug stores selling Western medicines also carry patented ayurvedic drugs and health products. Many of these drugs do not require medical prescriptions and are readily available over the counter. Although the government policy prohibits prescribing Western drugs for ayurvedic practitioners in most of the states in India it is often not followed. However, there continues to be resistance towards integrated practice. Of those surveyed, 80% were against cross practice and only 15% were for it; of those against, 50% belonged to the *kabiraj* group. However, 20% thought it important to understand other medical systems. While there is no separate hospital for doing internship for the undergraduate ayurvedic students in West Bengal state at the time of this fieldwork, the students inevitably did their internship training in the three Western hospitals. During housetop-ship (residency) they practiced Western medicine in an ayurvedic hospital.

3.4.2 Becoming a Doctor and Compete with the Practitioners of Western Medicine

This is a common tendency among students and young graduates to become a doctor instead of Chinese medicine or ayurvedic practitioner. In China, a large number of students come to study Chinese medicine college/Universities after having failed to enroll in a college/University of Western medicine. Their prime motivation is to become a medical doctor, not particularly a practitioner of Chinese medicine. Statistics from the survey revealed that 32% Students from the Henan University of Chinese medicine came to study Chinese medicine after having failed to enroll in a Western medicine college and 40% students would prefer to study Western medicine if they got a chance. At the same time 20% of the practitioners those surveyed also tried to enroll in a college of Western medicine. However, this statistics does not represent the true priority of choice among students and practitioners whether to study Western medicine or Chinese medicine. Students those study humanities in highschool can study Chinese medicine but not Western medicine. Because of this government policy students who have come to study Chinese medicine from humanity background did not have a chance to study Western medicine. The survey team could not distinguish who are the students from humanities and who are from science background because of their poor knowledge about admission system.

[15]Western medicine is called in India as allopathic medicine.

The admission requirements in India is more straight forward. Students who have science background during secondary education can only sit for the entrance exam in an ayurvedic college/University. 95% of the students surveyed in India in 2004–05 came to study ayurveda after failing to gain entry in colleages of Western medicine (Islam 2012: 519). Some of them sat entrance exam more than one time to get admission in a college of Western medicine. In the state of West Bengal where this study was conducted, there are two joint entrance exams to study medicine. First joint entrance exam is to study in the colleges of Western medicine and dentistry and second joint entrance exam is to study in an AYUSH college. Generally the joint entrance exam for study Western medicine take place earlier than to study AYUSH college.

The professionalization of indigenous medicine according to Western line has also caused a decline of the traditional apprenticeship system in China and India. Chinese medicine has been practice over the millennium through family line or apprentice system. However, very few students from modern colleges have any family attachment to Chinese medicine. Statistics revealed that 18% students have other members in the family who have studied or practices Chinese medicine and only 2% have a long family tradition or apprentice. At the same time 60% of the practitioners those surveyed have no other family member who practiced Chinese medicine and only 10% have long family and apprentice background. This statistics illustrates the gradual decline of family influence in Chinese medicine education and practice.

The scenario in India is more or less similar. In the apprenticeship system in India, most of the ayurvedic practitioners came from brahmin castes, but the majority of ayurvedic practitioners in recent times have come from non-brahmin castes. The government of Indian has promoted a caste-neutral admissions policy in recent decades in the ayurvedic colleges to ensure the enrolment of lower-caste students. Out of a total of 60 admissions each year at the J B Roy State Ayurvedic College and Hospital, 11 places are reserved for scheduled caste (lower caste) students. The rest of the places are distributed among: general students (39), government-awarded (5), and students from Tripura State (5). However, 90% of the *kabirajes* surveyed, who had learned ayurveda through the apprenticeship system, came from brahmin castes. On the other hand, of modern ayurvedic practitioners who had not had any experience of apprenticeship, only 25% of those surveyed came from brahmin families. This change has also brought a discrepancy between the view of traditional *kabirajes* and modern practitioners in their perceptions of ayurveda.

In 2003, the number of those with formal qualifications as ayurvedic practitioners increased to 333,742, nearly 3.8 times higher than it had been in 1980 (88,265). However, the number of those trained predominantly under the apprenticeship system (Non-Institutionally Qualified) had not increases proportionally, as in 1980 there were 83,893 apprenticeship-based practitioners and in 2003 only 98,883 (AYUSH 2003: 89). Apprenticeship-based ayurvedic practitioners were predominantly located in rural areas and often provided health care services where no other health care facility was available and living in the communities they served. Many of them produced ayurvedic medicine for treatment; while those with formal degree qualifications prescribed commercially-manufactured drugs to their patients. However, some apprenticeship *kabirajes* are very popular in urban areas and provide health care services for the middle class elite, although most of these have formal training in addition to that of the apprenticeship tradition. They usually come from traditional *vaidya* or *kabiraj* families, and today most are old.

3.4.3 Social Status and Prestige

Chinese medicine has been developed historically as individualistic practice where an individual practitioner opened a polyclinic and attend patients. This practice did not require a salaried job and the success of the polyclinic depends on the skill and fame of the practitioner. Individual knowledge, experience and skill are the key of success rather than qualification and training background (Islam 2016: 61). This is, however no longer been the case. Majority of the Chinese medicine graduates in contemporary China are rush to get a salaried job in private or public hospitals or big clinics instead of setting their own polyclinic. Private practices are shrinking and replaced by salaried job. Social and professional status, prestige, and material gain have become prime objective. One of the tendencies is to compare and compete with Western medicine practitioner. 40% students those surveyed from the Chinese medicine University consider their socio-economic status as lower than the student/graduates from Western medicine. They are far behind in some particular areas such as employment opportunities, income, professional skill, social attitude toward Chinese medicine practitioners, etc. For example, Chinese medicine graduates are not considered as doctor but health care professional from public point of view, they added. This is, however, not the perception of Chinese medicine practitioner those surveyed. Only 25% of the survyed practitioners think that their social status is relatively lower than the practitioners from Western medicine.

In India, the government has given similar status to both the Western practitioners and practitioners from AYUSH systems. However, those surveyed 80% students from ayurvedic colleage perceived there social status is lower than Western practitioners in real life. The general social view favoured Western practitioners which confirms higher status for a qualified Western doctor. Of those surveyed, 70% of the physicians realized that their status had been upgraded after taking part in the formal training program as a result of the modernization and professionalization of ayurveda, and there has been an increase in their interest in studying ayurveda. The status of the ayurvedic physicians and practitioners has risen considerably in recent years (Islam 2008: 160). In addition there is a greater availability of jobs for Western trained doctors. However, rest 20% students those surveyed think that status could be a relative issue and the educated people value ayurvedic practitioners. The superior status of Western doctors are confimed by the actual behaviour of moder ayurvedic gradauates. None of the ayurvedic practitioners surveyed, who hold BAMS degree, used the title of *kabiraj* or *vaid* on their visiting card or letterhead, preferring the use of the term, "Doctor", a term used by the Western practitioners (Islam 2012: 519).

3.5 Challenges of Professionalized Education and Practice

Professionalization of indigenous medicine and its transition from apprenticeship education and practice to moderninstitutional framework in China and India is not always smooth. The major challenges are link to the overall socio-economic and socio-political situations in both the countries. Although in 1929, the Central Government in China passed a bill to ban Chinese medicine in order to clear the way for developing medical work according to Western line the situation reversed after the 1949 revolution and formation of the People's Republic of China (Xie 2002: 118). The new Chinese government formulated official policies to protect and develop Chinese medicine. In 1950, it stipulated that "uniting the Chine medicine and Western medical professionals" as one of the guiding principles of health work (Ibid). The Constitution promulgated in 1982 and the present Constitution declared that the State should "develop both Western medicine and Chinese medicine" (Ibid: 119). However, critics say that the role of the government is not enthusiastic enough especially in the area of resource distribution and promotes a positive attitude toward this system. The total national health budget in 2013 was RMB 260,253 billion[16]while the budget for Chinese medicine was only RMB 0.858694600 billion.[17] Government statistics have revealed that only 0.330%[18] of the annual health budget was allocated for Chinese medicine in the same year. There are three types of hospital in China. Most of the big hospitals only provide Western medicine care whereas some of them have a window for Chinese medicine care. The later type is called as integrated hospital. There are also hospitals only provide Chinese medicine care. According to the Chinese Government Statistics, the number of Western medicine hospitals in the year 2012 is 19,724; number of integrated hospitals 312; and number of Chinese medicine hospitals 2886.[19] The number of registered doctors from Western medicine 1,782,057 whereas from Chinese medicine 356,779[20] in the same year. A year earlier i.e. in 2011 the number of beds available in Western

[16]Ministry of Finance of the People's Republic of China Web page. Retrieved from the http://yss.mof.gov.cn/ Accessed in March 22, 2014.

[17]Ibid.

[18]This calculation was done by the author based on the above figure.

[19]State Administration of Traditional Chinese Medicine of the People's Republic of China (中华人民共和国国家中医药管理局). (2012). The statistics of Traditional Chinese medicine. Retrieved from the following link:http://www.satcm.gov.cn/1999-2011/atog/2012/B02.htm. Accessed on March 19, 2014.

[20]Ibid.

Table 3.4 Comparison between Chinese medicine and Western medicine facilities available in contemporary China

Area of comparison	Total	Western medicine	Chinese medicine
Number of hospitals	24,720 including integrated hospitals and others[a]	19,724 in 2012[b] (79.8%)	2886 in 2012[b] (11.7%)
Number of hospital beds		3,167,200 in 2011[c]	477,100 in 2011[c]
Number of registered doctors		1,782,057 in 2012[d]	356,779 in 2012[e]
Doctor patient ratio		1: 760[f]	1: 3795[f]
Annual health budget	RMB 260.253 billion in 2013[7]	259.40 billion (99.67%)	RMB 0.858694600 billion in 2013[g] (0.330% in 2013)

[a]National Bureau of Statistics of China (2013). Statistical communiqué of the People's Republic of Chinaon the 2013 national economic and social development.Public health and social service column. Retrieved from the http://www.stats.gov.cn/english/PressRelease/201402/t20140224_515103.html Accessed on 30 March 2014

[b]State Administration of Traditional Chinese Medicine of the People's Republic of China (中华人民共和国国家中医药管理局). (2012). The statistics of Traditional Chinese medicine. Retrieved March 19, 2014 from: http://www.satcm.gov.cn/1999-2011/atog/2012/B02.htm

[c]The national bureau of statistics of the People's Republic of China.(n.d.). Retrieved from http://data.stats.gov.cn/search/keywordlist2?keyword=医院床位 Accessed on 20 March 2014

[d]China Statistical Yearbook. (2013). *21–2 Employed Persons in Health Care Institutions*. Retrieved March 19, 2014 from http://www.stats.gov.cn/tjsj/ndsj/2013/html/Z2102e.htm

[e]The basic situation for Chinese medicine doctors in China (2012). Retrieved March 19, 2014 from http://www.satcm.gov.cn/1999-2011/atog/2012/A07.htm

[f] This number has been calculated by the author through divided the total population by the number of registered doctors

[g]Ministry of Finance of the People's Republic of China Web page. Retrieved from the http://yss.mof.gov.cn/ Accessed in March 22, 2014

medicine hospitals 3,167,200 whereas in Chinese medicine hospitals 477,100.[21] Table (3.4) can show a comparison between Chinese medicine and Western medicine facilities available in contemporary China.

Apart from resource and budgetary allocation, public attitudes toward the Chinese medicine practitioners are not as positive as doctors of Western medicine. Chinese medicine practitioners are still treated as health worker if not medical doctor in public perception. This causes major setback for the graduates from Chinese medicine institutes to stay stick in their own system of practice. Increasing pressure of using standardized diagnosis and treatment methods and prescribe evidence based drugs force the practitioners to adopt diagnosis and treatment methods and modalities from Western medicine. Throughout its history Chinese

[21]Ibid.

medicine has developed as individualistic system of medicine which used to employ individualistic treatment method and prescription. However, the regulations from modern Chinese state obligate them to follow standardised treatment method and prescription which is a norm in Western medicine.

The contemporary practice of indigenous medicine in India encounters similar challenges to China which include lack of resource, public attitude, lack of government patronise, standardization according to the standard of Western medicine, etc. Furthermore, the lack of qualified and dedicated teachers and infrastructure, library resources also served to further alienate potential students from studying ayurveda. The fact of only small numbers of patients in the ayurvedic hospital hinders ayurvedic medical interns and students in their clinical practice. Although ayurveda focuses primarily on herb and plant-based medicine for its pharmacology, there was no herbal garden within the college campus where this study was conducted. As a result, many students could not identify the medicinal plants. All these factors led to frustration and disillusion on the part of the students, and many moved away from this form of training. According to the national statistics in 2012, although India produces around 30,000 doctors, 18,000 specialists, 30,000 AYUSH graduates, 54,000 nurses, 15,000 ANMs and 36,000 pharmacists annually absulate majority of the health budget goes to Western medical care.[22] The frollowing table shows the comparison between Western medicine and Indian systems of medicine about budget allocation in differnet years from the government (Table 3.5 and 3.6).

Table 3.5 Yearly estimated health budget and budget for the Department/Ministry of AYUSH (INR)

Year	Estimated Health Budget (INR)	Estimated AYUSH/ISM & H Budget (INR)	% AYUSH/ISM & H Budget
1998–99	23,616,900,000	500,000,000	2.11% (App)[a]
1999–20	24,491,700,000	591,300,000	2.41% (App)
2000–01	25,740,000,000	1,000,000,000	3.88% (App)
2001–02	27,471,200,000	1,200,000,000	4.36% (App)
2002–03	NA	1,500,000,000	NA
2003–04	29,219,500,000	1,500,000,000	5.13% (App)
2013–14	373,300 billion	10 billion	3.73% (App)[b]

Source AYUSH, 2003:225 and Ministry of Health and Family Welfare, Government of India webpage (http://mohfw.nic.in/reports/Performance%20Bud0506.pdf)

[a]The % calculation is made by the author with using simple calculator

[b]Retrieved from http://health.india.com/news/union-budget-2013-14-health-gets-rs-37330-crore/ Accessed on November 2013

[22]Kumar Anand (2013), India has just one doctor for every 1700 people, The New Indian Express, September 22. Retrived from the following link: http://www.newindianexpress.com/magazine/India-has-just-one-doctor-for-every-1700-people/2013/09/22/article1792010.ece Accessed on June 30, 2015.

Table 3.6 A comparison between Western medicine and AYUSH on medical education and health care facilities in India

Area of comparison	Total	Western medicine	AYUSH or Indian systems of medicine
Number of college/ University		355[a] (MCI, 2011–12:11)	510 in 2011 (AYUSH, 2011:2)
	Private sector	194 (MCI, 2011–12:11)	NA
	Government sector	161 (MCI, 2011–12:11)	NA
Number of admission facility available for undergraduate and postgraduate study	Undergraduate study	44,050 in 2011–12[b]	26,790 in 2010–11 (AYUSH, 2011:26)
	Postgraduate study	22,850 in 2011–12[b]	2384 in 2010–11 (AYUSH, 2011:26)
Health care facilities	Number of total medical and health institutions including general hospitals, township health centers, community health service centers, clinics, village clinics, epidemic disease prevention centers, and health monitoring institutions	48,366 sub-centers, 24,049 PHCs and 4833 CHCs (According to health statistics 2012)[c]	3277 hospitals, 24,289 dispensaries, 2942 CHCs, and 9559 PHCs in 2010 (AYUSH, 2011:1–2, 26)
	Number of beds available in hospitals/clinics medicine hospitals	NA	62,649 in 2010 (AYUSH, 2011:26)
Health service delivery	Number of registered doctors/practitioners	8,53,195 in 2012[d]	785,185 in 2010 (AYUSH, 2011:2)
	Doctor/patient ration	1:1800 (Deo, 2013:632)[e]	
	Number of Drug Manufacturing units for Ayurveda	NA	8898 in 2010 (AYUSH 2011: 2)

[a]Medical Council of India (2011–12). *Annual Report (Amended) 2011–12*. New Delhi: Medical Council of India. Retrieved from http://www.mciindia.org/pdf/Annual%20Report.pdf Accessed on November 2013

[b]Medical Council of India (2011–12). *Annual Report (Amended) 2011–12, p. 2*. New Delhi: Medical Council of India. Retrieved from http://www.mciindia.org/pdf/Annual%20Report.pdf Accessed on November 2013

[c]Kumar Anand (2013), India has just one doctor for every 1700 people, The New Indian Express, September 22. Retrived from the following link: http://www.newindianexpress.com/magazine/India-has-just-one-doctor-for-every-1700-people/2013/09/22/article1792010.ece Accessed on June 30, 2015

[d]Medical Council of India (2011–12). *Annual Report (Amended) 2011–12, p. 6*. New Delhi: Medical Council of India. Retrieved from http://www.mciindia.org/pdf/Annual%20Report.pdf Accessed on November 2013

[e]Deo, Madhav G. (2013) "Doctor population ratio in India: The reality". *Indian Journal of Medical Research*, 137, April 2013, pp. 632–635. New Delhi: Indian Council of Medical Research

While the students were dissatisfied with the slow rate of change, the practitioners found the professionalization of ayurveda to their advantage. Of those surveyed, 70% of the physicians realized that their status had been upgraded after taking part in the formal training program as a result of the modernization and professionalization of ayurveda, and there has been an increase in their interest in studying ayurveda. The status of the ayurvedic physicians and practitioners has risen considerably in recent years.

3.6 Reviving Indigenous Medicine and Replicating Western Hegemony

One of the strongest arguments for professionalizing Chinese medicine according to Western line was to recover "national sovereignty" (Andrews 2014: 3). While after the 1911 revolution many players in the newly formed nationalist government in Republican era wanted to legislate Chinese medicine banned on the grounds that it was superstitious, unscientific, and unhygienic which can potentially cause a threat to the health of the nation-they encountered so much opposition that the nationalists ended up capitulating and eventually supported the foundation of the Institute of National Medicine in 1931 (Ibid: 4). The Mao era further fueled the nationalistic development of Chinese medicine inspired by the nationalist cultural sentiment where medicine was mixed up with nationalist cultural politics. By 1980s, the Ministry of Health in China already adopted 'three paths' of medical practice in China: Western medicine, Integrated medicine, and Chinese medicine (Ibid: 5). The nationalist sentiment still exists among contemporary Chinese medicine students and practitioners although problematically. Western medical science became integral part to form a modern state and increasingly being utilized in the regulation and standardization of Chinese medicine. This trend continued during the post-reform era and Western medical science has been used to define the boundaries of Chinese medicine in contemporary China (Chen 2005: 107). Those surveyed 82% of the students perceived Chinese medicine as part of Chinese national culture apart from medical practice and only 8% considered Chinese medicine as a completely medical system. At the same time 95% of the practitioners those surveyed noted that Chinese medicine is directly linked to the Chinese national culture, language, geography and philosophy. This trend has formed a development paradox in the practice of Chinese medicine. There is enormous effort to integrate Chinese medicine with Western modalities and majority of the students and practitioners are in favor of this trend. Simultaneously, they perceive Chinese medicine as part of national cultural treasure and pride.

There is another paradoxical claim brought by the practitioners and students those surveyed about the impact of Western medicine on contemporary Chinese medicine practice. When asked whether Chinese medicne will grdaually dilute and replaced by the Western medicine because of the adoption of integrated education and practice, 85% practitioners and 76% students consistently claim that this will never happen. Chinese medicine has disadvantages which needs to be scrutinize and modernize through following Western medicine path. At the same time there are wellknown advantages of Chinese medicine which kept it survived over the milleniums, they added. Only 15% practitioners and 12% students perceived that the dilution of Chinese medicine is already on the way because of the the new experimental and integrated education and practice. Remaining 8% students were not sure about the future of Chinese medicine and 4% did not give any answer. I have quoted the following two different opinions given by two practitioners about the impact of Western medicine on contemporary Chinese medicine:

Chinese medicine will neither replace nor dilute because of integrated curriculum. This is an old question which came forward before the 1949 revolution. Chinese medicine was almost abolished by the nationalist government after the 1911 revolution and formation of the Republic of China. The debate continued during post Mao revolution era. It has been more than half a century of integrated education and practice going on but Chinese medicine still being survived. Chinese medicine will never be replaced by Western medicine. More and more people are willing to practice Chinese medicine is recent time and all most all big cities have Chinese medicine school. Also, Chinese medicine has its' own specific advantages specially treating chronic disease such as liver disease, tumor, rheumatoid, etc. *Western medicine is unable to curethese diseases. Some companies are bringing new patent drugs in the market which is a new invention in Chinese medicine. Other companies also follow classical formula or preparing drugs. However, there are also many patent drugs manufactured by the thought of pharmaceutical factories where some elements of Western medicine is added such as Niu Huang Jie du pian.*[23]

Our current society has taken Western medicine more seriously. General people sometimes cannot understand Chinese medicine theories because many of the terminologies are written in classical Chinese with ancient form. That forces me using Western theories to provide any explanation to patient and public. That's why I need some knowledge on Western medicine. Also, some patients come to us after having failed to get curefrom Western medicine. They would talk about how Western medicine practitioner diagnosed them. So we have to know some Western medicine knowledge. I think we need a book containing all the Chinese medicine knowledge for the practitioners. This book should be used as reference during the practice, which is different from the textbook. Because for us, we feel that we just recite the knowledge in the textbook and we don't know the exact meaning of them. After a longtime's reciting, we may understand them gradually. The teachers in the college are not really qualified Chinese medicine doctors because some of them even don't have any clinical experience. They just teach the knowledge from the textbook. As you can see some of the folk clinics, which have the old famous Chinese medicine masters are very popular in the public simple because they have

[23]Name of the practitioners has not disclosed because of the privacy policy.

their own typical and effective formula and experience. Like our hospital, all diseases have their systematic routines. We have to follow these Chinese medicine routines to cure different diseases. It is hard to say whether Chinese medicine will replace by the Western medicine in future. Firstly, there is some limitation of integrated education and practice. Second, the new knowledge taking in by us is also limited. After work, the knowledge you use will be in a particular area. Thus what you do in work is becoming more and more different than what you study. I think apprentice system is very important because the old master can teach you the Chinese medicine knowledge in a specific area that depends on what you want to learn, such as acupuncture. Some knowledge cannot be taught just by the textbook. It needs to be taught by practice of old master. The knowledge in the textbook is just the general idea. If you want to understand it deeply, learning from the old master will be better. Each time you read the classical Chinese medicine books, you will have a new and different understanding. If you learn Chinese medicine from some old masters such as learning their typical formula, you can learn some experience form them and then put them into practice in your later clinical practice. For Chinese medicine, I think it's more about experience.[24]

In India, nationalism was born during the colonial rule and became a part of anti-colonial resistance. British imperial authority, in order to justify its legitimacy, applied two techniques, which were fairly common in the colonized countries. First was the incorporation of the indigenous economic system into the global network of capitalism through the restructuring of the production and exchange sectors; second, introduction of the procedures of law and administration and institutionalization of the "rational bureaucratic norms" developed in Europe during the enlightenment period (Chatterjee 1994: 81–82). Gradually, those institutional norms were shared by increasingly large sections of the urban middle class and became a hegemonic project of the colonial state, in which Western education was used as chief instrument (Ibid: 83). The professionalization of ayurvedic medicine in India during the British colonial rule was a hegemonic project first lounged through introducing integrated medical curriculum by the colonial state. This was gradually accepted by the Indian middle class and in fact many traditional ayurvedic families sent their children to study integrated medicine and learn Western treatment method and modality.

The debate on whether colonialism was an asset or liability towards the ayurvedic medical system of India continues today. Professional ayurvedic groups are still divided over the impact of colonial rule on ayurveda. 40% of the ayurvedic practitioners surveyed in this study considered that British colonization had played a negative role on ayurveda, as the health administration subjugated ayurveda and imposed Western medicine; while 20% considered the British rule as having played a positive role for ayurveda (Islam 2008: 91). There are various explanations given by present day practitioners concerning the negative impact of British colonization on ayurveda. Firstly, the British administration promoted the Western medical

[24]Name of the practitioner has not been used because of the privacy policy.

system. Indigenous practitioners felt discriminated against and undervalued because their skills were not regarded as of equal status to those of Western trained physicians. Furthermore, many of the ayurvedic physicians did not speak English, which had become the language of the elite. In this sense, they were seen as less modern than their English-speaking counterparts. Thirdly, the colonial administration which established ayurvedic colleges adopted an integrated education curriculum, combining ayurvedic and allopathic training, thereby diluting the ayurvedic contents. Finally, colonial rule promoted the use of the English language, resulting in decline in the use of Sanskrit, which was essential for ayurvedic texts that were written in Sanskrit (Ibid).

After decolonization, India became independent and emerged as a nation state in 1947. Efforts were made to revive ayurveda with state backing which included adopting policies and changing strategies to provide better health care services and integrating ayurvedic practitioners into mainstream health (Ibid: 94). Since the 1970s, the Indian state has attempted to revive ayurvedic medicine, with both the central and state governments taking positive initiatives in recent decades. Different offices and directories have been established, and redistribution and restructuring of the ayurvedic practitioners within the ministry have occurred. The Indian Medical Council Act was adopted and introduced ayurvedic medical education.

In 1970s, the Indian government established primary health centres and under this scheme the Western, ayurvedic and homoeopathic practitioner work under the same hospital structure. In the state of West Bengal each primary health care centre has two Western practitioners, one homoeopath, and one ayurvedic practitioner. However, many physicians those interviewed were careful about integration for a variety of reasons. They emphasised the practical difficulties of integration because of diverse and different principles and modes of operation in different medical systems. And another difficulty of integration is methodological incompatibility. Different systems imply different methods during diagnosis, albeit with the common objective of curing the patients. The mode of actions involving drugs and the procedures to understand physiological facts in various systems are different. There is also the fear that given the popularity of the Western medical system, an integrated medical curriculum will lead to students' opportunity to study Western medicine to the detriment of ayurvedic medicine (Islam 2008: 100–104).

Any endeavour to write about and examine the ayurvedic practices in contemporary India is impossible without discussing the British colonial intervention. The coming of the British to India marked the entry of the Western medical system in the subcontinent and the beginning of the subjugation of existing indigenous medical systems. It has been claimed that the British medical policy in India was clearly subservient to the imperial rule. However, the post-colonial state has supported a revival of ayurveda although problematically. If the revival of ayurveda by the post-colonial Indian state is a nationalist project 60% of the ayurvedic practitioners those surveyed noted that the post-colonial government did not give much attention to the development of ayurveda in the immediate years after independence. The professionalization of ayurveda in modern India, however, is under threat through a process of modernization in the hands of India's emerging elites. The revival of indigenous medicine, ayurveda in particular, in the post-colonial state has become an issue of professional and group interest. In modern India, the majority of ayurvedic practitioners perceive the role of British colonial rule negatively, despite the fact that they follow Western method and framework to revive ayurveda.

3.7 Conclusion

Chinese medicine, ayurveda and Western medicine have own theories, methods and history which cannot be readily integrated. The theories of *dao* (the universe), *qi* (vital energy), *yin-yang* (two complementary phase of the *dao*), and five phases (wood, fire, earth, metal and water) from Chinese medicine do not fit with the theory of microorganism in Western medicine. Similarly the theories of three bodily humors *vata-pitta-kapha* (air/wind-bile-phlegm) from ayurveda do not easily fit with the theories of Western medicine. Any attempts to integrate these theories with the modalities of Western medicine can only cause the loss of epistemological authority for Chinese medicine and ayurveda over Western medicine. Since Western medicine readily suit with modern lifestyle which gives it advantages, young graduates of Chinese medicine and ayurveda will be very reluctant to follow the theories of their own system of medicine.

Professionalization of Chinese medicine and ayurveda according to the Western line caused the decline of traditional apprenticeship and family education. Today the training and research of Chinese medicine and ayurveda have moved out of the traditional apprenticeship system and into the formal education system. More specifically, students are able to study Chinese medicine and ayurveda from a tertiary institution and are awarded formal degree qualifications for their training. This formalization and professionalization has led to a revival of interest at various points. There has been a popularization of interest in obtaining Chinese medicine and ayurvedic qualification by college-going students. At the same time, the professionalization of Chinese medicine and ayurveda and the formal training program have created an avenue for graduates to do back-door Western medicine practice because of nature of their education curriculum. Most students come to study Chinese medicine or ayurveda after having failed to enrol in colleges of Western medicine. The major trend of education and practice in Chinese medicine and ayurveda today is the integrated medicine which combines Chinese medicine and ayurveda with Western treatment modalities. As the statistics has revealed that students and graduates from Chinese medicine and ayurvedic colleges are eager to learn Western medicine and use Western diagnosis and treatment methods apart from prescribing Western drugs. However, this trend has raises serious concern about authenticity. This would not be surprising if Chinese medicine and ayurveda only exist as a brand name to sell Western medicine practice and products if this integrated education and practice continued.

Chapter 4
Commodification and Commercialization

4.1 Introduction

Commodification of indigenous medicine across Asia through a process of commercialization is not new. Burmese Chinese herbalist Aw Chu Kin whose father was a herbalist in Xiamen city of modern China developed Tiger Balm-a secret herbal formulation commonly used as tropical cream to treat inflammation and muscle aches in 1870s in Rangoon, Burma.[1] By 1920s Tiger Balm became a well established brand of Chinese herbal medicine and marketed commercially all over South and Southeast Asia including British India, Singapore, Malaysia, etc. Founded in 1669, Beijing Tongrentang is another prime example of commercializing Chinese medicine across China and beyond. Since its inception during the reign of emperor Yongzheng in Qing Dynasty, Tongrentang has supplied Chinese medicines not only to Chinese imperials family but also peoples around the globe.[2] In India the commodification of ayurvedic drugs and health products started when the large ayurvedic drug manufacturers started to link commercially-prepared ayurveda to, and as a symbol of, Indian civilization, with a revivalist inspiration (Nichter and Nichter 1996: 292). With this process, drug manufactures have promoted traditional ayurvedic drugs with a modern sophisticated outlook. The establishment of Dabur India Limited, popularly known as Dabur in 1884 by Dr. S.K. Burman in Kolkata and the establishment of Shree Baidyanath Ayurved Bhawan (p) Ltd. in Kolkata, popularly known as Baidyanath in 1917[3] are the frontrunner of commercially viable produce of ayurveda in India. Both of these ayurvedic companies were founded when India was under the British colonial rule and at the time when nationalist movement for independence was in height.

---

[1]Retrieved from the https://en.wikipedia.org/wiki/Tiger_Balm and accessed on October 26, 2015.
[2]Retrieved from http://www.lookchem.com/Company/120/ and accessed on January 26, 2015.
[3]Retrieved from the http://www.baidyanath.com/about_baidyanath.php and accessed on October 26, 2015.

M.N. Islam, *Chinese and Indian Medicine Today*,
DOI 10.1007/978-981-10-3962-1_4

In recent years, there have been intense debates on whether Chinese herbal medicine and ayurveda related products should be regarded as a medicine or a commodity for public consumption. This chapter explores how indigenous medicine in China and India, Chinese herbal medicine and ayurveda in particular, have shifted from a home-based medicine and or small scale manufactured health product to become a health commodity for domestic and global consumption. Not only patients but also the mass people who may not have any symptom of disease or illness become the ready consumers. The chapter also explores how large pharmaceutical companies have appreciated both the Chinese herbal medicine and ayurveda and have commodified them for profit maximization. In this process of commodification, these drug manufacturers redefine the nature of Chinese herbal medicine and ayurveda and the production process because of commercial interest. At the same time, this chapter also explores how these drug manufacturers are creating new brand under the banner of indigenous medicine and targeting new consumers. Final part of this chapter examines the perception of indigenous medical practitioners and consumers about this commodification process. Beijing Tong Ren Tang from China and Dabur India Limited from India are used as case study.

4.2 Indigenous Medicine as a Health Commodity in China and India

Since China adopted an open door policy in late 1970s there is a significant rise of pharmaceutical companies manufacturing Chinese herbal medicine with creating new patens and brands. Some Western medicine companies in China also opened unit preparing Chinese herbal drugs, health products and patent medicine. Indigenous pharmaceutical companies also went through a process of modernization and innovation and cater various new products including drugs, health products, diet supplements, beauty products, and cosmetic. The major herbal medicine China exports are: Angelica, Rehmannia, Coptis, Scutellaria baicalensis, Astragalus, Atractylodes, Chuanxiong, white peony root, Codonopsis, pseudo-ginseng, Campanulaceae, Poria, rhubarb, Radix, Bupleurum, Licorice, Angelica, and wolfberry. China also imports some of the herbal medicines from International market, mostly from South East Asian countries and those includes—Millettia, Dinggong vine, Homalomena, Semen sterculiae lychnophorae, Radices sophorae subprostratae, Small ring grass, Yellow vine, Tsaoko amomum fruit, and Gynostemma. In the year 2009, Chinese exports of Chinese medicine were $2.03 billion (Xuefeng 2012).[4]

[4]Retrieved from the following link http://english.jl.gov.cn/Investment/Opportunities/Industry/MedicineandBiotechnology/201208/t20120810_1256011.html and accessed on February 16, 2016.

One of the noteworthy features of modernizing indigenous herbal drugs in post-Mao China is the entry of consumerism and ignores classical formulas. Traditionally, Chinese herbal drugs are prepared by the practitioner with the help of own pharmacist which follows the formula invented by the practitioner or written in the classical texts. For example, *Bencao Gangmu* comprises 52 volumes and describing 1892 drugs where 1094 floral drugs, 444 fauna drugs, and 354 mineral drugs (Li 2012: 33–34). Under this traditional practice individual patient is given individual drug and the formula could vary from patient to patient even though they experience similar symptom. However, modern drug manufacturers are reluctant to follow traditional procedure and manufacturing generic drugs or health products rather than individualistic drugs.

4.2.1 Beijing Tong Ren Tang: An Oldest and Largest Chinese Herbal Drug Manufacturer

Founded in 1669, and with a history of nearly 350 years, Beijing Tong Ren Tang is one of the largest Chinese herbal drug manufacturers in China. According to the English Webpage of the company it promotes traditional Chinese culture through preserving one essence: "Serving the people and cultivating benevolence" and two commandments: "no manpower shall be spared, no matter how complicated the procedures of pharmaceutical production are; and no material shall be reduced, no matter how much the cost is" and "We do things with our sincerity and trustworthiness even without supervision from others, because God sees".[5] The company has become one of the top ranked foreign exchange earners in China since the beginning of 21st century. Tong Ren Tang has supplied health care service and medicine to the imperial families since the first year of the reign of Emperor Yongzheng in Qing Dynasty, and served eight emperors over 188 years timeframe. Today, the company has established more than 10 joint ventures, solely invested companies and 20 pharmacies in China and the world including Hong Kong, UK, Australia, Thailand, Malaysia, Indonesia, Canada, Macao, United States and Republic of Korea. Tong Ren Tang produces more than 800 products of 24 types of formulation and owns two listed companies and more than 500 drug stores at home and abroad. Its products are being sold in more than 40 countries and regions[6] and recognized by various agencies. Beijing Tong Ren Tang has been recommended as one of 16 Chinese enterprises with the strength to become world famous brands by China Federation of Industrial Economics and China Top Brand Strategy Promotion Committee. It has been awarded the "famous time-honored brand" by

[5]Retrieved from the following link http://www.tongrentang.com/en/abouttrt/culture.php and accessed on January 10, 2015.

[6]Beijing Tong Ren Tang English Webpage, Retrieved from http://www.lookchem.com/Company/120/ and accessed on January 26, 2015.

Fig. 4.1 Entrance of a Beijing Tong Ren Tang outlet. *Source* Photos were retrieved from the following links and accessed on March 23, 2016: http://www.tongrentang.com/en/, https://www.google.ca/search?q=Beijing+Tong+Ren+Tang&biw=1280&bih=687&source=lnms&tbm=isch&sa=X&ved=0ahUKEwi7ybXM5NfLAhUBX5QKHePTAj0Q_AUIBygC

the Ministry of Commerce, and has been awarded the honorable titles of "2005 CCTV—My Favorite Chinese Brand," "China Top Ten Brands with Strongest Influence Power of 2004," "Ten Brands Influencing the Daily Life of People in Beijing" and "China Famous Export Brand." In 2006, Beijing Tong Ren Tang Traditional Chinese Medicine culture was listed in the National Intangible Cultural Heritage Directory.[7] Until now, Beijing Tong Ren Tang has established three business sectors under the overall framework of the group: modern pharmacy, retail business and medical services. It has also established 10 companies, 2 bases, 2 institutes and 2 centers, out of which there are 2 listed domestic and overseas companies, over 800 retail stores at home and 28 overseas joint ventures (stores) over 15 countries and regions (Figs. 4.1 and 4.2).[8]

In India there has been a significant rise in the number of ayurvedic or herbal companies over the last decades manufacturing and marketing both classical ayurvedic medicine and patent ayurvedic medicine, or health products for mass consumption. Medical representatives of large ayurvedic companies have engaged in aggressive marketing campaigning, just as medical representatives from Western drug companies have (Islam 2010: 781). In many instances medical representatives of ayurvedic drug manufacturers offer attractive benefits to ayurvedic and Western medical practitioners if they prescribe drugs from their companies (Nichter and Nichter 1996: 292–93), visiting Western physicians door to door with comprehensive 'package incentives' and insisting they prescribe their drugs or health products. Large producers of indigenous medicines in India "offer financial incentives to encourage retailers and chemists to raise the sales of their products".

---

[7]Retrieved from the http://www.tongrentang.com/en/abouttrt/profile.php and accessed on January 26, 2015.

[8]Retrieved from the http://www.tongrentang.com/en/abouttrt/profile.php and accessed on January 26, 2015.

Fig. 4.2 Beijing Tong Ren Tang logo. *Source* Photos were retrieved from the following links and accessed on March 23, 2016: http://www.tongrentang.com/en/, https://www.google.ca/search?q=Beijing+Tong+Ren+Tang&biw=1280&bih=687&source=lnms&tbm=isch&sa=X&ved=0ahUKEwi7ybXM5NfLAhUBX5QKHePTAj0Q_AUIBygC

About 80–90% of ayurvedic and unani pharmaceutical products, such as patent medicines, health products, beauty products, food additives, etc., are sold directly to consumers by retailers such as ayurvedic and unani shops, chemists, small grocers, medical representatives, supermarkets and beauty parlours (Bode 2001: 185–186). There is no clear regulation governing the sale of ayurvedic health products in India until now.

4.2.2 Dabur India Ltd: One of the Largest Ayurvedic Drug/Health Product Manufacturers

Established in the year 1884 by Dr. S.K. Burman in Kolkata as a small pharmacy to produce and distribute ayurvedic medicine, "Dabur Indian Limited is the fourth largest FMCG Company in India" today, with INR 2233.72 crore (US $546.12 million) in yearly turnover. It has adopted mottos such as "Being dedicated to health and well-being of every household" and "Health is Wealth" (Dabur India Limited 2015: i–iii). Dr. Burman founded Dabur in Bengal when Bengal was a single province of British India. His intention was focused on providing affordable and effective treatment for the masses at a minimal cost, as cures for various epidemic diseases of the time such as cholera, malaria, plague, etc. Because of the growing popularity and enormous success of his company in the ayurvedic field Dr. Burman expanded the commercial uses of Dabur by establishing a manufacturing plant for large scale production. In 1936, Dabur became a full-fledged company and renamed it 'Dabur India (Dr. S.K. Burman) Pvt. Limited. Later it was shifted from Kolkata to Delhi, in 1972. Dabur became a public limited company in 1986 and was renamed Dabur India Limited. It made its first public share issue in 1994 (Dabur India web page). A significant number of members of the company's board

Fig. 4.3 Dabur India logo. *Source* Photos were retrieved from the following links and accessed on March 23, 2016. https://www.google.ca/search?q=dabur+india+limited&biw=1280&bih=687&source=lnms&tbm=isch&sa=X&sqi=2&ved=0ahUKEwjs0rf36dfLAhUI6GMKHf76DHsQ_AUICCgD&dpr=1#imgrc=wH2Xeq4H-I0AjM%3A

Fig. 4.4 Dabur India products. *Source* Photos were retrieved from the following links and accessed on March 23, 2016. https://www.google.ca/search?q=dabur+india+limited&biw=1280&bih=687&source=lnms&tbm=isch&sa=X&sqi=2&ved=0ahUKEwjs0rf36dfLAhUI6GMKHf76DHsQ_AUICCgD&dpr=1#imgrc=wH2Xeq4H-I0AjM%3A

of directors, including the Chairman and Vice-Chairman, came from the Burman family, although they handed over the management to professionals in 1998 and hired a CEO (Dabur India web page) (Figs. 4.3 and 4.4).

Today, the Dabur group has 8 manufacturing plants producing a range of 450 products. The range of Dabur ayurvedic medicine and health products includes "health and beauty care products, foods and food additives, toiletries, bulk drugs, pharmaceuticals, diet supplements, natural gums, and animal health products" with some popular brand, such as Dabur Amla, Dabur Vatika, Dabur Chyawanprash, etc. (Dabur Therapeutic Index 2004: ii). In 2004 the company had, nation-wide, over 5000 distributors covering both urban and rural India. Dabur products for health care, skin care, oral care, hair care, foods, etc., are also being exported overseas and are available in more than 50 countries, particularly in the Middle East, South-East Asia, Africa, the European Union and America. Apart from its various products, Dabur also produces classical (*Shastriya*) ayurvedic preparations and the number of such medicine is more than 350 (Dabur Therapeutic Index 2004: ii).

4.3 Post Open Door Development

China has adopted open door policy in 1978 whereas India took same initiative 13 years later in 1991. India is the world's second most populated country followed by China. Around 2020 India is likely to surpass China to become the planet's most populous country (Bose 2013: 1–2). At this moment China is the world second largest economy whereas India stands third. The adoption of open-door policy has significant impacts on the rapid economic development of both the countries. China and India are experiencing an intense process of globalization and integrated to the global economy. With the rise of globalization the countries have produce an emerging middle class who are ready consumer for new products and services. In order to cater the need of this middle class large pharmaceutical companies in both the countries brought new products under the banner of indigenous medicine. This trend has several noteworthy features in the process of manufacturing and marketing indigenous medicines and health products such as: creating new brand, rise of new products, rise of subsidiary companies, mass marketing and entering global market, and advertising in the mass media.

4.3.1 Creating New Brands

Through taking the advantage of globalization and open door policy large pharmaceutical corporations in China and India have intensified their production, marketing and sale of indigenous medicine, health products and services. In the last few decades, local large Chinese herbal medicine manufacturers such as Beijing Tong Ren Tang or ayurvedic pharmaceutical companies such as Dabur India Ltd. have started producing various health products together with drugs for all kinds for mainstream diseases and illnesses through creating their own brand. In addition, they have also produced health supplements, beauty products, toiletries and cosmetics. Beijing Tong Ren Tang has the largest local and overseas market share of the Chinese herbal medicine market so as to Dabur India limited for ayurveda.

Beijing Tong Ren Tang produces 5 types of products with 22 types of formulas. The product categories are: medicines, health care foods, foods, cosmetics, and prepared slices of Chinese herbs. The formulas manufactured by this company are: big honeyed pills, small honeyed pills, water-honeyed pills, medicinal wines, tablets, mixture, troches, capsules, granules, glues, soft capsules, syrups, watered pills, plasters, aerosol, smeared films, pasted pills, liniment, tincture powders, concentrated pills, dripping pills, and concentrated decoctions.[9] Beijing Tong Ren Tang has established 25 production bases all over China and it has 70 production lines with the capacity of production of 24 forms of drugs and more than 1000 types

[9]Retrieved from the following link http://www.tongrentang.com/en/medicines/psearch.php and accessed on February 22, 2014.

of products.[10] By the end of 2008 Beijing Tong Ren Tang already had 894 business terminals including 32 overseas terminals in 16 countries, 295 domestic large pharmacies, 571 shops in 30 provinces, cities, autonomous regions and 75 districts.[11] Beijing Tong Ren Tang's famous new products includes Angunguhwanghwan, Tongren Niuhuang Qingxin Wan, Tongren Da Huoluo Wan, Tongren Wuji Baifeng Wan, Zixue, Guogong Jiu, Zhuanggu Yao Jiu, Yufeng Ningxin Pian, Jufang Zhibao Wan and Zaizhao Wan. These products are called as the "Top Ten Trumps" for Beijing Tong Ren Tang. There are also top ten famous medicine list manufactured by Beijing Tong Ren Tang and posted in their English webpage. These are: Niu Huang Jie Du Pian, Xiao Xuan Zai Zao Wan, Sai Long Feng Shi Jiu, Gan Mao Qing Re Ke Li, Jing Zhi Ke Sou Tan Quan Wan, Gou Pi Gao, Er Tong Qing Fei Kou Fu Ye, An Shen Jian Nao Ye, Pian Tan Fu Yuan Wan, Gu Ci Xiao Tong Ye.[12]

Similarly, Dabur India Limited no longer been just an ayurvedic drug manufacturers but is a leading Indian consumer goods company manufacturing hair care, oral care, health care, skin care, home care, personal care, consumer health-ethical, Guar Gum and foods. The company has invented and developed several popular brands of consumer products over the decades including Dabur Amla hair oil, Vatika hair care, Vatika professional, Dermoviva USA skin care, FEM, FEM professional, Dabur herbal tooth paste, Dabur Miswak, Dabur Chyawanprash, Hajmola, Real, Dabur honey, and Dabur Gulabari premium Gulab Jal (Figs. 4.5 and 4.6).[13]

According to Dabur India Limited Annual Report 2014–15 the market capitalization of Dabur has reached to INR 46,653 Crore in 2014–15 financial year and profit after tax amounted INR 1066 Crore. The sales volume at the same financial year accounted INR 7806 Crore nearly double than in the financial year 2010–2011 (Dabur India Limited 2015: 2–3). Table 4.1 shows the trend of increase market capitalization, sales volume and profit after tax for the last five financial years for Dabur India Limited.

Today Dabur India Limited claims itself as the world's largest ayurveda and natural products marker with a portfolio of over 381 trusted products spread across 21 categories (Dabur India Limited 2015: 7). Three of Dabur's famous brands-Vatika, Amla, and Real have crossed the INR 1000 Crore sales mark globally by 2015 (Dabur India Limited 2015: 13). Table 4.1 also shows the steady growth of Dabur India Limited in the area of sales volume and profit increase. Apart from beauty and consumer cares the company also produces 35 categories of ayurvedic

[10]Retrieved from the following link http://www.tongrentang.com/en/fellowsub/production.php and accessed on January 26, 2015.

[11]Retrieved from the following link http://www.tongrentang.com/en/fellowsub/business.php and accessed on February 25, 2014.

[12]Retrieved from the following link http://www.tongrentang.com/en/medicines/medicines.php and accessed on January 6, 2016.

[13]Retrieved from the http://www.daburinternational.com/index.php/en/front/home and accessed on January 5, 2016.

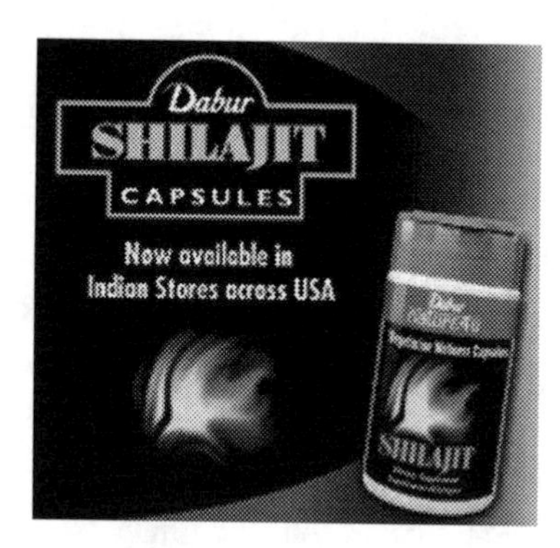

Fig. 4.5 A Dabur India Limited manufactured impotence product. *Source* Retrieved from the following links and accessed on March 24, 2016: https://www.google.ca/search?q=dabur+shilajit&biw=1280&bih=687&source=lnms&tbm=isch&sa=X&ved=0ahUKEwitv-exp9nLAhUC42MKHTpqDygQ_AUIBigB#imgrc=UOSuTepscIVlQM%3A

Fig. 4.6 A Dabur India Limited manufactured health product. *Source* Retrieved from the following links and accessed on March 24, 2016: https://www.google.ca/search?q=dabur+shilajit&biw=1280&bih=687&source=lnms&tbm=isch&sa=X&ved=0ahUKEwitv-exp9nLAhUC42MKHTpqDygQ_AUIBigB#tbm=isch&q=dabur+stress+com

Table 4.1 Financial highlights of Dabur India Limited

Financial highlights	2011 (FY) INR Crore	2012 (FY) INR Crore	2013 (FY) INR Crore	2014 (FY) INR Crore	2015 (FY) INR Crore
Market capitalization	16,722	18,536	23,887	31,310	46,653
Sales volume	4077	5283	6146	7073	7806
Profit after tax	569	645	763	914	1066

Dabur India Limited (2015: 2–3)
Source This table is prepared by the author from the data presented in Dabur India Limited Annual Report 2014–15 under the column of financial highlights

medicines for illnesses that range from specialized drugs for diabetes and high blood pressure to non-prescription drugs for common colds, flues, headaches, etc. (Dabur Therapeutic Index 2004).

4.3.2 Diversification of Business and Rise of Subsidiary Group Companies

Diversification of business under the core company name is another key features developed over the decades by indigenous drug manufacturers in China and India. This is a trend brought by globalization where profit maximization and increase the portfolio is the main objective. Beijing Tong Ren Tang own seven sister companies under the brand name Beijing Tong Ren Tang including: Beijing Tongrentang Co. Ltd., Beijing Tongrentang Technologies Co. Ltd., Beijing Tongrentang Health-Pharmaceutical Co. Ltd., Beijing Tongrentang Chinese Medicine Co. Ltd., Beijing Tongrentang Medicinal Herb Co. Ltd., Beijing Tongrentang Pharmaceutical Co. Ltd., and Beijing Tongrentang Biological Co. Ltd.[14] Beijing Tong Ren Tang also established more than 10 joint ventures, solely invested companies and 20 pharmacies. Some of these companies are listed under Hong Kong stock market. For example, Beijing Tong Ren Tang Technologies Company Limited, a Hong Kong stock market listed company with an annual revenue of RMB 2,910,749,000 in 2013 and profit after tax is 503,163,000 in the same year. Table 4.2 shows the financial highlights of the Beijing Tong Ren Tang Technologies Company Limited for the last five years.

Table 4.2 also illustrated a steady growth of the company during the last five consecutive years in all the areas including revenue, profit after tax and total assets.

Table 4.2 Financial highlights of the Beijing Tong Ren Tang Technologies Company Limited (year ended 31 December)

Category	2013 RMB'000	2012 RMB'000	2011 RMB'000	2010 RMB'000	2009 RMB'000
Annual revenue	2,910,749	2,439,002	1,899,551	1,578,914	1,352,202
Annual profit after tax	503,163	399,548	281,494	224,726	190,119
Total assets	5,148,192	3,179,671	2,829,373	2,179,082	1,930,967

Source Financial highlights, Beijing Tong Ren Tang Technologies Company Limited, a summary of the consolidated results of the company and its subsidiaries for each of five years, 2014 (The above table was prepared by the author from the data the company posted in her webpage. Retrieved from the following link http://www.tongrentangkj.com/en/investor_info.aspx?id=45 and accessed on January 16, 2016.)

[14]Retrieved from the following link http://www.tongrentang.com/en/fellowsub/business.php and accessed on January 26, 2015.

Dabur India Limited in recent years also has set up subsidiary group companies across the world, including Dabur Foods, Dabur Nepal, Dabur Egypt, Dabur Oncology, Dabur Pharma, Dabur UK, Hobi-a Dabur Enterprise, NewU, SUNDESH, Dabur North America, Dabur International, etc. The company has set up three strategic business units; consumer care business, international business, and others. 66% of the company business has contributed by consumer care whereas 31% by international business and 3% from others. Within the consumer care business unit, hair care business contributed largest part 23% followed by food 19% and health supplements 18%. Within the International business unit there is regional distribution and Middle East generated 32% of their business followed by Africa 23% and Asia 17% (Dabur Annual Report 2014–15: 8). A summary on the business diversification of Dabur India Limited has been presented in Table 4.3.

4.4 Commodifying Indigenous Medicine in China and India: Common Trends

As stated before that the commodification of Chinese herbal medicine and ayurvedic drugs and health products started several decades before. With this process, drug manufactures have promoted traditional Chinese herbal drugs and ayurvedic drugs with a modern sophisticated outlook. They also created new brands, invented patent drugs and many health, beauty and cosmetic products. As a result indigenous medicines have been transformed into modern health products for middle class over the last few decades under the banner of globalization in China and India. Recent features of commodification could be found in two levels: commodification of drugs and health products, and commodification of health services. Commodification of drugs and health products refers the quick development of patent medicine, health supplement, diet supplement, beauty products and toiletries, etc. Commodification of health related services includes the rise of wellness and spa culture, rejuvenation therapies, massages services, cupping, etc. under the brand name Chinese medicine or ayurveda. Three major features could be found under this process of commodifying indigenous medicine: **firstly**, mass marketing; **secondly,** use of mass media; and **finally,** lack of drug standardization and quality control of the health products.

4.4.1 Mass Marketing

According to Chinese Patent Medicine Industry Report, 2012–15 the revenue for Chinese patent medicine industry has been increasing from RMB 142 billion in 2008 to RMB 360 billion in 2012 at a Compound Annual Growth Rate (CAGR) of 26.2%. Over the same period, the total profit maintained a CAGR of 26.6%, and the

Table 4.3 Business diversification of Dabur India Limited

Category									Total (%)
Consumer care unit	Skin care	Oral care	Home care	Hair care	Foods	Health supplements	Digestives	OTC Ethicals	
%	5	14	6	23	19	18	6	9	66
International unit	Africa	Americas	Asia	Europe	Middle East				
%	23	16	17	12	32				31
Others									3
Total									100

Source The table has been prepared by the author from the data published in Dabur India Limited Annual Report 2014–15

gross margin remained higher than the average level of the overall pharmaceutical industry. The report further noted that the twelfth Five-Year Plan on the Development of Traditional Chinese Medicine included various favorable policies and the new National Essential Drugs List published in March 2013 increased the number of Chinese patent medicine from 102 in 2009 to 203 in 2012.[15]

The overall situation in India is not that dissimilar to China. Across India, there are 8898 licensed pharmacies under AYUSH and were producing and manufacturing a wide range of ayurvedic, unani, siddha, and homoeopathy medicine, health products, and supplements (AYUSH 2011: 2). One of the foremost indicators of the rise of ayurvedic demand is the huge sales volume recorded by different companies. New companies are investing in the industry and many new drugs/health products are available in the market. A new consumer class has already been emerged and a large majority of consumers are purchasing and using ayurvedic health products and supplements.

Since Chinese herbal drug and health products and Indian ayurvedic products are aimed at the local and global market, in order to appeal to the consumers, the large pharmaceutical companies have adopted various marketing strategies. To make them appear modern, the drugs, health supplements, beauty and sex products, and diet supplements are packaged in attractive modern styles, with bilingual name or foreign sounding name such as combining Chinese and English name which is called Chinglish or combining English and Hindi or English and Bengali name in India. There are two reasons for the increasing popularity of English names for ayurvedic drugs and health products in India: firstly, "because of a general ascription of 'quality' attached to a new, modern and foreign sounding name"; and secondly, because many MBBS doctors and AYUSH graduates are reluctant to prescribe ayurvedic medicines with Sanskrit names (Nichter and Nichter 1996: 294–5)—probably because of their poor knowledge of, and fluency ing, Sanskrit. Simultaneously, a large number of Western medicine doctors, as well as young ayurvedic practitioners who wish to be seen as modern physicians, are enthusiastic to prescribe ayurvedic patent medicines and health products instead of classical (Shastriya) ayurvedic preparations.

In addition to specialized drugs for chronic diseases and common illnesses the rise of new health, beauty and sex products has further reinforced the commodification of Chinese herbal medicine and ayurvedic medicine. Most of the patent medicines and health products are new creations. It has been widely accepted that fashion is the central linkage among production, merchandising, and consumption in capitalist societies. The capitalist transformation in indigenous medicine industry in China and India under the banner of globalization has enhanced a market sphere with a fashionable presentation of products, and thus health has turned into a commodity. Today large and small Chinese herbal drug manufacturers and

[15]Summary version of this report has been retrieved from the following link http://www.reportlinker.com/p0361703/China-Chinese-Patent-Medicine-Industry-Report-2012–2015.html#utm_source=prnewswire&utm_medium=pr&utm_campaign=Drug_and_Medication and accessed on June 25, 2015.

ayurvedic drug manufacturers produce and market their products to address popular health concerns such as male impotence, women's skin care, mental distress, and physical lassitude (Islam 2010: 783; Nichter and Nichter 1996: 297).

Two categories of ayurvedic products—cosmetics and health supplements—are most popular in India. Within 7 days in September 2004, a total of 205 customers visited Dabur Ayurvedic Medicine Shop. The best-selling products were herbal-based cosmetics and essential oils—health tonics and capsules, male sex stimulus pills and capsules, remedies for common illnesses, remedies for stomach-related problems, headache and other pain remedies; and reproduction and skin disease-related medicines and health products were also purchased by significant numbers of consumers (Islam 2010: 784).[16]

How do the health service providers in both China and India perceive this new commodification strategy? There are similarities among the practitioners of Chinese medicine and ayurveda. Of those 20 Chinese medicine practitioners surveyed, 75% of them are not very optimistic about the current trend of commodification and the development of Chinese medicine health products, health supplement and diet supplement. They are afraid the manufacturers do not follow the Chinese medicine formula and the advertisement of those products over aggregated. This has driven by the market interest and caused a chaotic situation. If Chinese medicine health products still develop according to the current routine, the reputation of Chinese medicine will be ruined since many of these products are ineffective and expensive. The development of Chinese medicine health products should be directed by the traditional Chinese medicine theories. However, no department in contemporary China is doing so. The pharmaceutical companies produce the health products and advertised in television and other social media targeting particular group of consumers. People are confused about the concept of Chinese medicine health products. Many of the practitioners those surveyed do not consider health product or health supplement coming into the market under Chinese medicine banner as Chinese medicine. As one practitioner[17] commented that:

> Health products and health supplements which contain only Chinese medicine herbs are good but many of them are not. The companies claim that they only use Chinese medicine herbs because of commercial interest. The entire situation has been hyped by the insidious entrepreneurs and makes the bad reputation for Chinese medicine. The supervision from the Chinese government is not too strong. Thus, the market of health products is chaotic and people are quite often mislead. If some regulation exists to supervise the process, it will be better. Nowadays, many business are immoral. The government regulation perceives Chinese medicine health products should not have medical effect, however, many supplements available in the market are defined as the drugs and claim medical effect which can cure diseases. Many health supplements in pharmacy claims that they can cure the diabetes, hypertension, etc. Here is the dilemma.

[16]Participant observation was conducted in Dabur Ayurvedic Medicine shop selling ayurvedic medicine and products from 18 September to 24 September, 2004.

[17]Personal information about the practitioner is not disclosed because of the privacy reason.

Another practitioner commented that:

> The market is a wash with health and diet supplements and there are more low quality products than good ones. Most companies produce these products for their economic interest and play upon people's psychology that these supplements can help them keep in good health. In fact, the materials and ingredients of most supplement are false and their effects are overestimated by publicity. The sellers always propagate that their products have magical effect. At this points, I suggest the government should regulate the manufactures. Actually, it is good to develop these health products because they have a market and intended persons, and it is suitable for those with chronic diseases. There is a market niche here. I suggest that the government should regulate and legislate them, set a regulatory framework or drug surveillance system to restrict the abuse of patent drugs, health supplements and health products.

However, there were also 10% practitioners who do not have adequate knowledge about the market and commodification process of Chinese medicine. They never prescribed those health products or diet supplements to their patients. There are also careful comments make by few practitioners. One senior practitioners Dr. Zhang who is in his late 70s and does not mind to disclose his name commented that:

> Nowadays, there are different kind of Chinese medicine health supplements. There are always some advertisements shown in Television every day. However, the development of health supplements is a kind of market demand. With the development of peoples economic conditions, they would like to think about how to get a prolong and healthy life. Since Chinese medicine is more preventive its effect on health is better. From ancient time, food has been used as medicinal recipes and vice versa. Thus, the prospect of Chinese medicine supplements in general is good. There are also many kinds of CM supplement for different target groups such as the elderly, women, children, etc. I do not object the development of health and diet supplements. Although these may have some side-effect, they are not significant. Some health supplement has health benefit if it is properly used. For example, some health supplements in Guangdong province has to cook as soup and it does have health benefit. But the health products available in the market often say that they can make effect quickly and it is dangerous for patients. I think health products are useful if it is used correctly through following the Chinese medicine procedure.

Only a small fraction of the practitioners perceived the development of patent medicine positively. I have quoted the comments of another practitioner about the development of patent drugs by the modern drug manufacturers:

> There are many forms for Chinese medicine such as Gao(cream), Dan(pellet), Wan(bolus), San(powder) and Tangji(decoction). The patent drugs based on traditional formulas or modern formulas are all effective. For example, Liu Wei Di Huang Wan or Yun Nan Bai Yao are all effective since ancient time. These kinds of patent drugs are very good. We always use them. The CM patent drugs are very convenient which can be taken orally without decocting. However, the effectiveness of Tangji(decoction) is better than CM patent drugs. The formulas for Tangji(decoction) are more accurate because they depend on different patients. If the dose of Tangji(decoction) is larger, the effect of absorption will be larger, so that diseases will be cured faster.

The situation in India is slightly different. In present-day India there continue to be a small group of ayurvedic *kabirajes* who prepare their medicines for their patients, although the majority of ayurvedic practitioners now prescribe wholly commercially-produced ayurvedic drugs. Out of this small group of *kabirajes*, a large group of them those surveyed doubted the effectiveness of the commercially-produced drugs. However, the unavailability of various types of herbs made it difficult for the *kabirajes* to prepare their own health remedies. Another factor contributing to the decline in this practice is also the lack of knowledge and skills among the younger-generation ayurvedic physicians. Apart from the local market, there is also the development of an international market for herbal-based drugs, health supplements and beauty products. As a result of this global demand, many Indian drug companies, such as Dabur and Baidyanath, are mass producing and creating a large range of herbal-based drugs for the global market. Such mass production of ayurvedic drugs and products for global and local markets sometimes do not find support among the more traditionally-minded *kabirajes*. The traditional *kabirajes* surveyed are less dependent on commercially-manufactured ayurvedic drugs and health products produced with the help of modern technology and laboratory equipment. In addition to arguing that modern technology and large production do not consider the environmental condition of plants and herbs during collection and in preparing medicine, they worried that drugs manufactured commercially with the help of modern technology ignore the condition of the individual patient a consideration which is one of the fundamental principles in ayurveda.

4.4.2 Use of Mass Media

The use of mass media is a recent initiative launched by the drug manufacturers in both China and India to advertise their health products, beauty products and cosmetics. Many drug manufacturers have promoted beauty and sex products as a health alternative to synthetic cosmetics and Western drugs by emphasizing the herbal and organic content. They use media to widely advertise products that appeal to people's vanity, emotion and fears. Consumerism in modern Chinese and Indian society is increasing because of growth of advertisements for herbal health and pharmaceutical products promoted by various pharmaceutical companies.

In India, ayurvedic cosmetics, beauty and sex products advertisements are found on highway billboards, in various beauty competitions or fashion shows, on the roadsides in city, in city centres, in small ayurvedic shops, in super markets, and even at international scientific conferences where scholars of ayurveda are participating (Bode 2001). Popular and widely-selling magazines in West Bengal where this study was conducted such as *Anand Bazar, Anand Mela and Desh Patrika* carry such advertisements. The advertisements carry a range of herbal or ayurvedic products and beauty cosmetic products such as facial creams, essentials oils, hair products to toiletries and slimming products. They also featured sexual impotence products for men (Islam 2010: 787). As the big ayurvedic pharmaceutical companies turn their attention to the development of beauty products for women, ayurveda has been propagated as a natural healing system, and ayurvedic medicine/

Fig. 4.7 An ayurvedic impotence product advertised in the television in 2015. *Source* Retrieved from the following link and accessed on March 24, 2016: https://www.google.ca/search?q=mood+on+forever&biw=1280&bih=687&source=lnms&tbm=isch&sa=X&sqi=2&ved=0ahUKEwj89Py5qdnLAhUG5GMKHVy6CQgQ_AUIBigB#imgrc=mHVyFlEs00ppBM%3A

health products are featured as natural remedies. Advertisements, both in print and in the electronic media, have been broadcasted repeatedly concerning ayurvedic beauty products that are essential for 'beauty and natural care' for the body (Ibid). Besides sex products advertisement for men represents how ayurveda can boost men's sexual energy and ensure a conjugal happiness through satisfying their spouse. The power of the media has created a new taste and a new trend of consumption through the heart-rending fashions of product presentations. Below are few case studies of how various ayurvedic products are marketed through mass advertisement (Fig. 4.7).

> "Mood on forever-Extra mood just for man" is an impotence product that advertised in various television channels across the Indian subcontinent for more than 15 min every day during summer 2015. The product claims it as ayurvedic which combines 21 materials including silajit, shorno vasho, ashoghandha, etc. and after using this product a man in his 40 can feels the energy of age 24. The stories of different couples who have encountered conjugal difficulties because of the husband's sexual incompetence have been featured in various scene. These difficulties includes, conjugal infidelity and wife's extra marital affairs, wife's intention to divorce, bring shame for the family, distance between spouses, abundant or avoiding wife, depression, family violence, unhappiness, etc. Various emotional scenes repeatedly show how couples live a miserable life because of inadequate sexual performances. One scene shows that when a husband objects his wife's extra marital affair, the wife replies: "marital life does not mean only to live together, you cannot give the satisfaction I expect. Women might have some dreams which you do not understand". However, after using this product for a month the situation reverses and they begin to live a tension free and happy conjugal life with full of joy. In order to make the product more appealing, the advertisement use various statistics to prove that majority of the world

Fig. 4.8 An ayurvedic beauty product advertised in the television in 2015. *Source* Retrieved from the following link and accessed on March 24, 2016: https://www.google.ca/search?q=Ayur slim&biw=1280&bih=687&source=lnms&tbm=isch&sa=X&ved=0ahUKEwiR9e3UqtnLAhUP5 2MKHZOZAjEQ_AUIBigB#tbm=isch&q=Fair+look+gold&imgrc=ufx8NCeFhwhkRM%3A

> divorces are caused by incompetent sexual intercourse. The product claims it as "unique combination and safe selection of special herbs renowned for their spermatogenic properties. It is a powerful blood flow stimulator that pushes excess blood into the erectile chambers of the penis during arousal". There are three advantages of using this product written on the product packet: enhance pleasure and performance; natural and herbal; for vigor, vitality and stamina. The product has no side-effect, it claims.[18]

Another product named as "Fair Look Gold" and has advertised during the same time particularly targeted to middle class consumer. The product priced INR 3000 which is affordable for the middle class Indian. The advertisement in its various scenes shows how peoples are neglected in public sphere only because of unfair skin. Even someone who owns INR Crore also suffers from inferiority complex because of unfair skin. The same person finds very positive attitude towards him after using this product. Another scene shows that a woman has offered second honeymoon by his husband after using this product. The product claims it as an unique ayurvedic formula for beauty and fairness which can make the face and entire body fair by using few weeks. One of the noteworthy features of this advertisement is that it has promoted fairness not only for women concern but also for men in contemporary India (Figs. 4.8 and 4.9).[19]

An online shopping facility providing company is WWS which has marketed four health products as ayurvedic-based products and has advertised them for about 15–45 min on several Bengali language television channels during 2004–05. The products are: *Ayu Slim* (ayurvedic slimming powder), *D Care Plus* (for diabetes), *Danpury* (ayurvedic tooth powder) and *Rup Amret* (ayurvedic fairness cream). WWS has an expanded advertisement program. In Bengali, *rup* means fairness and

[18]This advertisement was broadcasted in a Bengali language TV channel in August 2015.

[19]This advertisement was also broadcasted in a Bengali language TV channel in August 2015.

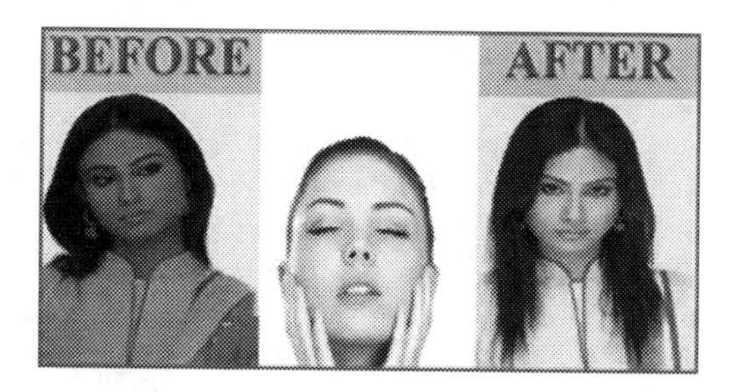

Fig. 4.9 An ayurvedic beauty product advertised in the television in 2015. *Source* Retrieved from the following link and accessed on March 24, 2016: https://www.google.ca/search?q=Ayurslim&biw=1280&bih=687&source=lnms&tbm=isch&sa=X&ved=0ahUKEwiR9e3UqtnLAhUP52MKHZOZAjEQ_AUIBigB#tbm=isch&q=Fair+look+gold&imgrc=ufx8NCeFhwhkRM%3A

amret means magical honey, so that and *Rup Amret* means a magical honey for fairness. The glamour of these products is reinforced by commissioning actors and actresses to appear in the advertisements. The slimming and diabetes products are priced expensively, in the Indian context, and only affluent people can afford to purchase them. The drug company offered a 100% money back guarantee if their products did not work. They provided online shopping facilities, toll free phone call service for any inquiry, and retail sale from their office or distribution units.

One of the common themes of all the four advertisement is to increase physical attraction and promote a sense that obesity, bad teeth, lack of fair complexion and diabetes cause the loss of physical attraction of a spouse, boyfriend/girlfriend, colleague, boss, subordinate or friend. However, the situation reverses dramatically after the use of these health products. For example, the WWS Company spent large sums of money on advertisements broadcast on several satellite television channels that focus on selling slimming products. One of the selling and advertising strategies was to promote the idea that ayurvedic products do not have side-effects. Thus, *Ayu Slim* slimming product states that "indigenous technology, natural procedure and no side effect is the key features of *Ayu slim*. This product is made using 52 types of roots and plants. It saves time, reduces weight, builds muscle and creates perfect look" (Ayuslim television advertisement 2004).[20] The advertisement also portrays women as satisfied customers who have benefited from the product, and men as approving such products for their wives or girlfriends (Islam 2010: 787).

Today, because of the booming cosmetic industries and various beauty-related products, women's health concern has been largely replaced by beauty concern, and ayurvedic brands have been used as a "lucrative market strategy" (Selby 2005: 121). However, beauty, fair skin in particular is no longer been a women's concern alone in contemporary Indian society. As the advertisement of *Fair Look Gold*

[20]This advertisement was broadcasted on the Bangla television channel 'Alfa TV Bangla'.

clearly illustrated how a well establish man feel social negligence and suffer from inferior complex because of his unfair skin. Besides men's health has been symbolizes as power and manufacturing power boosting energy pills has become a lucrative choice for the ayurvedic and or herbal pharmaceutical companies in India. In participant observation conducted during September 2004 in an ayurvedic medicine shop, out of a total 134 customers observed, 'oil and cosmetics' was the best-selling category, purchased by 33 customers. 120 customers were male and only 14 were female. 51 male customers purchased health products for their wives, children or other female relatives. The best-selling cosmetic products were hair oil, hair tonic, hair massage and facial cream.

How do the ayurvedic practitioners perceive the role of media advertisements to promote ayurveda in India and overseas? Of the 30 surveyed, 70% of the ayurvedic practitioners felt that drug companies had misled Indian women by redefining body and beauty. They have influenced the perception of body and beauty as synonymous with the consumption of ayurvedic beauty and health supplement products. In this sense, women purchase cosmetics products not for medical needs but for beauty and health concerns because of their growing fascination towards what are considered the ideals of body and beauty such as fairness, slimness, etc. Today there is also another perception, which equates 'herbal' with ayurveda, and people often misunderstand herbal products as ayurvedic products. Ayurveda perceives the human body for medical reasons and proceeds with the treatment of diseases and illnesses. By contrast, with global commodification, the human body comes to be seen as part of the 'beauty and health' industry, where beauty becomes an essential part of healthy life and can be affected by ayurvedic treatment. Ayurvedic products have thus been promoted as essential elements contributing towards the maintenance of beauty and health of the human.

4.4.3 Drug Standardization!!

Drug standardization in indigenous medicine is one of the major topics discussed from various corner in contemporary China and India. From government policy makers to general practitioners, every corner is very much concern about drug standardization. Many new companies have launched their businesses in recent decades and manufactured patent drugs without quality control. As Chinese herbal medicine and ayurvedic products became popular in both the local and international market, these products are subjected to closer scrutiny and regulation, especially from regulatory agencies overseas. National Policy on Chinese medicine was first issued in 1949 followed by the pharmaceutical regulations in 1963. The national office to monitor Chinese medicine was established in 1949 under the Ministry of Health. By the year 1998, the State Drug Administration became responsible for regulatory issues relating to Chinese medicine. Chinese herbal medicine is regulated as prescription and over the counter medicines (OTC), self medication, dietary supplements, health foods and functional foods (WHO 2005: 130). Safety assessment requirements for herbal medicines include the requirements applying to conventional pharmaceuticals as well as special requirements of traditional use without demonstrated harmful effects on people's health (Ibid). There are more than 9000 registered Chinese herbal medicines in China by the year 2002, and 1242 of them had been included in the national essential drug list. In China, herbal medicines are sold in pharmacies as prescription and over the counter medicines (OTC), in special outlets and by registered practitioners.

Practitioners in China have different views on drug standardization. Some of them are very concern about the role of the drug manufacturers particularly during the era of globalization whereas others are careful about the idea of drug standardization. They raised the applicability of Western drug standardization for Chinese medicine. Chinese medicine has own theory, philosophy and methodology which are unique. From the historical time, different Chinese medicine practitioners prepared drug differently through using different herbs, plants and materials to treat similar symptom and modality. Chinese medical texts such as *Bencao Gangmu* also acknowledged various prescriptions provided by different physicians about same drugs. Whether Western medical style drug standardization is necessary for Chinese medicine, they raised this question. One practitioner commented:

> Chinese medicine is a kind of philosophy, humanistic thought and experience passed on from generation to generation. It has its own theory rather than the scientific view such as data or standardization. Chinese medicine is a kind of self-development, so that it can be easily duped. Unlike Western medicine, Chinese medicine cannot be counterfeited because it does not need to use data to prove that it is not fake. I have learnt many CM formulas to cure the same disease and I didn't know which one would be more effective. After working many years I will gain some experience about which one is more effective. So, every CM practitioner has his/her own way to practice CM. For me, if a CM practitioner has long experience and kind-heart, he or she is a good practitioner. Nowadays many CM patent drugs are being westernization and few CM theories is used in those patent drugs which is not a healthy trend.

Many of the practitioners those surveyed acknowledge that the present Chinese medicine is not as effective as before. In the past, the practitioners collected the natural CM herbs from the mountain whereas CM herbs are cultivated nowadays. Practitioners in modern days use more quantity of herbs than before which symbolizes the reduction of efficacy because of the cultivated herbs. The following comments was made by one practitioner who came from a traditional Chinese medicine family and learned CM through an apprentice system:

> The present Chinese medicine herbs are totally different than those used by my family to prepare drugs during my childhood. In the past, 5 to 10 pieces of Chinese herbs were enough while 15 to 20 pieces are used now to get an effect. In the past, herbs are wild whereas herbs are cultivated with pesticide and chemical fertilizer today, so that the production cycle can be reduced. Thus, some drugs are not as effective as before and their properties have changed. Today, CM practitioners and CM drug manufacturers are separated. CM practitioner only writes prescriptions and people who take charge of drugs will only get in touch with the drugs. Some of the prescriptions written in the past by CM physicians and cured disease successfully. However, the same prescriptions and drugs are now considered as harmful to patients because the property of drugs is changed.

Some of the practitioners also added the complexity of drug standardization for Chinese medicine and few of them were not aware whether there is any specific policy or programs on drug standardization in contemporary China. They found the entire situation of marketing Chinese medicine is a mess. Instead of counting percentage I have quoted some of the views from the physicians those surveyed in the following section:

> One of the meanings of drug standardization is to use the similar drug for similar symptom which contradicts the principle of Chinese medicine. I think some media mislead people through propagate a view that same drug should be used for similar symptoms. However, different people have different situation even their symptoms are same and the same drug may not be suitable for everybody. That is the unique philosophy of Chinese medicine.

> All the herbs grew in the past naturally whereas large quantity of herbs are artificially cultivated today within a small piece of land. Thus the property of herbs is definitely different and the efficacy has reduced. For example, Fu Zi, a root of the plant which usually grows in the mountain of North China where temperature is very low. Thus, its character is cold-resistance. However, Fu Zi has been cultivated in the plain land of South China recently and I dought if it is still cold-resistant? The theory of Chinese medicine is good but the efficacy of drug is different today. For example, Huang Qi-a famous herbs and using 10 caps could provide best effect in the past. However, nowadays the doctors use 20 caps but not as effective as before. My mum worked in the CM herb field for long time. According to her, if a herb is transplanted from north region to the south we have to observe its efficacy for at least 3 years before using it for drug manufacturing. The herbs are artificially cultivated now because the supply of natural herbs are not enough to satisfy the market demand. I use some 'Niuhuangqingwei pills' to treat patients. The niuhuang available in the market is not authentic and the treatment periods is longer than before since the quality of herbs has decreased. The farmers use manure to increase the yield and decrease the growth time of herbs for the benefits. So the quality of natural herbs and artificial herbs are different. Modern Chinese patent drugs follow Western approach.

There are also several positive aspects noted by the practitioners on the development of patent drugs and drug standardization. Firstly, patent drugs suit with modern lifestyle. Some patients cannot use decoction for various reasons. Some may develop vomiting syndrome after taking decoction. Not all user have time to go through decoction. People want to develop Chinese medicine with a fast speed although this is contradictory with the principle of Chinese medicine. Secondly, large quantity of herbs is required to respond the current depend. Population has risen fast and sometimes the combination of Chinese medicine and Western medicine can provide better result. Thirdly, the issue of drug standardization and the development of patent drug is more related to market demand and profits get the priority. It is necessary for the survival of the drug manufacturers.

In India, the first national policy on indigenous medicine including ayurveda was introduced in 1940 and the national regulation of ayurveda came in effect in the same year under Drugs and Cosmetics Act. Ayurvedic medicines are regulated as prescription and over the counter (OTC) medicine and dietary supplement and may be sold with medical, health and nutrient content claims. The National laws and regulations were also issued in 1940, and updated in 1964, 1970 and 1982. The national office named as the Indian System of Medicine and Homeopathy was established in 1995 as part of the Ministry of Health and Family Welfare (WHO

2005: 121). This office was later renamed as Department of Ayurveda, Yoga, Unani, Siddha, and Homeopathy (AYUSH) in 2002. AYUSH became an independent ministry in 2014. Ayurvedic drug manufacturing regulatory requirements include adherence to information contained in pharmacopoeias and monographs and the same GMP rules required for conventional pharmaceuticals (Ibid). Drug licensing, inspection and testing personals are employed to ensure compliance with these requirements. Safety requirements include those required for conventional pharmaceuticals, as well as special requirements of traditional use without demonstrated harmful effects and reference to documented scientific research on similar products (Ibid: 122). There are 315 ayurvedic herbal medicines on its essential drug list and medicines are sold in pharmacies and outlets as prescription and over the counter medicines without restriction.

Although India has long history of regulatory mechanism to ensure the quality of ayurvedic medicine and safety of patients many drug manufacturers and outlets those sell ayurvedic and or herbal drugs, health products are reluctant to follow the regulation strictly. The National Policy on Indian Systems of Medicine & Homoeopathy 2002 also recognized the fact of poor quality control in their policy report. The report stated that although "drugs manufacture and related matters are covered under Drugs & Cosmetics Act, 1940 and Drugs & Cosmetics Rules, 1945, the safely, efficacy, quality of drugs and their rational use have not been assured" (National Policy on Indian Systems of Medicine & Homeopathy 2002, Article 5.1). The report further stated that although there were several enforcements mechanisms advised in the Act, they still remain ineffective because of poor implementation of the enforcement laws. There was still reluctance among a large number of ayurvedic drugs manufacturers in various parts of India to maintain standard manufacturing practices and ensure the quality of their medicine or health products (National Policy on Indian Systems of Medicine & Homoeopathy 2002, Article 5.1). However, the patients in contemporary India are less concern about the issues of drug standardization. Of those surveyed, 89% of the patients had no ideas about drug standardization. They depended on faith in the function and effectiveness of the ayurvedic drugs they used. Many ayurvedic physicians were also frustrated at the poor quality control of ayurvedic drugs.

4.5 Conclusion

Today, a larger number of consumers in China, India and overseas use Chinese herbal and Indian ayurvedic health products, medicine, health supplement, diet supplement, and cosmetic products coming into the market under the banner of herbal or ayurvedic. The biggest Chinese herbal and ayurvedic companies are promoting aggressive marketing campaigns all over the world. Chinese herbal medicine and ayurveda has been transformed from indigenous medical systems to a global health commodity for mass consumption. Their natural and herbal content has been stolen and commoditised by these manufacturers for profit maximization.

Many modern graduates of Chinese medicine and ayurveda are paying less attention to considerations of person, place and time in providing medicine or medication, which means ignoring a fundamental principle of their medical systems. The demand for natural and herbal products has risen significantly because of lower toxicity, more advertising, changing outlooks of medicine and products, failures of Western medicine to cure chronic diseases, etc. Consumers across the globe are also used to this new consumer marketing of these products. The entire advertising industry has promoted health products and cosmetics in ways other than medical. All these appearances boost the uncertainty as to whether the current Chinese herbal medicine and ayurvedic medicine are indigenous medical system or global commodity for mass consumption. The commodification process of these indigenous medical systems is contrary to their principle of 'restoring health' through prevention or preservation.

Chapter 5
Manufacturing Magic Bullets

5.1 Introduction

Indigenous drug manufacturers in both China and India are bringing large number of products into the market related to particular sex. The major selling points for these products are natural and herbal content and no side-effect. For man, most of these products are related to power and energy, sexual energy in particular. Many products are focusing men's premature ejaculation, impotence problem, erectile dysfunction, vigour and vitality, quick recovery from weakness, and boosting energy through revitalizing body. Through the process of manufacturing energy boosting products these drug companies are problematically masculinising indigenous medicine. At the same time, there is huge development of women related products particularly focusing body and beauty. Women's body has been transformed from a medicalized to a natural body for beauty by these drug manufacturers. They are instrumental in redefining women's body from a reproductive to a beautiful body which equate beauty with health. The major products line for women ranges from beauty related cream to sliming products, hair care, body care, tooth care and skin care.

This chapter examines how Chinese herbal medicine and ayurveda has been used as brand name to sell sexual and beauty products which is contextually different than their representation in the classical texts. While men's impotence discussed in Chinese medical text *Huang Di Nei Jing* as deficiency of kidney *qi* and virilisation therapy discussed in the ayurvedic text *Susruta Samhita* requires following a routine and lifestyle change to enhance sexual energy, modern drug manufacturers are reluctant to follow such requirements in promoting impotence products. The pharmaceutical companies this seeks to redefine masculinity with reference to sexual power. Besides this section also explores how women's bodies were represented in Chinese and Indian medical texts as primarily reproductive, and how this female reproductive body has been transformed into a beautiful female body in the contemporary Chinese and Indian context. The large pharmaceutical

M.N. Islam, *Chinese and Indian Medicine Today*,
DOI 10.1007/978-981-10-3962-1_5

companies are thus instrumental in redefining the female body in order to establish a market niche for various cosmetic and beauty products.

5.2 Textual Representation in China

According to Chinese Medical texts as *Huang Di Nei Jing*, erectile dysfunction or impotence is primarily caused by two factors, firstly, a deficiency of kidney *yang* energy, and secondly, blood stasis in the lower abdomen. The text has mentioned men's impotence problem in several occasions. In Chap. 2 of *Ling shu* (spiritual pivot) the text discussed the circulatory process of *yang qi* or the *yang-energy* and states how it reaches into kidney through various channel and finally communicate with the external genitals (Bing 2010: 595–596). In Chap. 1 of *Su Wen* (plain questions) of the above text also discussed men's sexual ability with reference to their reproductive ability. The chapter explicitly denotes how kidney energy developed, reach to peak and decline again in different ages during a lifecycle of men. For example, the text notes that men's kidney energy becomes prosperous by the age of sixteen and if conducts sexual intercourse with a woman, he might have child. Next paragraph states that:

> *by the age of twenty four man's kidney energy is well developed to reach the state of an adult. However, by the age of forty, man's kidney energy turns gradually from prosperous to decline and by the age of forty eight kidney energy declines even more. As the kidney energy is the source of yang energy, yang energy also begins to decline at this age. By the age of fifty six, man's liver energy declines in the wake of the deficiency of the kidney energy. Finally at the age of sixty four man's kidney energy become very weak and he losses reproductive ability (Bing 2010: 9–10).*

Kidney energy is the congenital energy of human body, but it can only bring its functions into play when it is nourished by the postnatal energy, the chapter concludes (ibid). Apart from acupuncture treatment discussed in *Huang Di Nei Jing* text to recover from impotence problem, Chinese text *Bencao Gangmu* provided several herbal prescriptions and drugs to treat erectile dysfunction. The text comprises 52 volumes, describing 1892 drugs with 1109 illustration (Li 2012, volume 1: 35). These drugs are categories under 16 categories and some of the categories related to herbs, animals and minerals those are link to impotence remedies. For example, *Yin Yang Hui* is a drug described in this text which grows in the north of *Xichuan* (Western Sichuan) province. After taking this drug, the patient tends to have love affairs more often. Tao Hongjing-a famous Chinese medicine physician from old time mentioned that there is a kind of sheep which likes eating this drug a lot and mates often, even 100 times within a single day (Li 2012, volume 1: 281–83). Lei Xiao, another old time Chinese medicine physician discussed the preparation of the drug and mentioned that the flowers around the leaf of the plants should be removed during processed the drug, blend one *jin* of the leaves with four *liang* of sheep's fat and stir-fry the mixture until the fat is exhausted. Another physician Xu Zhicai suggested processed the drug with wine for stronger efficacy.

Li Shizhen, the author or editor of *Bencao Gangmu* provided the indications of the drug through saying that this drugs treat impotence due to exhaustion and damage, with pain in the penis. It reinforces physical strength and invigorates willpower. However, long-term taking of the drug will make the man prolific (Ibid: 285–87).

Another drug suggested by *Bencao Gangmu* to treat impotence problem or enhance man's sexual energy is called Fu Zi. It is grows in the mountain valleys of Jianwei and Guanghan and the lateral root has to be collected in winter (Li 2012: 1683). The therapeutic effects of this drug vary according to the seasons it is collected (Ibid: 1687). The text also provided various preparation methods of this drug suggested by different physicians. Han Baosheng-an old time physician suggested the following preparation for getting best result:

> *The drugs have to be soaked in Shengshutang (mixture of boiled and fresh water) for half a day, and then take them out and wrap them with lime. Change the lime several times to make the drugs dry for best efficacy.*

Li Shizhen in his book Fuzi Ji described this drug as the devil of drugs and suggested the following preparation method:

> *Soak the drug in vinegar and keep it in a sealed room. After soaking the drug for over a month, take it out and dry it in the sun. At the time when the drug is taken out from the vinegar, a piece of the drug as big as a fist may shrink into a piece that is smaller than the palm can hold after it is dried in the sun. After processing, a piece weighing more than one liang is a scarce find (Ibid: 1693).*

Physician Tao Hongjing also suggested to use other drugs such as Gancao, ginseng root and Shengjiang together with Fuzi which can detoxify the toxin of Fuzi (Ibid). As it effect, Physician Zhang Yuansu said that the drug diswarms the spleen and stomach, disperses invading pathogenic humidity in the spleen and warms the cold in the kidney. Thus it enhances male sexuality, and consolidates the muscle and bone (Ibid: 1701). All the above prescriptions of Chinese herbal drugs discussed in the text *Bencao Gangmu* to treat man's impotence or enhance sexual energy requires to follow a systematic preparation method and rule during intake.

5.3 Contemporary Situation in China

Modern drug manufacturers producing impotence pills are reluctant to follow the systematic rules described in the text. They are more eager to manufacture quick fix pill to solve impotence problems as much as Western drug manufacturers do. During my winter holiday in 2016 I went for window shopping in the underground market of Gongbei Immigration Check point of Zhuhai City bordering the Macao Special Administrative Region of the People's Republic of China. That market is famous for the tourists from Macao who enter mainland China for relax or bargain shopping. When I was crossing a drug store, a mid-age Chinese woman was chanting; "Chinese medicine …Chinese medicine", and asking me to get inside the store. Once I entered the store she shows a large pool of impotence pill line up on the shelf from different drug manufacturers with different price level. Most of these impotence products package contain an English or combination of English-Chinese name such as Dragon Power Capsule, Tiger King, Double Dragon Pills Herbal Supplement, etc. These were manufactured by different companies from Hong Kong and mainland China. The erotic layout of packages gives clear impression of their ability to boost sexual energy. For example, Dragon Power Capsule package contains 3 capsules. The layout of the package shows two dragons sitting face to face with a romantic mood. One is in aggressive face and clearly represent male whereas another with gentle face. At the top of the package it is written that "natural herbs" and at the bottom "made in China". I have purchased one pack among them cost CYN 15 and contains 10 capsules. After opening the packet I have found an English-Chinese flyer inside which mentioned the name of the capsule as "Santi Bovine Penis Erecting Capsule". The flyer gave product introduction, materials and ingredients, work mechanism, function and indications, usage and dosage, specification and storage, and caution. It mentioned under product introduction that "this product has been made, based on the theory of traditional Chinese medicine, applying modern production technology of medical science". Materials that are used include "penis of cattle, pilose antler and ginseng, schisandra fruit, the fruit of Chinese wolfberry, semen cuscutae". About the usage and dosage the flyer mentioned that taking 3 capsules orally 1 h before sexual intercourse for the best effect. Patients with heart disease or diabetes mellitus shall take 1 capsule per time, once a day and with boiled water orally before going to bed or in the morning. It also provided caution through saying that "the product has strong effect, be careful when using in patients with serious cerebrovascular disease and consumption disease".

After I came back home I have visited the web page of this product. This product is manufactured by Anhui Santi Medical Health Products Company. The product list posted in the English website of the company queues a total seven products with their photos and description. These are: Santi Scalper Penis Erection Capsule (Two colours package with two types of pills), Santi Scalper Baois Erection Capsule, Santi Scalper Penis Adam Tonic Solution (Two colours package with two types of tonic), Jianwei Xiaoshi Weiganpian, and Jian Bbao Xin Oral Liquid. All these products are sex enhancement products. The company also mentioned that their products are exported and very popular in the USA, Japan, and other Southeast Asian countries apart from Hong Kong, Macao and Taiwan.[1] All the products listed under product list are man's impotence products giving a clear indication that these products contributed large share of their business and profit margin. It is not surprising that many small drug manufacturers in China only produce impotence and beauty related products exploiting the natural and herbal content of Chinese medicine.

Beijing Tong Ren Tang has also manufactured and marketed various impotence products. During my visit in one shop of Beijing Tong Ren Tang in Zhuhai city we

[1]Retrieved from the following link http://www.ah-santi.com/index.htm and accessed on January 24, 2016.

have found eight types of energy boosting products particularly targeting to enhance vitality and increase man's sexual energy. The products include Shenrong Sanbian Wan, Suojing Wan, Shenrong Wan, Yishen Qiangshen Wan and Eangshuai Yishou Wan (two packs within same box), Bushen Qiangshen Pian, Wuzi Yanzong Wan, and Jinkui Shenqi Wan. The price also varies from product to product ranging from RMB 15 a pack to RMB 1000. For example, Wuzi Yangzong Wan 60 gm prices RMB 22 whereas Yishen Qiangshen Wan and Eangshuai Yishou Wan (two packs within same box) priced RMB 999. Generally those products contain herb and plant based material are less expensive than those use animal materials. One Packet Bushen Qiangshen Pian contains 60 pills and priced RMB 16. The ingredients written inside the flyer of Bushen Qiangshen Pian packet includes epicedium, cuscuta Chinese Cherokee, Rose Fruit, Glossy Private Fruit, and Rhizoma Cibotii. Yishen Qiangshen Wan and Eangshuai Yishou Wan contain materials such as poria, astilagalus, membranaceus (fried with honey) honey, semen euryares (stir-baking with bran), prepared rehmannia root, black sesame, cacumen biotae, sealwort (stir-frying with wine), black soya bean, Chinese yam, fossil fragment (calcine), amber, placenta hominis, pearl, polygram, English walnut seed, asparagus, radix ophio-pogonis, etc.[2] This product priced RMB 999. The procedure to take this product mentioned in its flyer is "orally 20–30 pills in the morning for increase kidney and help firm body and take another 20–30 pills in the evening from another bottle for anti-aging and lengthen one's life"[3] (Figs. 5.1 and 5.2).

Another drug store located next to Beijing Tong Ren Tang shop and sells both Chinese herbal and Western medicine also have various impotence and sexual energy boosting products manufactured by other companies such as Shengfa tablets, Liuweidihuangjiaonang, Qiangsheng, Zhibao sanbian wan, etc. It is thus clear that manufacturing sexual energy boosting products, particularly for man has become one of the major product lines for drug manufacturers in contemporary China.

5.4 Vedic Representation of Male Sexuality and Recent Development

The situation in India is not different than China where most of the small and big ayurvedic and or herbal pharmaceutical companies are manufacturing various sex products targeting sexual weakness, impotence, pre-matured ejaculation and erectile dysfunction. Masculinehealth in pre-modern India was linked to the problem of physiology and semen, as distinct from a generalised symbolization of power and

[2]These materials were listed in a flyer for this product found in one of the outlet of Beijing Tong Ren Tang.

[3]Ibid.

Fig. 5.1 An impotence products manufactured by Beijing Tong Ren Tang. *Source* Retrieved from the following links and accessed on March 27, 2016: https://www.google.ca/search?q=Yishen+Qiangshen+Wan+and+Eangshuai+Yishou+Wan&biw=1280&bih=687&source=lnms&tbm=isch&sa=X&ved=0ahUKEwj6kNmcu-DLAhUP0WMKHUNeAfsQ_AUIBygC#tbm=isch&q=Shenrong+Sanbian+Wan&imgrc=B4vLg_OU5-7ZcM%3A. https://www.google.ca/search?q=Yishen+Qiangshen+Wan+and+Eangshuai+Yishou+Wan&biw=1280&bih=687&source=lnms&tbm=isch&sa=X&ved=0ahUKEwj6kNmcu-DLAhUP0WMKHUNeAfsQ_AUIBygC#tbm=isch&q=Wuzi+Yanzong+Wan&imgrc=RtNDVpIGSkjcyM%3A

Fig. 5.2 An impotence products manufactured by Beijing Tong Ren Tang. *Source* Retrieved from the following links and accessed on March 27, 2016: https://www.google.ca/search?q=Yishen+Qiangshen+Wan+and+Eangshuai+Yishou+Wan&biw=1280&bih=687&source=lnms&tbm=isch&sa=X&ved=0ahUKEwj6kNmcu-DLAhUP0WMKHUNeAfsQ_AUIBygC#tbm=isch&q=Shenrong+Sanbian+Wan&imgrc=B4vLg_OU5-7ZcM%3A. https://www.google.ca/search?q=Yishen+Qiangshen+Wan+and+Eangshuai+Yishou+Wan&biw=1280&bih=687&source=lnms&tbm=isch&sa=X&ved=0ahUKEwj6kNmcu-DLAhUP0WMKHUNeAfsQ_AUIBygC#tbm=isch&q=Wuzi+Yanzong+Wan&imgrc=RtNDVpIGSkjcyM%3A

thus linked to the, production, retention, and internalized flow of semen (Alter 2008: 178). In ayurvedic curative practice, *vajikarana* (virilisation) is regarded as one of the eight branches of ayurveda. *Vajikarana* can analyse and purify 'polluted' sperm; enable sexual ejaculation, competence and sperm reproduction; and enhance the strength of men (*Susruta* 1999, *sutro sthana*, Chap. 1, and paragraph 11). The *Caraka Samhita* text also described the causes of sexual weakness for men in intercourse, especially, the problems of elderly men, and provided potential medical remedies to recover sexual ability (*Caraka* 2003, *chikitsha sthana*, Chap. 2, paragraphs 4–6). The text suggests behavioural change in men during sexual intercourse, such as concentration on sex during intercourse and taking a bath and drinking milk with meat after intercourse and before going to bed. Following such a routine would cause further stimulation for sexual intercourse (*Caraka* 2003, *chikitsha sthana*, Chap. 2, paragraphs 2–8). Another paragraphs from the *Caraka Samhita* text informs those who aspire to longevity that they should avoid sexual intercourse before the 16th and after the 70th year of age and noted the causes of loss sexual power which includes stress and anxiety, fear, suspicion, distrust, wet dreams, immature ejaculation, loss of sexual desire for wife, suspicion about wife's sexual life, affliction, etc. (*Ibid*). The *Susruta Samhita* text also prescribes the procedure of preparing and manufacturing remedies for male sexual enhancement in the *Khinbolio Bajikaron* (weak virilisation) chapter. The text notes that "sesame, enamel, winter rice, etc. should be mixed with sugarcane drink and cooked with pig fat. The mixture then should be cooked with ghee and eaten before sexual intercourse" (*Susruta* 1999, *chikitsha sthana*, Chap. 26, paragraph 3). Alternatively "sesame should be mixed with goat milk and cooked with dolphin meat. Whenever a man eats this mixture, he can prolong sexual intercourse" (Ibid, paragraph 4). Ayurvedic text *Astanga Hrdayam* written by Vagbhatas also suggested following a seasonal routine during performing sex for better sexuality. For example the text suggested that a man should perform sex daily as much as he likes after making use of aphrodisiacs and obtaining strength during the *hemanta and sisira* (snowy & cold seasons), once in three days during *vasanta and sarat* (spring and autumn season), and once in fortnight during *varsa and grishma* (monsoon and summer season) (Vagbhatas 2009, Volume 1, Chap. 7:119–121).

Thus, the classical texts suggested certain habits, routines and behaviour for better sexual performance. However, the current development of sexual energy-boosting products and impotence pills under ayurvedic and or herbal brand names has no connection with the behavioural motivation and lifestyle-related activities that ayurvedic texts suggest (Islam 2013: 420). One is unlikely to find any flyer advertising ayurvedic impotence pills or sexual energy-boosting tonics suggesting behavioural changes, instead, flyers give precautions about side effects as much as Western medicine flyers do. For example, *Jaubon Shakti* (power of youth) is a dietary supplement advertised several television channels across the Indian subcontinent in August 2015. The product claims itself as "alternative name of manhood" and "if it comes to a man's life he will enjoy the true pleasure of making love". The product package contains one bottle of powder and one bottle of oil. The procedure to use this product as mentioned in the advertisement is "to take one spoon powder with hot milk twice a day and massage the oil gentle on penis 5–7 min before performing sex". The product priced expensively in Indian context as INR 2990 and could be delivered within 24 h of purchase through teleshopping.

The ayurvedic pharmaceutical companies in modern India have been quick to establish and exploit a market niche for their products. During my fieldwork in 2004–2005 in Indian eastern city of Kolkata there were at least 22 brands of male impotence products including capsules, pills, penis massage creams, penis sprays, etc. found in one ayurvedic store which uses the logo of ayurveda or 'herbal', with impressive packing and with erotic layout. The selling points for these products are again the herbal contents, the minimal side-effects and the effectiveness of these products. The packaging and the names given to most male sex products, such as Patton Power Caps, Vita-Ex Gold, Keep On, VIGO MAX, 303, Shaiwal Power House, Titanic-K2, etc., give the impression of the ability to enhance power. By using either English or Sanskrit or combination of the two languages names for these sex products (such as Love Care for passionate night, and Kamakshi), the ayurvedic companies hope to attract male customers from various classes to purchase sexual power. Out of the 22 male sexuality-enhancement products in the Dabur Ayurvedic Medicine Shop, 19 had English or combined English-Sanskrit names. Most of the bigger and smaller ayurvedic drug manufacturers in contemporary India such as Dabur India Limited, Himalaya, Baidyanath Ayurved, Arya Vaidya Sala, etc. produce various sex-enhancement products for men. For example, Baidyanath Ayurved has manufactured and marketed the Vita-Ex Gold sex-enhancement product, Dabur India Limited manufactured and marketed Shilajit Gold Capsule, Shilajit-Es Capsules for Extra Strong, and Himalaya Herbal Health Care manufactures and markets Tentex Royal capsules for man's impotence problem (Ibid: 20–21)[4] (Figs. 5.3 and 5.4).

How did the consumers and patients in contemporary China and India accept this massive rise of impotence pills under the brand name of Chinese herbal medicine or ayurveda? The Chinese medicine practitioners those surveyed have mix feeling about the role of drug manufacturers and quality control of the sex products they manufactured. 60% of them think that this is not a positive initiative launched by the drug manufactures whereas 20% admitted that it is necessary to bring the actions of drug manufacturers under control but the task is very difficult. Rest of the practitioners gave various answers. I have quoted several comments in the following section made by some of the practitioners:

Manufacturing sex or beauty products have own advantages and disadvantages. The advantage is that it can be easily accepted by the public. The weakness is that it does not obey the principle of Chinese medicine theory such as dialectical therapy. Regulating the production of these products is important. Otherwise, Chinese medicine will never spread out of the China. State Administration of Traditional Chinese Medicine is trying to do this but it is a hard job. As I said before, the principle of traditional CM theory is based on dialectical therapy where different patients require different treatments. How to develop a standardized product is a challenging task.

I have to say that it's impossible to control manufacturing these products. People always consider Chinese medicine as non-scientific. In my opinion, CM's theory cannot be explained by the modern medical theory. The development of CM is scientific. However, we cannot explain it with the help of current science. The thing you cannot see doesn't mean

[4]Some of the above data has been published in my article, The Promotion of Masculinity and Feminity through Ayurveda in Modern India, Indian Journal of Gender Studies [2013], Vol 20, No. 3, pp.415–434, Co-author K E Kuah-Perace.

Fig. 5.3 Some of the impotence products come under the logo of ayurveda or herbal in India. *Source* Photos were taken by the author during participant observation in an ayurvedic shop in September 2004

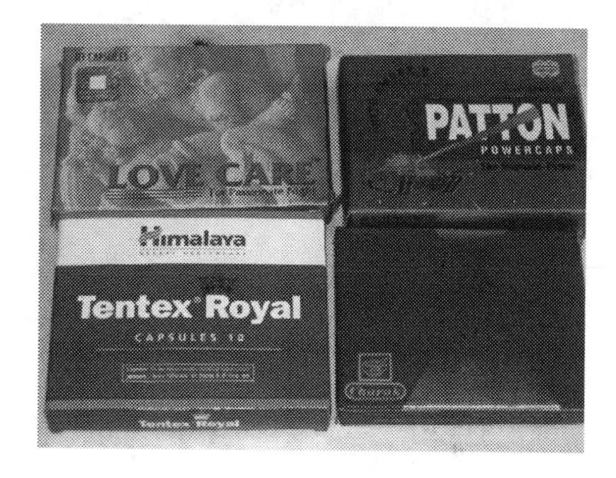

Fig. 5.4 Some of the impotence products come under the logo of ayurveda or herbal in India. *Source* Photos were taken by the author during participant observation in an ayurvedic shop in September 2004

that it does not exist. Drug standardization is a direction that we can make effort to but it's difficult. For example, Chinese medicine advocates individual differences among patients which is contradictory to the idea of standardization.

The effectiveness of Chinese medicine herbs depend on various factor such as place of origin, processing methods, etc. *Many drug manufacturers do not care about this and I think these things should be regulated. At the same time, Chinese medicine is a synthesize effect of many herbs, plants and materials and it is hard to define a standartised treatment or product. I encounter these challenges during conducting clinical trail. The quality of herbs can not be standardized by a simple way. Besides that, although the chemical component satisfies the requirements, we can not said it will make effect to the treatment. The scientific standard do not develop as fast as people believe. Something can not have a useful standardization now. The best to control the quality of CM is to provide more practice opportunities to students and improve the quality of doctors.*

Many bogus medicines and health products are available in the market under the brand name Chinese medicine. Actually, they are the combinations of Chinese and Western medicine. The government should take responsibilities to solve this problem. I am really opposed to fake drugs which ruin the name of Chinese medicine. Anyway, I believe many people trust Chinese medicine. This is also a key point why doctors of Western medicine underestimate us. The manufacturers add Western medicine which has lower quality and greater side-effect into the production of Chinese patent drugs. People don't know the truth and become ill after taking such drugs. Doctors of Western medicine, especially those in between 40–50 years age, feel annoyed when someone mentions anything about Chinese medicine to them.

In India, of those interviewed, 5% of the male patients had consulted an ayurvedic practitioner for problems related to premature ejaculation. Although many male patients are reluctant to consult ayurvedic doctors concerning sexual problems such as premature ejaculation, erectile dysfunction, impotence problems, etc., a significant number of male customers purchased impotence pills from ayurvedic shops. From participant observation conducted during September 2004 in an ayurvedic medicine shop, out of a total of 134 customers observed, men's impotence pills were the fifth highest-selling category and were purchased by 10 customers. A products-sold list from another ayurvedic shop for August 1–15, 2005 showed that men's impotence pills were purchased by 13 customers out of 187. It was also observed during participant observation that most of the customers left the ayurvedic shop quickly after purchasing impotence pills. This, however, was not the case for customers purchasing other health-related products or medicines, who usually asked various questions and information about the effective use of those products. Unfortunately I could not collect any primary data from any Chinese medicine shop. I have tried with the help of student assistants in an outlet of Beijing Tong Ren Tang in the city of Zhuhai in Guangdong province but failed to get permission from the shop authority to do participant observation or get any statistics. One of my student assistants also tried to collect the products sold list from other Chinese medicine shops in Shenyang city of Liaoning province but failed because of the non-cooperation from shop authority. However, we were able to interview Chinese medicine practitioners and explore their views on manufacturing these gendered products which I have discussed in the above section.

There are several reasons for the popularity of Chinese herbal and Indian ayurvedic or herbal impotence pills. Although various impotence pills prepared according to Western medical formulations were available in Western medicine drugstores, Chinese herbal and ayurvedic and or herbal impotence pills were preferred for various reasons. First, the natural and herbal content of the products inspires consumer perception of minimum side-effects. A large number of products that treat male impotence are advertised as natural or herbal and having minimum or no side effect logo. For example, Vita-ex Gold Plus manufactured by Baidyanath Ayurved is referred to in their flyer as, 100% natural ayurvedic powerhouse for richer, fuller and energetic life. Second, a doctor's prescription is not necessary to purchase Chinese herbal and ayurvedic impotence pills, Pill which is convenient for customers too shy to consult a doctor. Most of the impotence products sold in Chinese medicine drug stores contain a logo Over The Counter (OTC) which means anybody can purchase this products without a doctor's prescription. For example, Beijing Tong Ren Tang has manufactured several impotence products with OTC logo such as Jinkui Shenqi Wan, Bushen Qiangshen Pian, Wuzi Yanzong Wan, etc. and could be purchased from their outlet without a doctor's prescription. Various impotence products manufactured by the same company could be also purchased online without a doctor's prescription. For example, Souyang Gujing Wan manufactured by Beijing Tong Ren Tang could be purchased online with an average price RMB 18 for 10 pills. Another energy boosting related product Yangchun Koufuye (drink 6 bottle) manufactured by Beijing Tong Ren Tang could be purchased online with an average price RMB 136. Western medicine drugstores were not reluctant to sell impotence pill manufactured under Western medicine formula without a doctor's prescription given that some users could develop blood pressure symptoms or heart problem, or other complications. For example, Viagra-a famous brand of impotence pill manufactured by Pfizer through following Western medicine formula could not be legally purchased in China and India without a doctor's prescription. Finally, although some brands of Chinese herbal and ayurvedic and or herbal impotence pills were relatively expensive, they were cheaper than the famous Western medicine brands. The price of Chinese herbal impotence products could be varied according to the materials and ingredients they used. Generally those impotence products contain animal and mineral materials and ingredients are more expensive than those contains herb and plant based materials and ingredients. For example, one drug store in the city of Zhuhai in People's Republic of China which sells both Chinese herbal medicine and Western medicine has both Chinese herbal impotence pills and Western impotence pills.[5] One pack of Viagra from that store which is a famous impotence pill in Western medicine contains 1 g each 5 tablets priced RMB 495 whereas Shengfa tablet claimed as Chinese herbal medicine and each tablet contains 1.14 g of crude drugs priced RMB 496 for 180 tablets. The price of impotence pill manufactured under herbal or ayurvedic logo in India also varied significantly. For example, Love Care for Passionate Night (10 capsules), manufactured by Slim Care Herbal Products Pvt., cost INR 90, while Body Plus (six capsules), manufactured by Jay Pranav Ayurvedic Pharma, cost INR 540.

5.5 Women's Beauty as Ayurvedic Commodity

For women modern ayurvedic companies are manufacturing body-beauty related products ranging from slimming powder and pills to breast massage oils, reinforcing stereotypes gender roles. Beauty has become an exclusive commodity within ayurvedic domain, particularly for women, although recently for men as well, who spend a large amount of their incomes on body-beauty care. Beauty has been discussed in ayurvedic text as *Rasayana* (rejuvenation therapy) therapy procedure which is one of the eight branches of ayurveda. According to *Caraka Samhita* text rejuvenation therapy ensures prolonged lifespan, youthfulness, good health, fine voice and complexion, stoutness, intellect, power of retention and strength (Valiathan 2003: 233). The text provided a list of herbs and plants best for

[5]Exact location of the drug store is not disclosed because of the privacy reason.

preparing *rasayanas* such as *haritaki* (a fruit grows in Indian subcontinent) and *amalaki* (a fruit grows in Indian subcontinent). *Haritaki* promotes good digestion, youthfulness and strength of sense organs, the text added (Ibid: 235). *Caraka Samhita* text also suggested various prescription to prepare *rasayana* therapy for health benefit apart from beauty and youthfulness. For example, one prescription said: *amalaki* fruits, *vidari, jivanti,* and satavari should be processed according to a physician's direction and cooked with ghee and mixed with sugar and honey before intake the formulation. Following this prescription can promotes long life, strength, complexion, intellect, fertility, and gives a booming voice (Ibid: 327).

According to the above explanation beauty which could be achieved from ayurvedic rejuvenation therapy is not only women's concern but also men's concern since *rasayana* therapy is linked to improve other qualities. Women's health is presented in the classical ayurvedic texts in relation to human reproduction. In the *Caraka Samhita* text, women's bodily beauty is represented as necessary to gain appreciation from men. The text names five sensual attractions-beauty, smell, touch, fluidity, and flavor-highly appreciated by man, which he obtains simultaneously from woman's body. Women are also described in the text as more affectionate than men (*Caraka* 2003, *chikitsha sthana*, Chap. 2, paragraph 3). The text also considers men's desire for women who attract his miraculous powers by being pretty, youthful, glorious and obedient (Ibid, paragraph 1). The text further elaborates on womens problems, such as menstruation and the ideal time for sexual intercourse to enhance pregnancy, and prescribes treatments for particular women's problem (*Caraka* 2003, *sutra sthana*). In the *Caraka Samhita,* especially *sharir sthana*, women are associated with the qualities of breastfeeding, delivery, pregnancy and menstruation, etc. Here, the text considers as having "incomparable group physiology" (*otul gotrio sharir*), and explores womanly functions such as pregnancy, safe birth delivery, female fertility, birth and information on infants, foetus, twins, premature births, etc. The text also provides details on 'gynaecological physiology' and 'physiology for ideal pregnancy' and describes causes of pregnancy, growth of pregnancy, sages' views about the growth of pregnancy, background of pregnancy, foetus condition during first, second and third months, sex identification of the foetus, pains and pleasures of pregnancy, moods and emotions of pregnant women, foetus development, time determination for delivery, and causes of infertility (*Caraka* 2003, *sharir sthana*). The *Caraka Samhita* text (*sutro sthana*) also elaborated on "women problems" such as menstruation and ideal time for sexual intercourse to enhance pregnancy, and prescribed treatment for such women's problems (*Caraka* 2003, *chikitsha sthana*, Chap. 1, paragraph 1). The *Sharir sthana* (human anatomy and physiology) part of the classical ayurvedic text *Astanga Hrdayam* also contains chapters on women-related issues, such as chapters one and two, which describe gynaecology; paediatrics, and especially reproduction: pregnancy; sex determination; purity and pollution of sperm; menstruation; foetus condition during different phases of pregnancy; pre-natal, ante-natal and post-natal situations; labour pains; and related diseases and their treatments are all discussed (Vagbhatas 2009, sharir sthana, volume 1: 357–457).

Virilisation therapy, as discussed in the ayurvedic texts of *Caraka and Susruta Samhita*, was solely for men, while women's menopausal state was completely ignored (Islam 2013: 429; Shah 2006: 45). *Astanga Hrdayam* text suggested three major secrets of preserving health: food, sleep and non-celibacy. The text discussed the importance of avoiding celibacy and provided a list of women with whom a man should avoid sexual intercourse. This list includes: a woman who is not lying with her face upward; who is in her menstrual period; who is not liked; whose activities are displeasing; whose vagina (genitals) is dirty and troublesome; who is very obese or very emaciated; who has recently delivered and who is pregnant; the other woman (other than his wife); the nun; the other vagina of animals like the goat, buffalo, etc. (Vagbhatas 2009, Volume 1: 122). However, the text is silent about who are the men with whom a woman should avoid sexual intercourse. This clearly illustrates that sex is exclusively a man's affairs in ayurvedic text and women's role is secondary or only applicable to satisfy man's need.

Ayurvedic companies today problematically redefine women's health in relation to beauty concerns. Emphasizing the 'natural' content of ayurveda, pharmaceutical companies target women as potential consumers and present an ayurvedic feminization through associating women's bodies with beauty. The big ayurvedic pharmaceutical companies have attempted to redefine the woman's body—from a reproductive to a natural body. Female 'natural body' has been constructed according to a prime market strategy to promote and sell ayurvedic beauty and health products. Under this scheme, women's health has been replaced by the 'beauty paradigm', and natural beauty, which can be achieved through using ayurvedic products, has become an important part of Indian femininity. For example, Dabur India Limited -one of the largest ayurvedic drug manufacturers in India has three brands: *Vatika, Amla* and *Real*, crossed the INR 1000 crore sales mark globally by 2014 (Dabur India Limited 2015: 12). Out of the three brands, *Vitika* is primarily a haircare and skin care products brand, *Amla* is a hair care brand and *Real* is a health Care and food brand manufacturing primarily fruit juices and honey related products. According to Dabur International webpage which has three languages options, English, French and Arabic, Dabur *Amla* brand manufacturers four types of hair care products: Amla Shampoos and Conditioners; Amla Hair Oils; Amla Hair Creams; and Amla Snake Oils. Amla Shampoos and Conditioners include six items: Snake oil shampoo, Keratin Shampoo, Vitamin Shampoo, Snake Oil Conditioner, Keratin Conditioner, and Vitamin Conditioner. Similarly Amla Hair Oils series contain five items: Amla Hair Oil; Oil Amla Gold; Amla Jasmin; Amla Anti Dandruff; and Amla Cooling. Amla Hair Cream series includes products such as Hair Fall Therapy, Voluminising Treatment, Intensive Repair Therapy, Intensive Moisturizing, and Anti Dandruff Hair Cream, Amla Snake Oils series brought products such as Repair Therapy, Frizz Control, and Extreme Shine (Dabur International Webpage, 2016).[6] All the photos printed on the package of various

[6]Retrieved from the following link http://www.daburinternational.com/index.php/en/front/home And accessed on January 19, 2016.

Fig. 5.5 Ayurvedic Fair and Lovely package. *Source* Retrieved from the following link and retrieved on March 27, 2016: http://vanitynoapologies.com/fair-and-lovely-ayurvedic-care-cream-review-price-ingredients/

hair care products under Dabur Amla Hair Care series are female, clearly targeting women as their sole customers for those hair care products.

> *Fair and Lovely Ayurvedic Care is a cream brought under the Fair and Lovely brand. Although there are several products under Fair and Lovely brand such as Advanced Multi Vitamin Face Wash, BB Cream, Advanced Multi Vitamin Cream, MAX Fairness Multi-Expert Cream,* etc. *Fair and Lovely Ayurvedic Care is the only cream claimed as ayurvedic. The product in its package claims that it provides clear fairness for sensitive skin. The product claims in its package that it "infused with the goodness of Kumkumadi Tailam" and it contains 16 ingredients which are known to- Lodhra, Khas, Neelotpal – calm and soothe skin; Manjishtha, Kesar & Padmak—Clear marks & improve complexion; and Milk, Bargad, Wheat Germ Oil—Clear uneven skin tone. The product can provides "Clear Fairness even for sensitive skin", the product package claimed. The product package further claimed that it can "reduced skin darkening, marks, uneven skin tone plus, visible fairness for self perceived sensitive skin"* (Figs. 5.5 and 5.6).

> *A review on the product was posted online on February 25, 2015 by Vidhi as contributor. In her/his review the contributor wrote that "I have been using this cream for almost 2 weeks now and I didn't find any difference because I currently don't have any pimples nor I have uneven skin tone to find in difference in this regard. In case of fairness (I am already fair and don't wish to look white). I would say NO it will not give you permanent*

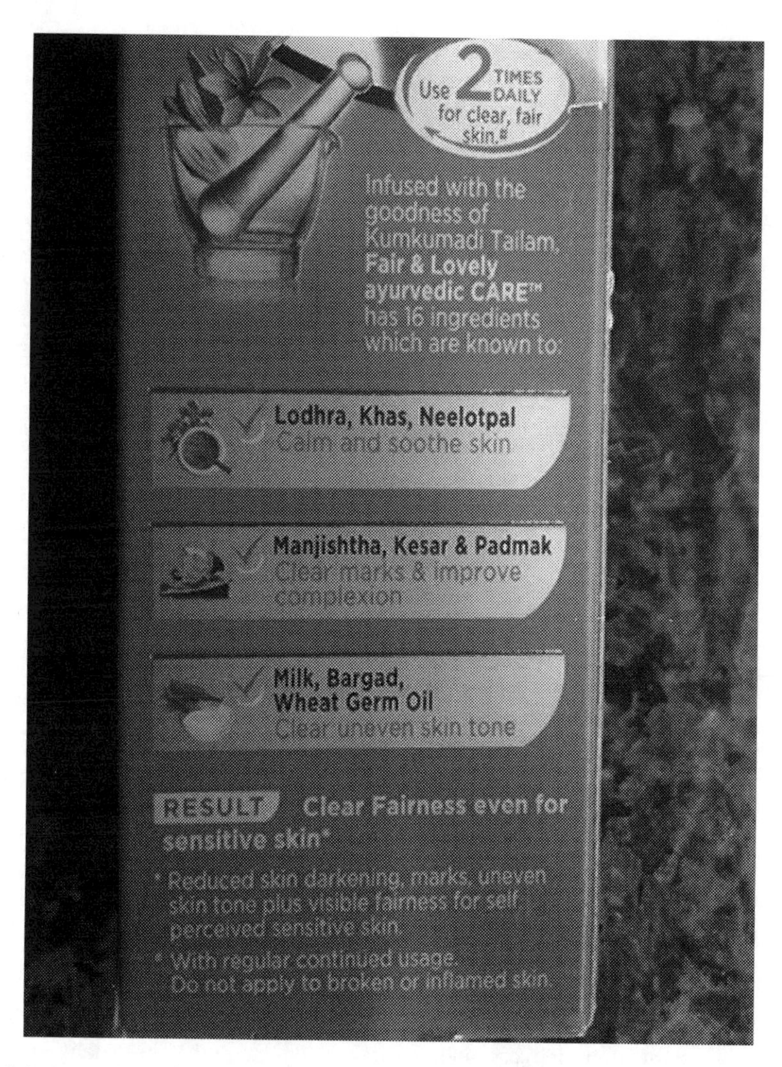

Fig. 5.6 Ayurvedic Fair and Lovely package. *Source* Retrieved from the following link and accessed on March 27, 2016: http://vanitynoapologies.com/fair-and-lovely-ayurvedic-care-cream-review-price-ingredients/

fairness in any way, it just brightens the face after applying the cream which all the fairness creams do"[7] *There are 14 comments posted on the review of the product and most of them perceived a negative view on the product. One comments was "I have used fair and lovely product ages ago, hated them". Another comment was "Fair and lovely products never works: (such a bad brand)".*

[7]Retrieved from the following link and accessed on March 27, 2016: http://vanitynoapologies.com/fair-and-lovely-ayurvedic-care-cream-review-price-ingredients/.

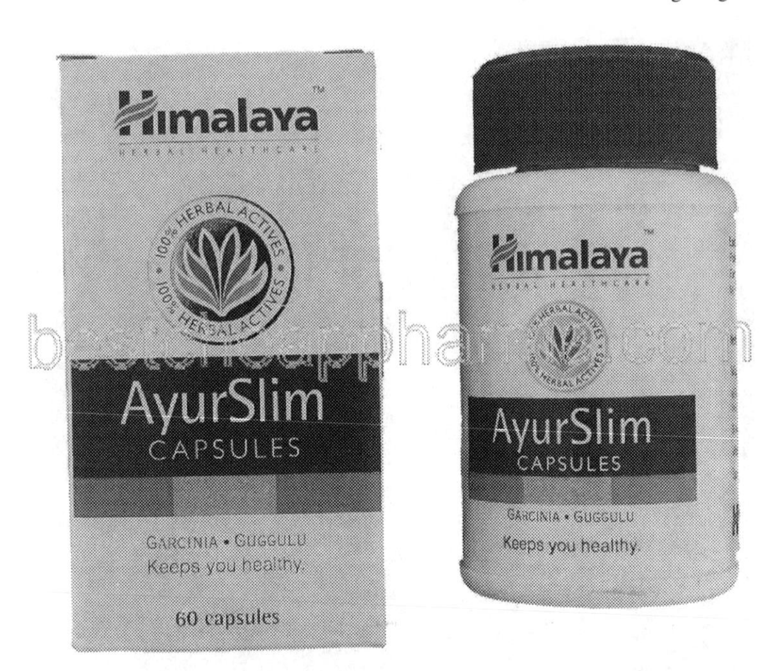

Fig. 5.7 An Ayurvedic sliming product package. *Source* Retrieved from the following link and accessed on March 27, 2016: https://www.google.ca/search?q=ayurslim&biw=1280&bih=687&source=lnms&tbm=isch&sa=X&sqi=2&ved=0ahUKEwio-siWueDLAhVO9GMKHULuAJMQ_AUIBigB#imgrc=buNERMLhvhFXVM%3A

One of the distinctive features of the entire ayurvedic feminization scheme in modern Indian society is the representation of social hierarchy in terms of categories of products, prices and naming. Six brands of slimming products found in one ayurvedic store during participant observation, four had English-sounding names, such as 'Oberid' weight loss capsules, manufactured by Ratan and priced at INR 350 for 30 capsules; Slim Fast, manufactured by Herbicure Private limited, priced INR 200 for 10 capsules; etc. For example, *Mritsanjivani Sura* ('For medical use only, useful after delivery and for increasing strength') post-delivery tonic manufactured by Dabur India Ltd. 375 ml is priced at only INR 60. Most of the expensive brand body-beauty-related products use English, or a combination of English and Sanskrit names targeted for middle-class elite women. However, most of the women's reproductive health-related products have Sanskrit names, such as *Ashokarishta* ('Health tonic for women') or *Dasmularishta* ('Reduces general weakness and restores energy in women after delivery') and are priced less aggressively. With this development, women's health concerns have largely been replaced by beauty concerns, and ayurvedic companies are capitalizing on the trend to increase their profits fourfold (Fig. 5.7).

5.6 Conclusion

Both for the Chinese and Indian drug manufacturers producing sexual energy boosting products such as impotence pill, penis massage cream, oil, etc. for male consumer have become a lucrative market strategy to boost their profit. Although statistics has revealed that only 5% of the male patients consulted ayurvedic doctors in India concerning sexual problems, a relatively large number of male customers purchased impotence pills from ayurvedic shops. Statements of patients who attended the out-patient department of the Central Research Institute (Ayurveda) in Kolkata, during the reporting period from 1st April to 31st March 2003–04 also shows that 4515 male patients attended the department for various diseases but that none of them attended a doctor for pre-mature ejaculation or erectile dysfunction. However, from participant observation conducted during September 2004 in an ayurvedic medicine shop, for a total of 134 customers observed, men's impotence pills were the fifth highest-selling category. At the same time, Beijing Tong Ren Tang one of the biggest drug manufacturers of Chinese herbal medicine in China also manufacture more than dozens of male sexuality enhancement products ranging from impotence pill to energy and vitality products. During observation, one outlet of the same company found selling more than eight types of power and energy boosting products directly or indirectly related to enhance man's sexual energy.

Another significant aspect of Chinese herbal medicine and ayurveda in modern world is the entry of women as consumers. Although there is no significant evidence to prove that Chinese herbal medicine or ayurveda were accessible to women as medical profession in the past, there is a dramatic shift in recent years about women entering as product customers. Both the classical Chinese and ayurvedic medical texts are male dominating and the representation of women in those texts relates to human reproduction. Contemporary drug manufacturers in both China and India are instrumental to redefine women's body and health. The propagation of cosmetics and health product as natural and makes women as target consumers symbolizes beauty as part of women's health. In this sense women's health has been replaced by beauty paradigm which is very dissimilar to women's representation in classical texts. The development of cosmetics, slimming and beauty products for women and sexual impotence products for the men is a way in which contemporary drug manufacturers feminize and masculinize Chinese herbal medicine and ayurveda.

Chapter 6
New Consumption: Rise of Health Tourism

6.1 Introduction

Health tourism has increasingly become popular in China and India over the last two decades with the rise of consumer capitalism. The economic boom brought by globalization, adoption of open door policy, rise of emerging middle class, and influx of foreign visitors are the major causes behind this development. The emerging middle class have found themselves taking on an array of technical, management and professional occupations that demand not only their skills but also long hours of commitment on the job. Accumulated stress and tension take a toll in such professions. The result is that many suffer from 'burn-out' syndrome, on both mental and physical levels (Islam 2008: 201–202). On the physical level, the stress and tensions are translated into muscle pain, backache, and mental lethargy. Recognizing the need to cater to the physical and mental needs of the middle-class, large corporations have explored different services and products to cater to them. Increasingly, the developments of services and products that focus on holistic lifestyle and traditional medicine have caught the imagination of big and small corporations as well as the middle class, who become ready consumers (Ibid).

The total number of health tourism companies offering treatments in China are 2 whereas in India 116. The number of health tourism companies based in China is just 1, whereas there are 89 in India (Connell 2011: 185–186). Chinese medicine and related health services such as massage, tuina, cupping, etc. have increasingly become popular among middle class consumers and overseas tourists who has disposable income. In India, ayurvedic lifestyle, yoga and various ayurvedic oil massage therapies are the popular health products consumed by the Indian middle class, Indian diaspora and tourists from abroad. The objectives of this chapter are to examine how Chinese medicine and ayurveda have been used as a brand name to cater various products and services to tourists, and the pattern of products and services offered under tourism program. This chapter examines the development of the notion of indigenous medicine and lifestyle related services and products in

M.N. Islam, *Chinese and Indian Medicine Today*,
DOI 10.1007/978-981-10-3962-1_6

response to contemporary demand. Besides, this chapter also explores the types of health products and services that consumed by the tourists from overseas. A couple of resort and establishment such as Ocean Spring Resort and Dragon Union Foot Massage Center from the Southern coastal city of Zhuhai in China were investigated and observed. In India, a case study on the Vedic Village located in the Eastern city of Kolkata was examined.

6.2 Defining Health Tourism

Health tourism involves a wide variety of interrelated domains and product niches, including medical tourism, wellness tourism, spa tourism, reproductive and fertility tourism, traditional medicine tourism, etc. It could be defines as "the attempt on the part of a tourist facility or destination to attract tourists by deliberately promoting its health-care services and facilities, in addition to its regular tourist amenities" (Goodrich 1994: 228). There are three major patterns of health tourism existing today: 'medication and therapeutics', 'pampering', and 'wellness' (Ibid). Medication and therapeutics tourism includes medical operations, continued therapeutics under the supervision of a physician (for purely medical or health reasons), etc., and this conforms to the idea of medical tourism. The most common medical, surgical and dental procedures medical tourists consume include heart bypass, heart-valve replacement, angioplasty, hip replacement, knee replacement, gastric bypass, hip resurfacing, spinal fusion, mastectomy, rhinoplasty (nose reconstruction), tummy tuck, breast reduction, breast implants, tooth crown, tooth whitening, dental implants, gastroscopy, cardiac surgery, hysterectomy, fertility treatment, cosmetic and plastic surgery, bariatric surgery (weight loss surgery), dermatological services including skin cancer checks and treatment; less frequent procedures include, anti-aging therapy, chronic disease care and treatment, high-end medical checkups, fitness exams, etc. (Department of Resources, Energy and Tourism 2011: ii; Herrick 2007; Khan 2010: 2; Neil Lunt et al. 2013: 34; Wanli and Zhihua 2012). 'Pampering' health tourism includes offering people an experience that makes them feel good (massages, herbal wraps, etc.). 'Wellness health tourism' includes services to help people to live a healthy lifestyle through preventing health problems, so that they stay well both physically and mentally. It focuses on activities such as medical check-ups to identify potentials problems, as well as classes or tutorials about healthy life, healthy diet, etc. (Bookman and Bookman 2007: 43–44, Goodrich 1994: 228). In both China and India, pampering and wellness health tourism have become overlapping domains, where the products and services constantly interact with each other (Islam 2014: 53). The 1983 World Tourism Meeting, referring to health tourism, stated that "the right to rest, a natural consequence of the right to work, must be affirmed as a fundamental right in terms of human ".[1] Thus health tourism is to fulfil some basic health needs for recovering mental, physical and spiritual well-being; and this is similar to the holistic definition of health by the World Health Organization (Islam 2008: 205).

Over the last two decades wellness health tourism particularly became popular in China and India where various forms of indigenous medicine have been promoted as a product and service niche. In Chinese medical thought, maintaining balance and harmony in and between the physical body and the natural environment is perceived to be the key to achieving good health and longevity. The theorization of the four major concepts used in Chinese medical philosophy, namely the *Dao*, *qi*, *yin/yang*, and the *five elements* (wood, fire, earth, metal, and water), places enormous emphasis on the balance between the internal body and the external environment (Kohn 2005). Besides, increasing numbers of life-style related chronic diseases such as diabetes and obesity, and those resulting from long working hours and poor working conditions for office workers due to rapid economic growth in China, have negatively affected the physical and mental well-being of her population (Tsui 2008). This chapter focuses on those wellness health related products and services coming under the brand name of indigenous medicine. The concept of wellness was first developed by the American physician Halbert Dunn in 1959; the concept combines individual well-being and fitness. The word 'wellness' refers to a lifestyle that an individual creates to achieve the highest potential for well-being. The concept of well-being requires initiative and determination, with everyone deciding for himself or herself whether to make a lifestyle change (Nahrstedt 2004). While Asian systems of medicine such as ayurveda, Chinese medicine, yoga, tai chi, etc., have recognized the wellness aspect of health from very outset, they also contain the seeds of the modern concept 'health and wellness'. Wellness is defined as "physical activity combined with relaxation of the mind and intellectual stimulus, basically a kind of fitness of body, mind and spirit, including the holistic aspect" (Schobersberger et al. 2004: 199–200). Wellness is also one of the prominent concepts of human health recognized by the World Health Organization's (WHO) definition: "health is a state of complete physical, mental and social well-being and not merely the absence of disease or infirmity" (WHO 1978, 2000).

6.3 Indigenous Medicine as Health Tourism Product Niche in China and India

Both the Chinese and Indian government are eager to promote health tourism under indigenous medical system for the visitors from overseas. A Chinese government report suggests that the existing underdeveloped health tourism industry is focusing on traditional Chinese medicine and therapies (Ministry of Health of People's

[1]Retrieved from the following link: http://www.medical-tourism-india.com/what_is_medical_tourism.htm and accessed on June 2007.

Republic of China 2007). In particular, spas and massage centers have become big business in China, which has an ancient tradition of offering massage, bathing, hot springs, herbal medicine and acupuncture (Heung and Kucukusta 2012). In India, the Central Council of Indian Medicine (CCIM) under the Ministry of Health and Family Welfare recognized the potential of ayurvedic tourism in the National Policy on Indian Systems of Medicine and Homoeopathy—2002, stating that "facilities for *panchakarma* and yoga would be encouraged to be offered in hotels. Indian System of Medicine parks would be developed in collaboration with state tourism authorities" (National Policy on Indian Systems of Medicine and Homoeopathy 2002, article 16.17). Apart from government initiative a massive growth of indigenous health resorts, spas and vacation housing under private initiative is also a significant trend. Many resorts are located at beaches and carry out aggressive marketing campaigns to attract local and international health tourists. People from the home and abroad come to various cities of China and India for different reasons but experience rejuvenation therapies, massage therapies, tuina, yoga, etc. offered by the massage centres, village circle clubs, wellness centres and other health tourist resorts.

In Chinese history the idea of wellness health tourism can be traced back to the Chinese medical classic *Huang Di Nei Jing* (Yellow Emperor's Canon of Internal Medicine). The text puts enormous emphasis on adjusting daily living, behavior, lifestyle, and food and dietary practice in accordance with the seasons and environmental conditions to preserve health and prevent diseases (Islam 2014: 54). *Huang Di Nei Jing* in its *Su Wen* (Plain Questions) part contains 81 chapters and 7 of them discussed how four seasons, nature, and the environment effect people's health (Bing 2010: 1–7). These includes chapter two on *Si Qi Tiao Shen Da Lun* (On preserving health in accordance with the four seasons), Chapter three on *Sheng Qi Tong Tian Lun* (On the human vital energy connecting with nature), chapter five on *Yin Yang Ying Xiang Da Lun* (The corresponding relation between the *yin* and *yang* of human and all things and that of the four seasons), Chapter nine on *Liu Jie Zang Xiang Lun* (The close relation between the viscera in human body with the environment of the outside world), and so on (Ibid). The physicians of ancient China had long recognized the impact of climatic factors such as sunlight, wind, dust and other elements of the natural environment; and also considered lifestyle factors such as food, behavior, morals, etc., as influencing the human body and health, and also as operative in curing diseases (Alter 2005; Islam 2014: 54). Following four seasonal regimens are the key secret to preserve health and prevent disease according to that text. The text suggested the ideal behavior, rules, and regulation people need to follow in their daily life to preserve health. For example, the text suggested the following paragraph about the spring season:

Spring is the season of birth and spread and people should go to bed when night comes and gets up early in the morning and breathe the fresh air while walking in the yard to exercise his/her tendons and bones, and loosen hair to make the whole body comfortable along with the generation of energy. People should also help surviving and not killing things, to donate but not to wrest, to award and not to punish so as to correspond the prosperity of spring energy and fit in the way of preserving one's health. Failing to follow such regulation can hurts someone's liver and can catch cold syndrome in summer (Bing 2010: 13).

Similar suggestions for the seasons of summer, winter and autumn are also provided by the text. Still many senior citizens in contemporary China try to follow such seasonal routine and do exercise, including *tai qi,* regularly in parks (Chapman 2007). *Huang Di Nei Jing* also contains several paragraphs in chapter five of *Su Wen* part on how landscape, desires, seasons, dietary practice, temperament, etc. affect *qi* and *yin/yang*, which are vital to keep balance and preserve health (Bing 2010: 35–38). The chapter divides China into five regions including the East, the South, the Central, the West, and the North and explain how peoples from different regions exposed to different lifestyle and dietary habit and experience different type of diseases which corresponds to their geographical location (ibid). For example, the text mentioned that the Western part of China is an area abundant with gold, jade, sand, and stone. The *qi* of heaven and earth is astringed there and people live alongside windy hills where water and soil are rigid. The peoples of Western China wear coarse clothes, lie on hay mats, and eat greasy and fatty foods. If diseases occur, people takes oral herbs which also came from Western part of China (*Huang Di Nei Jing* 2009: 271). Similar description can also be found on east, north, central and south China in the text.

Similar to Chinese medical texts, ayurvedic text *Astanga Hrdayam* contains chapter on daily regimen and seasonal regimen which suggested how to maintain health through following a daily and seasonal routine. In the chapter three of part one, there are six *ritu* (seasons) spelled out in the text: winter, spring, summer, rainy, autumn and dewy. The seasons are divided into *daksinayana* (southern solstice) and *uttarayana* (northern solstice), according to the movements of moon and sun. The rainy, autumn and dewy seasons are considered as southern solstice when the 'god moon' (the moon, which is considered a god) becomes stronger. Salt, food, and honey are produced in abundance and all living species become stronger during these seasons. Winter, spring and summer are considered as northern solstice when the 'god sun' (the sun, which is considered a god) becomes stronger, and bitter humours in nature increase and all living species become weaker (Vagbhatas 2009: 33–34). This text particularly emphasizes the condition of the natural environment in different seasons according to air, water and the location of sun and moon. It advises the duties of individual human to maintain their balance of health with nature during various seasons.

In the *Dinacarya Adhyaya* (desire for long life) chapter the text prescribes various rules and regulations to lead a healthy life on a daily basis which includes physical motivation, purification and postures for sleeping and waking hours; and for personal hygiene, physical exercise, and dietary intake. It also prescribes acceptable behaviour and moral and social values that individuals should uphold (Vagbhatas 2009: 22–23).

Based on the description on daily regimen/routine prescribed in the *Astanga Hrdayam* text daily regimen could be divided into four parts depending on the time of the day: morning regimen; afternoon regimen; evening regimen; and night regimen. The text denotes that since our body is governed by the sun and moon all activities related to our body are also related to the sun and moon. Every physiological functions of the body also run in accidence to the sun and moon. Table 6.1 has been prepared by the author about daily regimen presented in the text:

Many kings and elite group of the society in medieval India tried to follow the daily and seasonal regimen prescribed by the ayurvedic texts to preserve their health and prevent diseases. Kings and wealthy people in medieval India changed their domiciles frequently according to the season in order to lead healthy lives, and might build several palaces outside capital cities, using them as vacation houses for leisure and relaxation as well as for seasonal capitals. Most of the palaces were surrounded by big compounds, with lakes, flowers, gardens—and physicians. Such palaces survive in Udaipur, Jaipur, Sheikhawati, Alwar, Jodhpur, Jaisalmer, Bikaner, Simla, and Kashmir in the Himalayan foothills in Northern India; in Bhavnagar and Wankaner in Western India; in Orchha and Gwalior in Central India; and in Mysore, Ootacamund, Cochin and Travancore in Southern India (Sugich 1992). Jag Niwas or the Lake Palace in Udaipur, is a good example of a place where royal family members "listened to the tale of the bard and slept off their noonday opiate amidst the cool breezes of the lake" (Sugich 1992: 29). Although it was admired as a garden house for the recreation of the wealthy people, it was also used as a domicile for rejuvenation. The famous garden, Ram Bagh, was associated with Ram Bagh palace, which was used as the rest house of a maharaja outside the main city, and also as a hunting lodge and official guest house for royal visitors (Ibid: 21). Sariska Palace built during the late nineteenth and early twentieth century's by Maharaja Jay Singh, was surrounded by mountains and a huge garden that could accommodate 1000 people. Siliserh Lake and its palace in Bikaner, the Gulab Bhavan built by Maharaja Jari Singh on the bank of Dal Lake, and Woodville, the official summer residence of the Maharaja of Gondal, are also some of the best examples of such elaborate retreats (Ibid). This kind of 'health tourism' became institutionalized during the British colonial rule. The British set up places in mountains and on beaches as tourist destinations for health, relaxation and the enjoyment of the beauty of nature. The idea was to lead a 'natural' way of life outside the cities and get away from the pollution that had developed in them during that time. Darjeeling in West Bengal and places in Kashmir in northern India were perhaps the best-known examples of resorts, and were known as 'heavenly paradises' where wealthy people from both the British and Indian went for a change of environment and to restore health. Many physicians suggested their patients 'change air' (*bayu poriborton*) and visit Darjeeling or Kashmir, and affluent people gradually established vacation houses in those regions. Al Hilal Palace in Kashmir symbolises this effort; it was built in 1931 by the Nawab of Bahawalpur to escape the summer heat (Ibid).

Another type of rejuvenation and relaxation for wealthy Indian males in ancient and medieval India involved was the presence of harems or *zenanas*. The tradition of harems entered India during the Arab invasion of Sindh, and later Persian. The harems were really palaces or areas of palaces, usually located at a convenient distance from the public, so that the privacy of the elite could be maintained. Although these private places were easily accessible for the royal male elites they were clearly distinguished from their own private apartments. Women accommodated in the harem included some members of royal families, their servants, slaves,

Table 6.1 Daily routine to preserve health and prevent disease

Daily regimen		
Steps	Action and note	Comments/suggestions
Morning regimen	Wake up	The period of fourth quarter of the night
	At *Brahma Muhurta*	Ideally 48 min before the sun rise
		Kapha is going to reduce and *vata* starts functioning
	Evacuation Depending on the condition or digestion	Don't try to evacuate unless there is real pressure
		Don't suppress evacuation when there is a pressure
		Don't start another work before finish the existing one
	Oral hygiene	Use a branch or particular tree such as *Neem*, front part of the branch should be tweak and make it softer so that it does not hit the meat of the teeth
	Sense of organs purification Ear, nose, throat, skin, eye	Eye- put helpful liquid on eye to make it sharp and charming
		Nose-clear the nose
		Throat-smoking or tobacco consumption (forbidden for people with weak body, sick person, etc.)
		Skin-put oil on your body everyday basis (or at least every second day)
	Morning drink/beverage	A glass of water could be left with some ayurvedic leafs depending on the availability of the leafs in different area before go to bed This water has to be taken as morning drink No food/breakfast should be eaten immediate after wake up except morning drink because of the following reasons: Person's don't feel hungry unless it is pathological Metabolic activities has not been activated Gastric circulation did not start properly
	Meditation/ritualistic activities/prayers	Why meditation? To take control of mind To take the brain ready to start up daily activities To focus towards concentration and calmness
		Rules of meditation Should be done in a ritualistic setting such as religious activities Should be done in empty stomach and before eating any food because all the blood in our body goes downward when inject food in our stomach and there is less supply of blood into the brain
	Physical exercise *Vata dosa* person-less exercise *Pitta dosa* person-moderate exercise *Kapha dosa* person-more exercise	Exercise increase the productivity of physical labor Patients suffering from gas problem, or bile related problem or arthritis are forbidden to do exercise)

(continued)

Table 6.1 (continued)

Daily regimen		
Steps	Action and note	Comments/suggestions
	When a person finds sweating under arm that is the optimal point of doing exercise. It symbolizes that the body has generated sufficient amount of heat and circulated all parts of the body	Person younger than 16 years or older than 70 years or sick should not do exercise Winter and spring are the best season for exercise Do little exercise in other seasons Over exercise can cause thirst, tiredness, fever, cough or vomiting
	Put oil on body Put oil on your body every day basis (or at least every second day)	Help to increase the power of eye, nutrition of the body, longevity, beauty of the skin, good sleep, etc.
		Put oil particularly on head, ears and feet (person having some diseases such as asthma are forbidden to use oil)
	Do massage Do massage after exercise with *amloki* (*a form of fruit like olive*)	Massage can reduce the fat from body, make the body strong and make the skin glassy
	Take a bath Take bath with warm water without putting the warm water on head	Taking a bath with warm water increase the power of the body but reduce the strength of hair and eye
		Taking a bath after in taking meals is restricted
	Eating breakfast/morning meal	Ideally after three hours wake up from the bed When the sun has risen reasonably up Body activities of generating *agni* (fire) has start up Breakfast should be light form because the sun heat is not very intense during that time and the digestive capacity is not very strong It is easier for the stomach to digest light breakfast Take a rest for a while after finish breakfast and before to go work
	Regular activity of the day such as job, farming, etc. Starts	
Afternoon regimen	Lunch When the sun has risen up and reach at the top of your head Should be the primary and biggest meal of the day Eat maximum amount of food	Digestive capacity is very strong and large quantity of food could be digested easily Major source of energy to build body and grow bodily tissues Take rest for a while after finish meal
	Afternoon siesta/nap Regionalized and seasonal Longer siesta for a *vata* person Moderate siesta for a *pitta* person, ideally for about 30 min No siesta for a *kapha* person	Only recommended in summer season for every body type person (*Vata-Pitta-Kapha*) because the body cannot generate energy and conserve energy through siesta
	Some goes to continue work but others not	
	Recreational activities Enjoy recreational activities or hobby development exercise such as music, painting, sports, etc. Indulges family activities and develop affinity towards other people who are around you	Provides longer span of brain activities since brain has limited capacity Provide longer lifespan Do not lose grave to the situation or do not lose memory Create continuity of the activities happening into the brain

(continued)

Table 6.1 (continued)

Daily regimen		
Steps	Action and note	Comments/suggestions
	We usually try to ignore this and put more emphasis on work/job	
Evening regimen	Dinner Immediate after the sun set	Digestive capacity of stomach become very slow after sun set and food takes long time to digest There should be enough gap between dinner and go to bed ideally at least three hours Sleeping immediate after eating dinner causes obesity and heaviness in the body and mind because food has not digested properly If food does not digest properly it cause disturbance in the formation and production of stool
Night regimen	Amount of sleep It is individualized and based on the body constituent	It is essential for a *kapha* dominant person to sleep less as they tend to put on excess weight People with pitta *dosha* need medium amount of sleep such as 8 h *Vata dosha* person need large amount of sleep
	Night snacks/drink Drinking a glass of milk before go to the bed is recommended	Eating snacks before go to bed is not recommended because it disturb the digestive process of the dinner a person has eaten Eating snacks cannot be fully digested before sleep which may causes obesity problem
	Size and height of the sleeping bed	Size and height of the bed should be up to the knee of the individual person
	Sexual activities for the adult Sex has to be performed after the digestion of food/dinner Wash body or take a bath if possible after performing sex and before go to bed	Milk has to drink after taking bath if perform sex
Every day moral teaching	Piousness	There is no real pleasure without piousness; Everybody should be pious
	Companionship	Respect them who give you good advise Avoid the companionship of a person who helps you to do bad things and enjoy the companionship of a person who helps you to do good things
	Things need to be avoided	There are ten types of bad things divided in three categories need to avoid everybody: Physical such as jealousy (or violence), theft or robbery and unconstitutional sexual services Speech related such as language which divide peoples, hard words, lie and inconsistent statements Mental such as thinking about killing species, intolerance about others, good quality and atheism

(continued)

Table 6.1 (continued)

Daily regimen		
Steps	Action and note	Comments/suggestions
Restriction on over doing certain issues	Exercise, sleepless night, long walking, over indulgence of sex, laugh, speech, braveness	If a strong lion attack a huge elephant, she might cause her suicide, human also can collapse if they do more than limit the above things
	Taking meals	Take a meal after the digestion of previous meal Intake a limited quantity of food

Vagbhatas (2009: 22–32) (this table is a combination of the Sutrasthna of the Astanga Hrdayam text and author's understanding of reading the text. The text was translated by Prof. K.R. Srikantha Murthy and published by Chowkhamba Krishnadas Academy, Varranasi, India. Author also took help from some video files titled The Daily Ayurvedic Regimen and presented by Korde, Dr. Neelesh. The video files were retrieved from the following link: https://www.youtube.com/watch?v=NGV2FT9zAvs&list=PLy6afWEJ8MGeww-CuDOikciNbz_FUkVc2 and accessed on December 19, 2016)

maids and dancers. Entrance to the royal harems was tightly controlled and visitors were carefully watched (Michelle 1994: 52). Elite males often watched recreational performances of the women, and spent time drinking. All of this was considered to bring physical and mental rejuvenation to the male elites.

6.4 Health and Wellness in Contemporary China and India

This section presents our survey and case study data from China and India.

In our empirical study in the Southern Chinese city of Zhuhai we found that fifty-six percent of the survey visitors had come from Hong Kong including Hong Kong citizen of Chinese ancestor and foreigners, fifteen percent from the United States of America, thirteen percent from Singapore, and the rest from Japan, Korea, Germany, England, South Africa, Mongolia, Spain, Australia, Poland, Belgium, Iceland, Malaysia, India, Russia and Thailand. Sixty-three percent of the visitors were male and thirty-seven percent were female, in an age group of 18–80 years. The tourists represented diverse professional backgrounds, including those with Manager/CEO/Director level positions, students, office workers, technological professionals such as engineers, designers, technicians, entrepreneurs, English teachers, retirees, housewives, lawyers, etc. Eighty-two percent of the visitors had no special health problem and the rest of them had only minor health problems such as back pain, stress, tooth pain, blood pressure, knee ache, etc. Only one expatriate had entered China for medical treatment and to attend a Traditional Chinese Medicine practitioner combine with family visit.[2]

[2]Some of the above data have been published in my article Chinese medicine as a product filling the wellness health Tourism niche in China: prospect and challenges, International Journal of Tourism Sciences, Volume 14, No. 1, 2014, pp. 51–69.

Forty-two percent of the surveyed expatriates had visited China for business purposes and twenty-seven percent had visited for travel, holiday or sight-seeing. The rest of them had come China for a variety of reasons, including jobs, study, to visit relatives and family, to visit ancestral graveyards, etc. Eighty-two percent of the visitors had stayed in mainland China for less than a month and ninety-eight percent for less than a year. Forty-six percent of the respondents had never taken a health tour before or had never taken a tour only for health reasons, and fifty-four percent didn't consider themselves to be wellness health tourists during their current trips. However, six percent of respondents admitted they didn't have any clear concept about health tourism or wellness health tourism and couldn't say whether they were health tourists or not.[3]

In our fieldwork in India we interviewed a total of 10 clients at the Vedic Village. Two Indian clients had monthly incomes of INR 30,000; another, an income of INR 50,000, two more, INR 100,000; and another, INR 20,000. Of overseas clients, two had monthly incomes of INR 45,000 (US$ 1000); one, INR 44,000 (US$ 965); and one, INR 81,000 (US$ 1775). Two of these overseas clients had graduate-level educations and 2 were post-graduate students, while 5 of the Indians had bachelor's degrees and 1 had higher secondary education. In the Indian context, such Indian clients are considered as belonging to the middle class. Out of the 4 interviewed clients from abroad, 2 were from the USA, 1 from the UK and one from Spain.

Today many big corporations invested heavily in both China and India to develop various product and services under the niches of wellness health tourism using indigenous medical therapies as brand name. Service providers broadcast advertisements over various media repeatedly and portray a new image of wellness and the healthy life their clients enjoy. They offer a broad spectrum of choice, and packages include massage, tuina, cupping, physical exercise, tutorials about healthy life, yoga sessions, ayurvedic oil massage therapies, etc. Such advertisements for spas, resort, hot spring, and wellness centre "frequently portray images of slim, bronzed and fit people enjoying an active and outgoing social life" (Laws 1996: 202). Many advertisements and web pages for such resorts such as Ocean Spring Resort or - Vedic Village use actors and actresses from overseas, predominantly the Westerners. The medicine and medical knowledge used have originated and have been practiced in China or India and a significant number of consumers are also Asian, but the advertisements show Westerners (predominantly Caucasians) enjoying healthy lives, thanks to Asian medical systems (Islam 2008: 210). For example, Beijing Tong Ren Tang, one of the biggest Chinese herbal medicine manufacturers has developed Tong Ren Tang Wellness Corporation in partnership with Greater China Corporation which will develop spa-like wellness centers to provide treatments and products based upon Tongrentang herbal medicines. These

[3]Ibid.

treatment include acupuncture, massage, acupressure, tuina, tai-Chi, qigong, reflexology, etc. as well as a full line of herbal foods and health products.[4]

6.4.1 Ocean Spring Resort, Zhuhai, China

Ocean Spring Resort, one of the pioneers to offer wellness health services under the label of Chinese medicine is located in Jinwan District, Zhuhai, a coastal city of China's southern Guangdong Province. It is an enterprise developed by the China Travel Hong Kong (Zhuhai) Ocean Spring Co., Ltd. When I click the web link of Ocean Spring Resort, a video appears at the beginning, which promotes various images such as: crystal clear sea water with moderate wave; a Caucasian couple enjoying their relaxed holiday at a beach at sunrise; a Caucasian lady walking on the beach when suddenly a clear water wave hits her foot; a Caucasian guy coming forward with his water surfboard, and the Caucasian couple hugging during the sunset. In the next scene, the same Caucasian lady appears painting on the beach in a fashionable dress; then there are beautiful small swimming pools, with two Chinese ladies and the Caucasian lady sitting in the pool in swimming suits; and the Caucasian man playing golf, with a background song in English. The Caucasian lady appears in the final scene having Chinese massage therapy.[5] Such promotional video advertisements broadcast on webpage are not uncommon in China, where tourist resorts target foreign visitors and offer various physical, mental, social and spiritual wellness products for health rejuvenation and relaxation. They show how foreign tourists enjoy the mysterious beauty and teasers of China, including Chinese medicine products and services (Islam 2014: 59–60) (Fig. 6.1).

Covering several acres of flat land, Ocean Spring Resort includes various establishments and facilities, such as Ocean Spring Hotel, Ocean Hot Spring, Health Center, Fisherman's Wharf, and Mysterious Island. Among these, Ocean Hot Spring and the Health Center are the venues offering wellness health tourism products and services. Ocean Hot Spring is surrounded by various pools and includes steam rooms and springs with heated marble beds, Korean style dry steam rooms, a 'dead sea salt' pool, a Finnish style sauna, a wet steam room, a lovely fish pool, a swimming pool for children, a limestone cave spring, sliding-board pool, and areas with names such as 'Aegean Sea spring', 'Atami spring', 'Monica spring', 'Caesar palace bath', 'Turkish bath', 'Tang dynasty style spring', etc.[6] Ocean Hot Spring leisure center also offers various massage services, face care,

[4]Retrieved from the following link: http://www.prnewswire.com/news-releases/greater-china-corporation-forms-tongrentang-wellness-corporation-58599442.html and accessed on February 7, 2016.

[5]This video can be observed on the Ocean Spring Resort web page. Retrieved from the following link: http://www.oceanspring.com.cn and accessed on 25 December 2013.

[6]All this information comes from the printed flyer of Ocean Hot Spring, published by China Travel Hong Kong (Zhuhai) Ocean Spring Co., Ltd. The hard copy was collected in July 2011.

Fig. 6.1 Ocean Spring resort advertisement. *Source* Retrieved from http://www.oceanspring.com.cn and accessed on 25 December 2013

men's care, Traditional Chinese Medicine, spa treatment and special treatment. The partial massages they offer includes foot massage, head massage, shoulder massage, leg massage, foot trimming, ear cleaning, hand trimming, etc.; body massage services include Chinese style massage, Thailand style massage, Ocean Hot Spring classical massage, ocean style massage, Ocean Hot Spring fire treatment, etc.[7]

6.4.2 Dragon Union Foot Massage Center, Zhuhai, China[8]

The Dragon Union Foot Massage Center is another establishment and one of the most popular and prominent massage centers in Tangjiawan Town, a suburban area of Xiangzhou District in Guangdong. There are 37 massage service providers' in total, with 35 females and 2 males on duty during our visit. The center provides foot massage and body massage. It is open from about 11:30 a.m. to 3:00 a.m., although the busiest period starts after about 8:00 p.m. It provides membership cards that can be purchased for 60 RMB with a validity period of six months and can be further renewed. A member can enjoy a discount of 30% for an ordinary foot massage. Dragon Union foot massage center also offers various packages, such as Package A, which costs 108 RMB and includes whole body massage (60 min) + back caring

[7]All this information comes from the printed flyer of Ocean Hot Spring, published by China Travel Hong Kong (Zhuhai) Ocean Spring Co., Ltd. The hard copy was collected in July 2011.

[8]Dragon Union Foot Massage Centre has been closed at the end of 2014 and replaced by a Shopping mall.

with milk bath salts (60 min), which enhance body resistance, relieves muscle stress and promotes rejuvenation. Package B cost 98 RMB and includes whole body caring with milk bath salts (90 min), which effectively improve skin problems caused by polluted environments. It is said to relax the skin, prevent bacteria, enhance permeability of capillaries, and make one's skin healthy, naturally white and perfect. The center also provides foot washing and massage with Tibetan medicine, skin scraping with oil essence for leg nerves, etc. (Ibid 61–62).[9]

6.4.3 *The Vedic Village, Kolkata, India*

The Vedic Village has been developed by a private commercial enterprise based in Kolkata, the Sanjeevani Group and located in the suburban area of Kolkata city, the capital of India's West Bengal State. The well-appointed villas and rooms reflect character, culture and cater to upper-middle-class lifestyle requirements. Currently, there are 40 well-equipped villas available for health tourists to stay in. However, the target is to build approximately 500 houses inside the village compound and sell them to outsiders who aspire to such a lifestyle. The cost range is approximately INR 3,000,000–4,000,000 (US$ 75,000–100,000) in 2004–05, depending on the decoration and facilities available inside the house. One of the goals is to attract the upper middle classes to purchase these vacation houses (Figs. 6.2 and 6.3).

Many owners stay in the village for a period of time each year; at other periods the Sanjeevani Group manages the villas and fills them with tourists. As in many resorts with privately-owned housing units, this system guarantees a source of income for the owner, depending on the occupancy rate. The total village complex occupies 120 acre of land and is surrounded by lakes and ponds. Vedic Village is designed to rely on organic farming and natural therapies such as ayurveda, yoga, homoeopathy, and naturopathy.

The objective of the Vedic Village is to recreate a traditional Vedic way of life that focuses on simplicity of lifestyle—lifestyle that is in true with the natural environment in order to enable those living in it, however temporarily, to experience body-mind-sprit holism. To enable individuals to experience holistic living, the VedicVillage offer comprehensive ayurvedic medication program under its wellness plan. Beside ayurveda, homoeopathy, naturopathic medical consultation and yoga practices, the VedicVillage offer three types of alternative therapies, including, ayurvedic therapies, spa massages, and wellness therapeutics. All these three segments include different massages of various duration and price. Many health tourists are attracted because of the therapeutic services that Vedic Village offers in the tranquil environment for the services.

[9]This data was collected from a poster hanging on a billboard inside Dragon Union Foot Massage Center in July 2011.

Fig. 6.2 Vedic Village entrance

Fig. 6.3 Vedic villas. *Source* Photos were taken by the author during fieldwork in Vedic Village

6.5 Major Product Line and Services Under Wellness Health Tourism

6.5.1 Massage

Various forms of massage and related services have become one of the front line product for the tourist and affluent middle class in China and India coming under the brand name of indigenous medicine. Therapeutic massage has been used as a form of treatment in Chinese medicine and ayurveda since ancient times. The Chinese medical classic *Huang Di Nei Jing* (the Medical Classic of the Yellow Emperor) discusses the development and importance of massage as a therapeutic method (*Huang Di Nei Jing*, twelfth article, 2009: 271–272). According to the *Huang Di Nei Jing*, massage originated in central China, in relation to the patterns of landscape, disease, and peoples livelihood. The text denotes that the landscape in central China is "flat and damp, and living things are produced in abundance" by heaven and earth, and people eat a "wide variety of foods" and are not "over-worked" which caused the popularity of massage in that region (Ibid: 272). Various techniques, such as: moving the body's protective *qi* by pressing, kneading, pinching, rubbing, tapping, and brushing areas between the joints, and using the thumbs, fingertips, and knuckles, etc., are used in massage therapies (Islam 2014: 62–63). After the communist revolution and formation of the People's Republic of China (PRC) in 1949, massage became a popular practice, "whereas 'tuina' refers to the medicalized therapeutic massage" that has eventually become a part of the curriculum in the schools of Traditional Chinese Medicine (Zhan 2013: 327; Islam 2014: 62–63). Although Tuina was generally taught through the apprenticeship education system and some practitioners still learn through direct transmission from a family lineage or apprentice master, various educational institutions accredited by the relevant authority in China offer more institutionalized and professional Tuina courses for their students (Zhan 2013: 327).

Oil massage or *Abhyanga* has also been discussed in *Astanga Hrdayam* ayurvedic text as part of daily regimen (Vagbhatas 2009: 24). The text denotes that oil-massage and bath should be resorted to daily since it wards off old age, exertion and aggravation of *vata* (air/wind). Oil-massage also bestows good vision, nourishment to the body, long life, good sleep, and good and healthy skin. Massage should particularly be performed to the head, ears and feet (ibid). However, the text also suggested to avoid oil-massage if someone is going through certain medical conditions such as suffering from indigestion, aggravation of *kapha* (phlegm), undergoing purificatory therapies, etc. (Ibid).

Many other medical systems worldwide have also promoted the practice of massage, such as those of the Egyptians, Greeks, Japanese and Romans, for therapeutic reasons (Cavaye 2012: 43). Late 19th and early 20th century massage literatures reveal that massage was practiced by doctors and nurses as an "orthodox medical therapy" (Goldstone 2000: 69). However, massage achieved its modern therapeutic form from the hand of Pehr Henrik Ling, a late eighteenth to mid-nineteenth century Swedish physical therapist who used massage in association with exercises and specific movements such as medical-gymnastics (Holey and Cook 2003). As a continuation of this development, massage had become an acceptable medical therapy by the early 20th century "when the focus of care moved to biological sciences" (Islam 2015: 86; Cavaye 2012: 43; Saks 2005). Today, massage is no longer the mainstream healing method to treat chills or fever. With the rise of globalization and rapid economic development, massage has transformed into a new consumer product and presented under the brand name of Chinese medicine and ayurveda. The contemporary development of massage in various parts of the world could be seen as an outcome of various issues such as health rejuvenation, a rise in sub-health conditions, and a rise in the number and interest in relaxation therapies, etc. (Islam 2015: 86). It can also be seen as the rise of 'self-centered consumer capitalism'. In his latest volume Paul Heelas claims that new age spiritual movements are simply a product of self-centered consumer capitalism (Heelas 2008). The recent development of massage in China and India could be seen as a part of self-centered consumer capitalism and has been promoted by the private sector and supported by the government. Massage and related services are consumed by the middle classes for physical and mental relaxation, rejuvenation, stress reduction and relief from physical pain.

Today, Tuina and other forms of massage therapies such as foot massage, head massage, shoulder massage, leg massage, foot trimming, hand trimming, Thai massage, Tibetan massage, etc., can be found from mega-mall to small streets in China. All, or most all, of the three to five star hotels in various cities in China offer a large selection of massage choices, from full body massage of various kinds to different kinds of foot massage, and everything in between (Herzberg and Herzberg 2011: 61). Advertisements for every kind of imaginable massage therapy can be found in the hotel lobby or just next to the front desk. Massage centers and spas around the mega-cities, as well as in small townships in China, offer various massages and other health related products and services under the label of Traditional Chinese Medicine therapy. Statistics from the survey show that thirty-eight percent of the overseas visitors including HK citizens of Chinese ancestor surveyed purchase Chinese medicine products or visit a Chinese medicine practitioner/therapist during their stay in China, making Chinese medicine one of the best-selling health products in China for tourists. In addition, sixty four percent of the respondents visited various massage center and spas, making services for health rejuvenation and relaxation and pampering and wellness activities very popular among tourists[10] who enter China. The major reasons they mentioned for taking such health and wellness related services are reduce pain or stress, to relax and 'rejuvenate', to try new things that are not accessible or available in their own countries, etc. However, twenty-six percent of the visitors had also purchased Western medicine or been admitted to Western-medicine hospitals and had visited Western medical practitioners. They had done so with different motivations including some had suddenly fallen ill during their tour in mainland China or had had a medical checkup for the extension of their Chinese visas.

Empirical study in India also suggests that most of the clients received therapy for back pain or weight loss, or got facial massages in the Vedic Village Wellness Center. Their main concern was to undergo 'natural' treatment with minimum side-effects. For the months of January, April and July 05, 73% of the clients visited Vedic Village for ayurvedic oil massage therapy, 17% went for massages and relaxation services, and only 10% of the total of clients consulted an ayurvedic physician. The primary aim to visit the VedicVillage is for relaxation and stress reduction (Tables 6.2 and 6.3).

Statistics from the month of January, April and July 05 show that about 90% of the total income of the Vedic Village wellness centre is generated from ayurvedic oil massage therapies, 6% of the income from massages that are not part of ayurvedic therapy, and only 4% of the income was generated from doctor's consultations. This is a clear indication that ayurveda is closely associated with 'relaxation therapy' and less with medical treatment options. Thus the response for wellness services has been overwhelming. There has been a consciousness in the number of people, both local and overseas visitors, visiting and using the various wellness facilities in the VedicVillage.

[10]Some respondents used more than one type of health related service.

Table 6.2 Pattern of services for clients attending Vedic Village wellness centre (numbers of clients)

Month	Medical consultation[a]	Medical consultation follow up[b]	Ayurvedic oil massage therapy	Massage	Total
January 05	13	5	185	37	240
April 05	12	4	123	26	165
July 05	15	6	110	33	164
3 months total	40 (7%)	15 (3%)	418 (73%)	96 (17%)	569

Source Client register notebook from the Vedic Village wellness centre in August 2005
[a]Medical consultation mean 1st medical consultation
[b]Medical consultation follow up mean repeat medical consultation

Table 6.3 Vedic Village wellness centre's income from various sources

Month	Medical consultation (INR)	Medical consultation follow up (INR)	Ayurvedic therapy (INR)	Massage (INR)	Total (INR)
January 05	6800	1500	286,425	12,164	306,889
April 05	6300	1200	119,936	11,700	139,136
July 05	7500	1800	136,510	13,600	159,410
3 months total	20,600	3500	542,871	37,464	605,435

Source Monthly statistical maintenance book from the Vedic Village for August 2005 (un-published and maintained by the Director)

6.5.2 Holistic Healing and Wellness

Besides massage, holistic healing and wellness packages are major form of products promoted under the brand name of Chinese medicine and ayurveda. Ocean Hot Spring Center from the Ocean Spring Resort offers a number of Chinese medicine treatments such as shoulder and neck treatment, abdomen treatment, waist treatment, acupuncture, scraping, cupping, royal fumigation health keeping therapy, nephric ridge fumigation health keeping therapy, etc. Apart from this, they also offer various form of spa treatment such as peeling care, egg treatment, face care such as "Israeli organic earth with fruits cosmetology", golden Chinese peal-leaf crabapple oil moisturizing nursing, etc., and men's care such as de-toxin face care, purifying treatment for oily skin, etc.

Vedic Village Wellness Center also offers various healing packages including one-hour Wellness Therapy, one-day *dinacharya* package, one-day Sanjeeva healing package, and the Sanjeeva Glow one-day package, Dead sea mineral mud wrap, Reflexology, Sanjeeva mud wrap, Detoxifying body wrap, Sanjeeva facials, Kerala-ayurvedatherapy, *Abhyangam* (a traditional Kerala-*Panchakarma* therapy),

Abhyangam and *shirodhara, Abhyangam&patrapinda awedana, Shiro lepa,* Herbal face pack, *Ayurvedamrita,* Cellulite breakdown, Meridian stretching exercises, Hair nutrition, etc.[11]Patients visited the Vedic Village to consult the ayurvedic physician over a range of diseases, such as Irritated Bowel Syndrome, gastritis, ischemic heart disease, neurological degeneration, stomach cancer, skin disease, diabetes, sexual dysfunction, digestive disorder, mal-absorption syndrome and infantile autism. Nearly one third of the total number of patients who had medical consultations in the Vedic Village for various diseases during the month of July 2005 came from overseas, including from the UK, the Arab Emirates and Bangladesh.[12] Out of 10 clients interviewed, 7 engaged in ayurvedic therapies for relaxation and rejuvenation 5 Indians and 2 from overseas.

6.5.3 Ayurvedic **Dinacharya** *(Daily Regimen)*

One of the unique features of commodifing ayurvedic service in modern India is the promotion of *dinacharya* (daily regimen) package. As I mentioned earlier that following a daily routine is one of the key conditions to maintain health and prevent disease described in ayurvedic texts. Many health tourist resorts in India are instrumental in marketing ayurvedic *dinacharya* concept through a process of commodification. In the Vedic Village, the *dinacharya* regimen focuses on personal hygiene related to the mind and body for "rejuvenation". The health tourist is required to wake up with a small prayer in *brahma muhurta*, the period of 48 min before sunrise. *Dinacharya* consists of several sessions starting with the *Brahma muhurta*. A photo of the Hindu god hangs on the wall of a small therapeutic room in the VedicVillage, in front of which clients pray. After the prayer, *vaktra shuddhi,* or oral hygiene, begins—a neem twig is crushed at one end and used as a toothbrush, with herbal tooth powder, the entire process being called *dantadhavana*. After cleaning the teeth and washing the mouth, the client or tourist is given a freshly prepared herbal infusion with pure honey as a morning drink. Afterwards, clients take a sunrise walk and assemble at the Yoga Hall for a Yoga session. Yoga is a different healing system originated in India to unite body-mind-spirit and relatively dissimilar to ayurveda. Ayurvedic *dinacharya* concepts presented in the text book suggests to do exercises depend on various conditions such as seasons, individual body condition, state of disease, etc. Because of the popularity of Yoga across the globe, ayurvedic resorts in India are incorporating Yoga within the ayurvedic concept of *dinacharya*.

The Vedic Village *dinacharya* regimen also promotes *abhyangam shirodhara*, an oil massage therapy where a traditional Kerala therapy (a type of massage

[11]These wellness packages were listed in Vedic Village wellness service price list.

[12]This information has been calculated from the Vedic Village Wellness centre patients' registration book.

therapy from the Indian state of Kerala) is given. A trained ayurvedic massage therapist starts the massage with the head and gradually extends it to all parts of the body from head to foot, in a synchronized manner. After continuing this oil massage session for an hour the therapist asks the client to take a bath with herbal soap, which is called *snana*. The therapist helps to put soap on all parts of the body. Again the concept of massage described in ayurvedic texts suggests putting oil on human body daily basis (or at least every second day) which helps to increase the power of eye, nutrition of the body, longevity, beauty of the skin, good sleep, etc. The texts also suggested to put oil particularly on head, ears and feet (person having some diseases such as asthma are forbidden to use oil) and do feet massage with another person's feet. The massage has to be performed after exercise with *amloki (a form of fruit like olive) to* reduce the fat from body, make the body strong and make the skin glassy, the text further suggests (Vagbhatas 2009: 24–25). However, Vedic Village *dinacharya* package is reluctant to follow all such regulations partly because those regulations do not suit with contemporary lifestyle or in an artificial setting which they have been marketing.

After the oil massage and cleaning session the purification sessions start under the Vedic Village *dinacharya* package. Here the principal sense organs—the eyes, ears, nose and throat—are purified, beginning with the *karnapoorana* session, when warm medicated herbal oils are dropped into the ears. This act is considered good for the prevention of headaches and ear infections. Again, a few drops of herbal oil are applied, this time deep inside the nostrils, and this act is intended to enhance the senses. *Anjana,* or *kajal,* follows, to clean the eyes. Here, a *colliriyum* (special paste) made from soot of turmeric and pure ghee is used to clean the eyes. *Dhoomapaana* is the final session to purify the sense organs. Clients are asked to inhale an antiseptic smoke generated from a burning wick made of pure turmeric. This is one of the more difficult sessions for the client who has not been exposed to the strong smell of burning turmeric. In the final sessions of *dinacharya*, the client consults an ayurvedic practitioner concerning a healthy lifestyle.[13] The commodified version of *dinacharya* offered under ayurvedic packages and promoted by various resorts is relatively dissimilar to their textual representation. This is an initiative brought by globalization where Indian medical heritage has put into the market for profit maximization. The Indian entrepreneurs are also very instrumental to redefine the ayurvedic concept to boost their profit fourfold.

6.6 Who Are the Service Providers?

Tourists in China those surveyed were generally unaware of the professional background of the service providers or the authenticity and standardization of the Chinese medicine they purchase. As the data shows, seventy-two percent out of 100

[13]Author has a personal experience of taking part in the *dinacharya* program. A detail description of the *dinacharya* (daily regime) program is also mentioned in the Vedic Village flyer.

of the respondents didn't have any idea of the professional qualification/background of their service providers. Unavailability of information about the professional background of the service providers or the fact that the available information was in the Chinese language made it difficult for expatriates to understand what they were purchasing or what intervention were going on their bodies. They simply put their faith in the service provider, or in Chinese culture, with an assumption that Chinese medicine and related products have no side-effects. The language barrier also made non-Chinese speaking clients frustrated when they read doctor's prescriptions and they depended on a translator.

In the Vedic Village Wellness Center in India there were 2 institutionally trained physicians with the Bachelor of Ayurvedic Medicine and Surgery (BAMS) degree working during our fieldwork in 2004–05. Apart from this, 3 institutionally trained homoeopathic practitioners with some experience of naturopathy also provide health care services. The largest number of service providers is that of the ayurvedic-trained therapists who hold a diploma degree in ayurvedic therapy. In addition, there is 1 yoga practitioner, and there are 2 massage therapists, providing yoga training postures and massage services, respectively.

6.7 Price and Satisfaction

It was a general feeling among the service recipients that the quality of service and the price of treatments were acceptable. The data from our survey shows that sixty-eight percent of the service recipients were satisfied with the quality, relative to the price. They praised the sincerity and kindness of the massage and related service providers, but did not praise the medical doctors. Generally, they hadn't encountered any problems while consuming wellness related services, and reported that the service providers tried their best to satisfy the needs of the clients. Sixty-six percent of the respondents spent from RMB 100 to 500 per session or massage or other wellness related services; only fourteen percent spent above RMB 1000. The vast majority of them also thought that the prices they had paid were reasonable and acceptable in relation to their satisfaction. Forty-four percent respondent considered China an ideal place for the services they had consumed. They also said they thought China can offer competitive prices for the best possible satisfaction of clients for health and wellness related services. However, thirty-two percent of our respondents didn't consider China an ideal place for health related services they had taken, and some of them had doubts about the quality. They felt that, although the services they had received had been acceptable, there were places in other parts of Asia for better services. Unfortunately the research team was unable to make any qualitative interview to collect intensive data or do case study among the tourists those have received wellness health care in China under authentic Chinese medicine practice.

The costs of various service packages and treatments provided by the Vedic Village wellness centre in India are expensive in the Indian context and only affordable for middleclass and upper middle class professionals or elites. The Sanjeeva Spa treatment price ranges from INR 1000 to INR 1500 for one hour; the Kerala Ayurvedic Therapy ranges from INR 1200 to INR 3000 for one hour. In addition, clients have to pay an additional 10.2% service tax. One-hour Wellness Therapy costs INR 1000. In a special offer, a one-day *dinacharya* package was priced at INR 3000[14]; a one-day Sanjeeva healing package cost INR 2500, and the Sanjeeva Glow one-day package cost INR 2500. A one-time medical consultation fee was INR 500. All these prices were applicable in the year 2005.

A male Indian visitor, Sri Apurbo Kumar Roy,[15] visited Vedic Village for relaxation therapy to reduce muscle pain. Mr. Roy is one of the leading industrialists in Kolkata and owns a group of electronic goods manufacturing companies. Mr. Roy commented that:

> I heard about the VedicVillage several times but I didn't have the opportunity to visit here because of my business. I only visited here another time a fortnight ago and this is the second time. I think it is still underdeveloped as far as other housing projects concerned. But once you enter here, it is a nice place with nice environment.
>
> I took both Ayurvedic medication and massage here. Generally I went in Bombay and Kolkata city for Kerala massage. In Bombay, there are some massage centres and I used to visit there. In Kolkata, I usually visit Tali club because that is conveniently located. I took ayurvedic massage therapy here not for illness of disease but for shoulder pain. That pain first came quite some time back and I started to take this massage one and half years before. I took some Western medicine and radiation therapy before but it gave temporary relief. I also took homoeopathic once but it is not effective. Ayurvedic massage ensures an overall blood circulation in the body and I basically take ayurvedic therapy for blood circulation, joint pain and back pain. My wife also came to the VedicVillage for the first time for ayurvedic massage therapy. In Bombay, I paid INR 700 and here in the VedicVillage, the charge was INR 750.
>
> Here, I personally tried to come once a week and it is rejuvenation for me. Vedic Village is not at all a poor man's luxury. It is a luxury. It is really expensive for the poor men. I also saw in the Vedic Village that it should be synchronise. Here the massage is given by one man but in Bombay and Ahmadabad they give two men. Synchronize means two person will give the massage at a time, one on left side and another on right side which is more effective. If two persons give massage together for an hour, it rejuvenates the body more effectively.
>
> Vedic Village can be seen as one of the ways to attract tourism because it is a good place for satisfaction and rejuvenation. The most important thing is to teach people how to lead a healthy life. People are looking for longevity. So, some people are staying here for 10–15 days to experience a healthy life and that is wonderful idea. All they need to do here 10–15 days is learn to relax and lead a healthy life. We need to train people for this industry.

It seems that improvement of the quality of services, professionalism of the service providers and standardization/accreditation of the services may be key requirements for the further development of this sector in China. Other challenges include dispute over tips given to service providers; poor environmental, hygienic

[14]Sanjeeva Spa price list.

[15]Original name has not been used.

and sanitary conditions; and the use of old equipment. Some of the respondents were also disappointed at the lack of information about the appropriate center to get their expected wellness related services. Statistics show that sixty-two percent out of 100 of respondents had been recommended to the designated service receiving centers by friends, translators, hotel staffs or business partners.

Similarly, with clever marketing in media, the Vedic Village has begun to gain a reputation overseas as a reputed wellness provider which provides holistic therapeutic treatments in a safe natural environment and at reasonable cost. Such a reputation has led to a steady stream of foreign visitors to the Vedic Village for alternative treatments and lifestyle experiences. As the findings have shown, local visitors to the Vedic Village are mostly Indian middle class professionals or wealthy business persons who come for relaxation therapy. Their main objective is to rejuvenate themselves and/or to relive stress. The majority of the Indian visitors do not consider Vedic Village as a place for ayurvedic medical treatment but one for massage therapy, spa treatments for rejuvenation and removing stress.

6.8 Conclusion

As data from our survey shows that most of the overseas tourists including Hong Kong citizens of Chinese ancestor had consumed pampering and wellness related services for health rejuvenation and relaxation. The vast majority of these tourists were short term visitors and had consumed Chinese herbal medicine, body massage, hot spring baths, foot massage, and spa activities for health rejuvenation and relaxation. This trend has made Chinese medicine a prime label for promoting various health products and services as wellness tourism. The major reasons for tourists' consumption of such Chinese medicine appear to be to reduce stress, relax, reduce pain, and try new things which are not accessible or affordable in their own countries. Favored by the Chinese government's intentions and entrepreneurs' initiatives, this trend will continue. China's competitive advantages to develop wellness health tourism lies in competitive price, low labor cost and consumers. At the same time, lack of regulation and monitoring, lack of professional training for service providers, and inadequate information about the best places for getting services are key for further development of this sector. Although very few of the overseas health tourists raised the issue of authenticity about the Chinese medicine-related services they had consumed, authenticity could also be a major issue for the systematic development of this sector. The government and related bodies should address and handle these issues carefully for the sustainable development of wellness health tourism in China. At its present state very few of the expatriates were aware of the professional background of the service providers and had little knowledge about Chinese medicine. Thus, Chinese medicine has been used as a label to cater to tourists, where the prime selling points are Chinese culture, minimum side-effects, and stress reduction.

At the same time this chapter has shown that ayurvedic wellness therapies has become popular in recent decades in India for several reasons. Ayurvedic wellness under the development of various spas has become popular in the West to cater to middle-class consumers in search of treatments for health rejuvenation and relaxation. As a result of globalization, this has also attracted middle class professionals and entrepreneurs in India. For entrepreneurs, using ayurvedic concepts to develop products and service niche under wellness health tourism is a way to make money. Likewise, for the Indian government, the creation of ayurvedic health tourism brings much-needed foreign currency into the Indian economy. Although ayurvedic texts contain chapters on *dinacharya* (daily regimen) and *ritucharya* (seasonal practices), *onnopanbidhi* (daily dietary habits), etc., and Vedic Village claims to promote those concepts. However, it is a big investment to build such an artificial Vedic infrastructure, and investors generally have the attitude to recover their investments as soon as possible. Thus the content of ayurveda becomes a consumer product. Consumerism has already rooted in the promotion of ayurvedic wellness program, and ayurveda takes the form of a commodity rather than as a means of restoring health.

Chapter 7
Conclusion

China and India are the few countries having millenium old medial systems and traditions. Some of these systems date back to several thousand years B.C. Indigenous medical heritages become a part of the common peoples culture in China and India. These systems correspond to various aspects of peoples everyday life including politics, religion, belief, food and diatary practice, lifestyle and so on. At the same time, various medical systems and practices also went under cultural assimilation, interaction, and changes over the time for various reasons: external political and military occupation, human migration, religious influence, commercialization, etc. Thus the idea of the existence of authentic indigenous medicine in China and India are always debatable. Nonetheless, both the countries have oldest surviving medical texts which systematically documented medical procedures including diagnosis, treatment, and prescriptions. *Huang Di Nei Jing, Bencao Gangmu, Caraka Samhita, Susruta Samhita, Astanga Hrdayam*-all are the living treasures in China and India. These texts also provided guideline on how to leave a healthy life, preserve health and prevent diseases which inspired one of the major health slogans in modern world-"prevention is better than cure".

Although indigenous medical systems in China and India were dominant medical practice for over a millenium and served much peoples health need it was the nineteenth century when major set back come through the introduction of Western medicine. Christian missonaries began to provide Western medical care in big cities such as Beijing, Guangzhou, Shanghai, etc, during the late Qing dynasty. Western medicine began to expand further in Chinese society through getting state patronaze after the formation of Republic of China by the hand of Sun Yat Sen who was trained as Western physician. By the middle of tweenth century Western medicine already consolidated dominance and became primary mode of healing in Chinese society because of the negligency to indigenous medical systems by the government. In India Western medicine was brough by the European colonizers during late eighteen to early nineteenth century and imposed by the British colonial administration to consolidate their power. Christian missonaries also played a vital role in promoting Western medicine in India since medicine was one of the few

M.N. Islam, *Chinese and Indian Medicine Today*,
DOI 10.1007/978-981-10-3962-1_7

means to enter Christian values in Hindu-Muslim majority Indian society. Missonaries were particularly active in South India to convert religiousless peoples or lower caste Hindus to Christianity apart from providing medical services. By the end of nineteenth century, Western medicine became the only recognised medical system in India by the British Raj.

The nationalistic revival and commodification of indigenous medicine in China and India in recent decades is caused by two reasons: firstly, although indigenous medicines should be regarded as an important part of national cultural heritage and treasure their revival is largely caused by economic necessity. The monopoly in health care delivery created by the Western pharmaceutical companies and practitioners become unaffordable to mass peoples. Many multinational drug manufacturers have power to control the price of their drugs and unwilling to dispense to people unless people can pay the price they demand. As a result, people have seek alternative and to fall back on indigenous medicine. Secondly, because of the hegemonic presence of Western pharmaceutical companies and their patent drugs indigenous medicines face challenge of survival. Commodification of indigenous medicine is an attempt of commercial exploration from the indigenous drug manufacturers for survival. This can be seen as new way of economic exploration during the new era of medical technology. People often views indigenous medicines are being too philosophical, metaphysical, and less high-tech which gives Western medicine an advantage.[1]

There are few similar features developed both in China and India after the political intervention in medicine and promotion of Western medicine. As I discussed in Chap. 2 that Western modernity was officially adopted in China after the 1911 revolution and Western science and technology became prime tool to develop the country. As a result, the adoption of the diagnostic method and treatment modality that developed in Europe with the rise of western medical science became key strategy in Chinese health care delivery. Since indigenous medical systems in China have different history, theory and method they were not suitable with this new trend of medical development. The development of clinical micro-biology, modern biochemistry and pharmacology contributed favourable for the further growth of Western medicine. The identification of micro-organism with the help of clinical microbiology and the invention of anti-biotic with the help of modern pharmacology to kill microorganism helps Western medicine gaining reputation and success. Because of the quick curable power Western anti-biotic drugs were capable to handle epidemic diseases overwhelmingly existed across China and India during early to mid-twentieth century. Western medicine gains attention and confidence from both the mass peoples and government. Indigenous medicines were treated as non-scientific or lack of evidence based practice because of their lacking to cure patients having emergency medical condition.

---

[1]This is a feedback given by one of my colleagues Prof. Chris Lam during a seminar I gave at the United International College in 2014. The seminar was a part of GEO Coffee Clutch-a lecture series for the GEO faculties from the United International College, Beijing Normal University-Hong Kong Baptist University, Zhuhai, China.

As indigenous medicine was developed historically as knowledge based science and the proof came through individual case study they were unable to develop standardised drugs to cure particular symptom. In principle, indigenous medicines support individualistic treatment method and prescrition in treating different patients with similar symptom. They believe that every human is unique and the causes of similar symptom may be different. Indigenous medicine practitioners usually follows individualistic or person based mode of treatment. This is also a major reasons why indigenous medical systems could not develop a particular standardised treatment, method and prescription for similar symptoms. It was, however, a serious set back for indigenous medical systems in China and India during the time when Western medicine expanded rapidly.

Late nineteenth to the middle of twentieth century is also the time when both China and India have transformed from a feudalistic mode of production to a capitalist production system. Incorporation of Western modernity in all spheres of civil life has become one of the preeminent features of the time. The individual states adopted a political, judiciary and education system similar to Western countries as part of their modernization. This has severe impact on indigenous medical education. From historical time to the end of nineteenth century, indigenous medical education was based on family education or apprenticeship which were relatively dissimilar to Western education. Once Western education was introduced in China and India indigenous medical education could not cope with this and eventually marginalized.

All these factors contributed disfavourable for the existance and further development of indigenous medicine in China and India. The systems still existed but as isolated and informal practice. As a result, a new idea of developing indigenous medicine emerged after the communist revolution in China and during the early tweenth century in India which is called 'integrated practice'. It was considered as a new initiative inspired by nationalistic sentiment with an precise objective of reviving indigenous culture. Under this initiative, indigenous medical systems were brough under modern education system and develop an integrated curriculam combining indigenous medical subjects with the subjects from Western medicine.

7.1 Integration

Integrated medical education and practice started in China after the foundation of four Chinese medicine College in four parts of China in 1956: Beijing College of Chinese medicine, Shanghai College of Chinese Medicine, Guangzhou College of China medicine, and Chendu College of Chinese Medicine. These newly founded colleges offered two programs: Chinese medicine (*Zhōngyī*); and Integrated Chinese medicine (*Zhōng xi yī*) for the students who intend to become Chinese medicine practitioner. Students from both the programs have to take a significant mumbers of courses taught in Western medicine.

Although graduates who study Chinese medicine are not allowed to practice Western medicine or prescribe Western drugs it is not uncommon that it happens in contemporary China. Our survey revealed that 86% students from the Henan University of Chinese medicine would prefer to do Western medicine practice apart from Chinese medicine regardless their training background. Besides, 90% of the practitioners those surveyed have noted that they prescribe drugs and use diagnostic methods commonly used in Western medicine.The only practitioner (5%) who does not prescribe Western drugs did not go through the professionalized education system and gained skill from apprenticeship. The major justifications are: their knowledge on Western pharmacology and pathology from their training; Western drugs are more powerful and have rapid curable power which can safe patients' life; Western diagnostic methods are more objective and accurate, etc.

Integrated medical practice started in India at the beginning of twentieth century through founding several ayurvedic colleges according to Western line. These newly founded ayurvedic institutions such as J B Roy State Ayurvedic College and Hospital in Kolkata, Vaidyaratnam P.S. Varier Ayurveda College in Kerala, and so on, offered integrated course curriculum where students have to study both ayurvedic courses and courses from Western medicine. As a result, they were allowed to practice Western medicine after graduation apart from ayurveda. Although this trend was not favored by the practitioners of Western medicine, a study after the Indian independence found that majority of the graduates from ayurvedic college practice Western medicine (Brass 1972: 349–358). After several decades of debate, the Indian government founded Central Council of Indian Medicine in 1970s to monitor ayurvedic education. Eventually they got rid from integrated education and introduced pure ayurvedic courses at the colleges of ayurveda. However, this trend was also not favored by many students. Most of the teachers those currently teaching at ayurvedic institutions are trained under integrated system and many of them in fact teach ayurveda from Western medical perspective. Students are also eager to learn Western pharmacology and pathology. Those surveyed 95% of the students from ayurvedic college came to study ayurveda after having failed to enroll at the college of Western medicine. Their major objective is to become a medical practitioner, not an ayurvedic *vaid* or *kabiraj* in particular. Although cross practice (prescribing drugs from Western medicine) is illegal in most of the Indian states it often happens under the table. Indian government has employed ayurvedic practitioners in Primary Health Care Center (PHC) which is the basic unit ofhealth care delivery in rural area but there is no supply of ayurvedic drugs in PHC. Since majority of the modern ayurvedic graduates are unable to prepare ayurvedic drugs by their own they entirely rely on Western drugs or patent ayurvedic drugs in their prescription. Last generation apprentice practitioners have already passed away or unable to practice because of the lack of institutional qualification which is mandatory for registration. Modern Chinese and Indian states are not eager to patronize or preserve the knowledge these apprenticeship practitioners have hold over the centuries as family secret.

As we can see that contemporary Chinese and Indian government adopted two different approaches to promote indigenous medicine. Chinese government is promoting “integrated approach” which tries to combine Chinese medicine with the modalities and methods from Western medicine. This initiative demands uniformity in education and practice, uniqueness in prescription, and standardization in drug preparation and manufacturing. However, this initiative causes serious challenge in keeping the Chinese medicine theory and method alive. Graduates from contemporary Chinese medicine institutionsare eager to use diagnostic methods from Western medicine and write Western drugs in their prescription. Besides, the Indian government got rid from integrated practice and adopted an approach in promoting “pure approach/ayurveda”. Under this initiative, students from ayurvedic colleges only need to learn subjects from ayurveda and practice ayurveda after graduation. However, this initiative does not suit with the contemporary socio-economic condition and social reality in India since many parts of ayurveda do not fit with modern Indian lifestyle. Students from contemporary ayurvedic colleges are also eager to learn Western medicine and do back door Western medicine practice after graduation. As a result, the outcome of “integrated approach” in China and “pure approach/ayurveda” in India is similar.

7.2 Commodification

China adopted an open door economic policy in 1978 and opened its market for foreign goods and services which was vertually nonexist during the Mao era. China also became a member of WTO in 2001. Because of the adoption of new policy and China‘s entry into global market various new products and services have emerged. Indigenous medical field was also inspired by the new trend and brought various products and services under the brand name Chinese medicine. Apart from existing Chinese herbal drug manufacturers many new investors also enter into the Chinese medicine market and manufactured various patent drugs, health supplements, dietsupplements, food addictives, health food, cosmetics, toilatories, beauty and sex products. Most of these products and services are new creation and fundamentally dissimilar to the traditional Chinese medical practices. Chinese medicine has been transformed from an indigenous medical system to a commodity for global consumption.

Large Chinese medicine manufacturers such as Beijing Tong Ren Tang or Yunan Baiwon have expanded business in various field and develop many subsidary companies under their brand name. Major share of their profit margin comes not from selling classical Chinese medicine formula but from other business. Beijing Tong Ren Tang today manufactured hair shampoo to various male impotence products such as hair nature and Bushen Qiangshen Pian which do not have direct relation with the textual presentation of Chinese medicine. Revenue of the big companies are growing stedly and profit maximization has become prime object. The development of Chinese medicine as a medical system has replaced by the growth of profit margin for the drug manufacturers.

Although India adopted open door policy in 1991, more than a decade later than China, the commodification of ayurvedic medicine started much earlier. Largest ayurvedic drug manufacturers such as Dabur India or Sri Baidyanath Ayurved began to manufacture commercially prepared ayurvedic patent drugs and health products immediate after decolonization. Today, large part of income for Dabur India comes not from selling ayurvedic drugs but from their famous cosmetic brand such as Vatica, Real, Fem, etc.

Contemporary development of indigenous medicine in China and India has made Chinese medicine and ayurveda as brand name to sell various health, cosmetic, and beauty products and services. This also caused uncertainty whether indigenous medical systems are capable to preserve health and prevent diseases according to their guiding principles. Besides, Chinese medicine and ayurvedic logo have been used in various spas, tourist resorts, hotels and massage centers to provide massage services and wellness packages. A perception is increasingly growing among mass people in China, India, and overseas that indigenous medical systems refer to health and cosmetic related consumer products and or massage therapies for relaxation and rejuvenation. The overall situation in both China and India are more or less similar. Thanks to globalization for making this homogeneity between China and India in the practice of contemporary indigenous medicine although they are politically and culturally different.

Appendix A

The University of Hong Kong

Department of Sociology

Project Title: Repackaging ayurveda in post-colonial India: Revivalism and global commodification

Questionnaire for the ayurvedic practitioners

1. **Background question**

   1.1 For how long have you been practicing?
   1.2 Why did you choose this profession?
   1.3 What types of training you do have?
   1.4 Do you have specialization in any particular area?
   1.5 What are the common problems you have encountered while attending to patients?
   1.6 For what kinds of problem do patients usually visit you?
   1.7 Do you charge any visiting fee? If yes, may I ask how much?

2. **Ayurveda versus Allopathic medicine**

   2.1 Do you have any professional training/knowledge about Western medicine?
   2.2 Do you think that your status is much like that of your Western counterparts?
   2.3 Have you ever discovered that after participating, in Western-style training programs, the status of indigenous medical practitioners had been upgraded?
   2.4 How do you perceive the Western style of training program?
   2.5 How do the patients behave towards a qualified and a non-qualified Ayurvedic practitioner?

3. **Colonizing the medicine**

   3.1 What kinds of impact do you think the British colonization made on Ayurvedic medicine? (Negative, positive, why and how)

M.N. Islam, *Chinese and Indian Medicine Today*,
DOI 10.1007/978-981-10-3962-1

Do you think that Ayurvedic medicine is now in a better position than during the colonial regime?

4. **Health policy, system and integration of Ayurvedic medicine**

4.1 Do you think that the government gave much attention to Ayurvedic medicine after the independence?
4.2 How do you perceive the integration of Ayurvedic medicine into the state health policy and systems?
4.3 Do you notice that the current state health policy has adequate avenues to provide Ayurvedic medical care?
4.4 What types of health services delivery do you expect (i.e.: market oriented, state owned, private, and public)?

5. **Ideology/politics**

5.1 Do you find any relation between communist rule in West Bengal and the practices of Ayurvedic medicine?
5.2 How do you correlate Ayurvedic medicine with Indian nationalism?

6. **Religion (cultural category)**

6.1 Do you find any relation between your religious belief and professional choice?
6.2 Do you prescribe some food as medicine or medicine as food or any behavioral taboo? (If yes, what kind of foods and how? Or do you suggest your patients follow certain behavioral taboos?)
6.3 How do you perceive the relation between *Ayurveda* practices and Hinduism in India?
6.4 Do you notice any relation between your caste and Ayurvedic medical choice?

7. **Gender and media**

7.1 Do you notice any relation between gender and healing/remedial choices?
7.2 Do you discover that Ayurvedic drug companies are feminizing Ayurvedic medicine, and/or provoking a new gender ideology?

8. **Market and capitalism**

8.1 Do you make any difference between branded and generic medicine during prescription? Why?
8.2 How do you get the ideas about a particular brand?
8.3 Do you discover more options to choose Ayurvedic medical products and services in the contemporary era?
8.4. Do you notice that new consumers are being created and that demands are rising for Ayurvedic medical products and services?
8.5 What are the key factors determining the consumption behaviour of Ayurvedic medical products and health services (affordability, accessibility and effectiveness)?

9. **Socio-economic status**

9.1 Was your professional choice influenced by your family background, socio-economic status?
9.2 Do you notice any relation among age, educational status and remedial choice?
9.3 Do you find any social hierarchy involved with the choice of healing (socio-economic or professional, and class differences)?
9.4 Do you feel that trained practitioners are more expensive than non-trained practitioners are?
9.5 Do you consider any difference between a qualified and non-qualified Ayurvedic practitioner? (How do you perceive their roles in health service delivery?)

10. **Globalizing Ayurveda**

10.1 How do you perceive the use of modern technologies and laboratories in Ayurvedic medical sectors?
10.2 What do you think about the standardization and patenting of Ayurvedic medicine?
10.3 Does media advertisement made any impact on your choice of Ayurvedic medicine?
10.4 Do you think that Ayurvedic medical practitioners should have knowledge about Western medical sciences?
10.5 How do you perceive cross-practice?

Respondent Number –

Respondent Category and number	
Date of Interview	
Respondent Location	
Name	
Address	
Date of Birth	
Profession	
Sex	
Education	
Religion and Cast	

Thank you very much

Appendix B

Beijing Normal University—Hong Kong Baptist University
北京师范大学- 香港浸会大学

United International College
联合国际学院

Project Title: Globalization and Health Tourism in China: Paradigm, Prospects and Challenges
课题名称:全球化和健康旅游在中国: 范式, 前景与挑战

M.N. Islam, *Chinese and Indian Medicine Today*,
DOI 10.1007/978-981-10-3962-1

Questionnaire for survey among visitor/tourists

Client Number **Location** **Date of Interview**

序号：采访地点： 采访日期：

Background Information:

背景情况：

Name: Nationality: Sex:

姓名：国籍：性别：

Age: Occupation: Monthly Income:

年龄：职业：月收入：

Main Purpose of Visiting China:

来中国的目的：

Duration of living China (this time):

本次逗留时间：

How many times have you been in China (including this one):

1st /2nd /3rd /4th /5th /more than 5

这是第几次来中国：1 次/ 2 次/3 次/4 次/5 次/多余 5 次

How often do you visit China: once a year/ twice a year/ every mouth/ every week/ others (please specify)

多久来一次中国：一年一次/ 一年两次/ 每月/ 每周/ 其它(请说明)

---

1. Where have you been in China?
   到目前为止, 你去过中国的哪些地方?
2. Have you ever received any health related service in China? Y/N, if yes (What type of service have you ever received?)
   (a) western medicine, (b) admitted in hospital, (c) Chinese medicine,
   (d) wellness center, (e) spa, (f) massage center,
   (g) others (please specify) (Chinese doctor/therapist)
   你有没有接受过任何与健康有关的服务呢?有/没有如果有, 请具体说明是说明服务?
   (a) 西医, (b) 正规医院承认的, (c) 中医, (d) 健康中心,
   (e) 温泉疗养, (f) 按摩中心, (g) 其它(请说明)
3. Reason for receiving the service:
   (a) suddenly ill, (b) relax, (c) reduce stress, (d) reduce pain,
   (e) try new things, (f) others (please specify)
   出于什么原因, 你接受了该项服务:
   (a) 突然生病, (b) 放松, 休闲, (c) 减压,
   (d) 减轻痛楚, (e) 尝试新事物, (f) 其它(请说明)
4. How do you evaluate the quality of service?
   你认为该服务的质量如何?
   What is your suggestion to improve the quality of service?
   有什么建议吗?
5. How much money do you spend for each time?
   你每次一般花多少钱?
6. What do you think of the cost of the service? If it's too high, what's the reasonable price for you?
   你认为这个花费合理吗?如果太贵了, 那在你看来, 什么样的价格才是合理的?
7. How often do you take a health tour?
   多久进行一次健康旅游?
   How much do you spend annually for health tour?
   你每年在这方面的花费是多少?
8. Do you have any special health problems or needs? If yes, what?
   你有没有什么特别的健康问题或者需要呢?如果有, 是什么?
9. Do you think the problem has been solved after the service?
   在接受了这些健康方面的服务后, 你是否认为你的问题得到了解决?
10. Have you ever encountered any problems during the service? Y/N (if yes, how did you solve it?)
    在接受这方面的服务时, 你有没有遇到过什么问题?有/没有(如果有,请说明)
11. Do you have any ideas about the professional skills/background of the service provider?
    你是否了解为你服务的人的专业水平?他们是否接受过专业训练/背景对你来说重要吗?

12. How did you know the service provider?
    你是怎么知道为你提供服务的机构的?
13. Do you think China is an ideal place for such kind of health service which you choose?
    根据你所接受的服务, 中国是否是你心目中的理想选择?
14. Do you consider yourself as a health tourist?
    你是否认为自己是一个健康旅行者?

Thank you very much for participating in this interview!
非常感谢您的参与!

Appendix C

Beijing Normal University—Hong Kong Baptist University
北京师范大学- 香港浸会大学

United International College
联合国际学院

Project Title: Globalization and Wellness Health Tourism in China (Zhuhai): Paradigm, Prospects and Challenges

Survey questionnaire for the client

Client Number: **Location:** **Date of Interview:**

Background question

Name (Name): Nationality: Sex: M/FAge:

Marital Status: Having children: Y/N Education:

Monthly income: RMB Profession:

Home town and province: Duration of living Zhuhai:

---

1. What type of service you are taking? (Please tick)
   (a) Hair wash, (b) Face wash, (c) Body massage, (d) Hair cut,
   (e) SPA, (f) facial beauty, (g) Foot massage, (h) Hair design,
   (i) Hair care, (j) Others (Please specify)———

M.N. Islam, *Chinese and Indian Medicine Today*,
DOI 10.1007/978-981-10-3962-1

2. How often you come here?
   (a) First time, (b) Once a week, (c) Once a month,
   (d) Every second moth, (e) seldom
3. Why do you choose here?
   (a) brand/chain enterprises, (b) other's recommend, (c) good service,
   (d) just picked this arbitrarily, (e) advertisement, (f) promotion and discount
   (g) Price is cheaper than others, (h) Location is convenient, (i) Others (Please specify)————
4. How do you evaluate this service?
   (a) For relaxation and rejuvenation, (b) stress reduction, (c) health benefit,
   (d) beauty, (e) body building, (f) Feelings comfortable,
   (g) Others (Please specify)————
5. How much money do you normally spend for this service each time?
   (a) <20 yuan, (b) no more than 50 yuan, (c) more than 50, less than 100,
   (d) more than 100, less than 200, (e) more than 200, (f) please specify if the amount is different————
6. What do you think about the price?
   (a) Just ok, (b) It is expensive, (c) It is cheaper, (d) Others (please specify)————
7. How much you spend for every month for this type of service?
   (a) less than 100, (b) more than 100, less than 200, (c) more than 200, less than 300, (d) more than 300, less than 500, (e) more than 500, (f) not fixed
8. Would you please describe your experience after the service?
   (a) feel energetic, (b) look good/better, (c) relaxed,
   (d) nothing change, (e) bad, (f) other (Please describe detail)————
9. Are you satisfied with the quality of service here?
   (a)Yes, (b) No, (c) So-so Because: (please specify the reasons)————
10. What is your suggestion to improve the quality of service?
    (a) better skill, (b) better product, oil, shampoo, etc., (c) better place,
    (d) better attitude of service provider, (e) better equipments, (f) better infrastructural environment,
    (g) others (Please specify)————
11. Do you have any idea about the professional training/ background of your service provider?
    Yes No I'll ask about that when necessary
12. Is the professional training for the service provider important for you?
    (a) Yes, (b) No, (c) Not concerned
    Why: (a) for my own sake: safety, effect, (b) does not matter as long as the outcome is good, (c) others (please specify)————
13. What are the problems you encountered during taking services?
    (a) outcome is not the same as they tell me, (b) does not fit my expectation, (c) bad temper, (d) product they use is not good, (e) other (please specify)————

14. What should be done to promote this sector in China?
    (a) ensure licensing, (b) better monitoring system from the government, (c) provide training for the service providers (d) increase/decrease price, (e) Better quality control mechanism, (f) Others (Please specify)———

Appendix D

Beijing Normal University—Hong Kong Baptist University

United International College

Project Title: Globalization and Wellness Health Tourism in China (Zhuhai): Paradigm, Prospects and Challenges

M.N. Islam, *Chinese and Indian Medicine Today*,
DOI 10.1007/978-981-10-3962-1

Interview Questionnaire (For Service Provider)

Client Number: **Location:** **Date of Interview:**

My name is ----------------------- , I'm a part of the above research team. If you agree I would like to interview you on your opinion and experience about these issues. This interview will last for about one hour. I would like to tape record it. No personal information will be asked/ or: any personal information is being kept separately from the main interview and is only accessed by our research team. I hereby declared that the information I am collecting will only be used for this particular research purpose. I will ensure the confidentiality of the informant and information and after completion of the research all the information will be destroyed. Do you have any further

questions concerning the study? May I interview you now/ shall I come back at a more convenient time?

---

1. Background question

Name (Name): Nationality:

Sex: M/F age: Marital Status: Having children: Y/N

Monthly income: RMB Profession:

Address (Optional):

Visitor/TR (Zhuhai)

Came from which province (Visitor/TR Zhuhai):

Duration of living Zhuhai:

2. Professional Training (Paradigm)

2.1 What type of service you provide?
2.2 What type of professional training you have to do this job? (Please describe your skill)
2.3 Do you think professional training/skill is important for this job?
2.4 How do you evaluate this service (for relaxation and rejuvenation, stress reduction, etc.)

3. **Job Satisfaction (Prospects)**

3.1 Why did you choose this profession?
3.2 For how long you are working in this profession?
3.3 Do you enjoy this profession?
3.4 Will you continue to work in this profession?
3.5 Have you signed a contract with the company?
3.6 How many clients you have to serve everyday?
3.7 What type of difficulty you usually encounter during providing service?

4. **Prospects and Challenges**

4.1 What are the difficulties to do this job?
4.2 Do you find any differences between male clients and female clients during providing services?
4.3 Do you find any difference between Chinese clients and foreign clients during providing services?
4.5 Does this job bring you any occupational risk/diseases? (If yes, does your company pay for treatment? Do you have health insurance? Who pay for you?)
4.6. What are the common occupational risks for this job?

5. **Health and Consumer Satisfaction (Prospects)**

5.1 Do you consider the service you provide having health benefit? (If yes, how?)
5.2 How do you evaluate the spa/wellness tourism in China (Zhuhai)?
5.3 Do you use any Chinese medicine/herb/CM therapy? (If yes, please describe the therapy)
5.4 Where did you learn about this therapy and for how long?
5.5 What improvement of this industry could make to provide better services for the clients?
5.6 What is your suggestion to improve the quality of service?
5.7 What are the other things you expect to provide better service but not available here?
5.8 Have you ever encountered any dispute with the clients? Y/N (If yes, how did you solve this?)

6. **Role of Government/Organization/Association/Policy (Prospects and Challenges)**

6.1 Do you think this sector should be promoted in China?
6.2 Are you familiar with the government policy/regulations about promoting wellness/spa/health tourism in China?
6.3 Do you think the government policy/regulation is favoring the development of this sector?
6.4 What the government/related authority need to do to promote the sector?

Thank you very much for participating this interview

Appendix E

Beijing Normal University—Hong Kong Baptist University
北京师范大学- 香港浸会大学

United International College
联合国际学院

Project Title: The Business of Chinese Medicine Today: Commodification and Paradigm

Client Number **Location** **Date of Interview**

序号： 采访地点： 采访日期：

Background Information:

背景情况：

Name: Gender:

姓名：性别：

Age: Occupation:

Monthly Income

年龄：职业： 月收入：

---

1. Why did you choose to study CM?
   请问您为什么选择学习中医？
2. Have you ever tried to get admission in a Western medical college? (If yes, how many times)
   您是否尝试过申请入读西医院校?(如果有, 是多少次)

M.N. Islam, *Chinese and Indian Medicine Today*,
DOI 10.1007/978-981-10-3962-1

3. What was your first priority of study either CM or WM?
   您的首选是研读西医还是中医?
4. Do you think your social status is lower than a student/professional trained in Western medicine? (If yes, why)
   您是否认为您的社会地位低于一位受过西医培训的专业人士或学生?
5. Are you/will you involve in cross practice (prescribe drugs from Western system)?
   您是否会有综合实践(如开西药处方)?
6. How do you compare CM with WM?
   您如果比较中医与西医?
7. How do you compare the traditional/apprentice CM education and contemporary education system?
   您如果对比传统的或学徒式的中医学习方式和当代的教育系统?
8. Do you have any family background on CM?
   您的家族是否有中医的背景?
9. What are the major limitations you encounter about contemporary CM education?
   在当代中医教育系统中, 您认为什么对您造成最大的限制?
10. How do you see the development of CM health products/commodity?
    您如何看待中药保健品的发展?
11. Do you think various drug manufacturers are misleading CM? (Please explain)
    您是否认为各种各样的药品生产企业正将中药引入歧途?(请解释)
12. Do you think CM has lost its authenticity because of the development of CM health products? (Please explain)
    您是否认为中医正因为中药保健品的发展失去它的可靠性?
13. Do you think CM will be replaced by WM one day because of the integrated education system?
    您是否认为将有一日中医会因为综合的教育系统而被西医取代?
14. How do you see the integrated Medical practice?
    您如何看待综合医学实践?
15. How do you see the relation between CM, Chinese nationality, culture, etc.
    您如何看待中医, 中华民族, 文化等之间的关系?
16. Do you consider CM as complete medical system or cultural practice?
    您认为中医师一个完整的医学体系还是一种文化实践?
17. Do you think drug standardization is a major concern for the quality control of CM?
    您是否认为将药品标准化是控制中医质量的一个重要因素?
18. In your opinion, what should be done do promote CM?
    为推广中医, 您有何建议?

Thank you very much

Glossary

Anti-colonial Someone or something who oppose the colonial rule.

Apprenticeship A education or learning system where students/trainees learn from a particular master/teacher for a long time. Apprenticeship system was the popular mode of education in ayurveda and Chinese medicine until the introduction of Western style education system in Twentieth century.

Astanga Hrdayam Title of the one of the major ayurvedic classical texts written by Vagbhatas. There are some similarities among this text and other ayurvedic classical texts such as *Caraka Samhita* and *Susruta Samhia*. This text is widely used in Southern part of India.

Ayurveda Ayu means life and veda means knowledge. Ayurveda is called as knowledge of life or science of life. It is one of the oldest medical systems originated in India. The root of ayurveda could be found in Vedic text *Atharvaveda*.

BAMS Refers to Bachelor of Ayurvedic Medicine and Surgery. It is the only recognized undergradute education in ayurvedic colleges in contemporary India.

Beijing Tong Ren Tang One of the oldest Chinese herbal medicine manufacturing companies founded in 1669.

Bencao Gangmu One of the oldest Chinese materia medicas widely used in Chinese herbal medicine preparation and written by Li Shizhen in 1578. It is popular as Compendium of Materia Medica in English speaking world.

Brahmanic One of the earliest religious traditions in India founded during the Vedic period.

Branding When something has been used as a brand name to sell various products or services.

Buddhist Some on who follows Buddism. Buddism is one of the oldest religions originated in the Eastern part of India.

M.N. Islam, *Chinese and Indian Medicine Today*,
DOI 10.1007/978-981-10-3962-1

Caraka One of the most popular and successful ayurvedic practitioners in ancient time who wrote the ayurvedic text *Caraka Samhita*.

Chinese Medicine The oldest medical systems originated in China. Chinese medicine may have different forms in contemporary China such as Acupuncture, Chinese herbal medicine, Tuina, etc.

Chronic Refers to long time disease which also needs long time treatment for cure.

Classical Well known and well accepted ancient book.

Colonial Administration When one country physically conquered and ruled another country by her own administration. In this book colonial administration refers the rule of East India Company and subsequently the rule of the British Raj in India Raj.

Commodification When some product or services become commodity for much consumption. Both ayurveda and Chinese herbal medicine has become commodity for much consumption today because of the profit maximization desire of the drug manufacturing companies.

Crore A money counting unit in India which is equivalent to ten million.

Curative Came from cure. The medicine which has the power to cure.

Dabur Name of the one of the largest and oldest ayurvedic drug manufacturing company in India.

Dao One of the major theoretical concepts used in Chinese medicine. It refers to universe and includes both the heaven and the earth. According to Chinese medicine everything belongs to *Dao*.

Demonology One of the eight branches of ayurvedic medicine. It deals with invisible creatures such as demon, ghost, etc. It also discussed about next life since ayurvedic text contain chapters about rebirth and next life.

Diabetes A popular chronic disease widely found among urban middle class in their mid or late age. It is widely believed and practiced that Asian medicine has better treatment and remedy to deal with diabetes.

Empirical Something which is observable. Empirical study is a popularly used research method in social science where a researcher do field work and gather data through various technic such as observation, fieldnotes, interview, survey, informal discussion, focus group discussion, etc.

Equilibrium The fundamental principle of both the Chinese medicine and ayurveda. It also called balance. The health and unhealth is determined according to the equilibrium of dosa in ayurveda and *yin/yang* in Chinese medicine.

Five Phase One of the major theoretical principles used in both ayurveda and Chinese medicine. In ayurveda human is a combination of five phases (earth, fire, space, air, water) and soul. In Chinese medicine *dao* (the universe) is formatted by five cosmic elements or five phases (water, wood, fire, earth, and metal).

Ghee A classified butter widely used in Indian household to prepare everyday meals. It is also used to prepare some ayurvedic drugs.

Gunagdong A province of China located into the Southern part of China.

Guangzhou The capital city of China's Guangdong province.

Healer Someone who has the power to heal or solve some health problems.

Hegemony A slow, less disputive or conflicting and inclusive process to establish authority which usually takes long time and also last long. Western medicine in Asia gains authority through hegemonic process.

Hindu Those who follow the religion Hinduism are called as Hindu.

Hinduism A form of religion originated and widely practiced in India. It is also called *Sanaton Dharma*. The European called *Sanaton Dharma* as Hinduism.

Huang Di Nei Jing The oldest Chinese medicine classic. It came to the reader as a conversation between the legendary Chinese emperor Huang Di and his doctor Qi Bo.

Humoral Came from humor. In Unani medicine there are four human which constitute human body: blood, black bile, yellow bile, and phlegm. Unani medicine is based on humoral theory. Humoral theory is very similar to balance theory since both the theories consider human health as balance between or among various elements.

Impotence A type of sexual weakness of man found during sexual intercourse such as erectile dysfunctioning, prematured ejaculation, etc.

Indigenous Medicine Usually refers the local system of medicine.

Integrated Medicine When various medical systems combined together that is called integrated medicine such as a combination of Western medicine and Chinese medicine or a combination of Western medicine and ayurveda. In contemporary China, many integrated Chinese medicine practitioner use Western diagnostic method to identify disease and prescribe Chinese formula/drugs.

Intercourse In this book intercourse refers as sexual interaction.

Kabiraj The title of ayurvedic practitioner in Eastern part of India, particularly in Bengal.

Kapha One of the three doshas (body constituents) used in ayurveda. Generally refers as phlegm.

Kolkata The capital city of India's West Bengal state.

Lingshu A part of Chinese medical classic *Huang Di New Jing*. *Lingshu* part mostly discussed about acupuncture.

Magic Bullet Something which has magical power to hill. The massive rise of ayurvedic impotence pill has been claimed as magic bullet in this book.

Mao The leader of China who lead 1949 revolution and founded People's Republic of China.

Microorganism Refers to germs such as virus, bacteria, etc.

Missionary Member of a religious group who promotes education, health care, justice, etc. apart from their religion. Christian missionaries were the earliest institutions brought Western medicine in China and India.

Mughal The longest Muslim empire in Indian subcontinent who expanded their territory around most part of today's South Asia. They rules India from 1526 to 1540 and from 1555 to 1857.

Nationalism Is a feeling which is used to unite a particular group of people within a particular territory and provide a common national identity to those people.

Non-celibacy Refers to sexual and other excitement related activities.

Ocean Spring A theme park with resort hotel located in the costal area of Zhuhai city, Guangdong Province, China.

OTC Refers to Over The Counter. Usually those medicine does not require a dontor's prescription to purchase carry an OTC logo.

Pharmacology A subject which deals with drug prescription/formula, preparation and manufacturing.

Pitta One of the three *doshas* (body constituents) in ayurveda. Usually refers to bile.

Pluralism/medical pluralism Refers to the coexistence of a variety of medical systems/traditions within a chosen content/society.

Qi One of the major theoretical principles used in Chinese medicine. Usually refers to energy.

Regimen Refers to routine. In Chinese medicine and ayurveda daily and seasonal regimen are key method to health preservation and disease prevention.

Revivalism Came from revival. Refers to bring back the old tradition which has declined.

Samhita In ayurveda *samhita* means compendium. The major two ayurvedic classical texts used this term at the end of the book title: *Caraka Samhita* and *Susruta Samhita*. *Caraka* and *Susruta* are the authors' name and *Samhita* means compendium.

Sanskrit One of the oldest languages in Indian sub-continent used by the Indo-Aryan. Many contemporary Indian languages came from Sanskrit language such as Hindi, Bengali, etc.

Spa An establishment where people visit for some relax and rejuvenating activities such as massage, body care, etc.

Su Wen The first part of classical Chinese text *Huang Di Nei Jing.*

Superstitious Refers to metaphysical world govern by the supernatural power. Both the Chinese medicine and ayurveda has some superstitious elements, particularly mythological origin.

Susruta One of the ancient ayurvedic physicians who were very skillfull on surgery. He wrote the book *Susruta Samhita.*

Tuina A method of Chinese medicine. Commonly known as Chinese medicine massage.

Vaid/Vaidya The title of ayurvedic practitioner.

Vata One of the three doshas (body constituents) used in ayurveda as theoretical principle. Usually refers to wind/air.

Vedic Village A tourist resort with hotel and housing complex. It is located in Rajarhat, Kolkata, West Bengal, India. There was an ayurvedic wellness center there and the author conducted research there.

Virilization A medical subject in ayurveda which deals with men's sexual weakness. It is also one of the eight branches in ayurveda.

Wellness Tourism A particular form of health tourism where people participate in living healthy life related activities such as following a ayurvedic daily routine, yoga, etc. and gain knowledge and skill on how to preserve health.

Western Hegemony Refers to the process under which Western value systems have been established in all spheres of daily life and become normal part of everyday living for people in contemporary China and India.

Yang/Yin One of the major theoretical principles used in Chinese medicine. Usually *yin* refers to shadow side and *yang* refers to bright side of health. *Yang* always stay as opposite of *yin* component. *Yin* and *yang* are two mutually interdependent but opposite component of health in Chinese medicine.

Zhuhai A costal city of China's Guangdong province. It is also an special economic zone in the pearl river delta region.

Bibliography

Abeykoon, Palatka., and O. Akerele. 2002. Development of training programmes for traditional medicine. In. *Traditional Medicine in Asia,* ed. Chaudhury, Ranjit Roy and Uton, Muchtar Rafei. South-East Asia: World Health Organization (WHO) Regional Office.

Ahluwalia, Sanjam. 2004. Demographic rhetoric and sexual surveillance: Indian middle-class advocates of Birth Control, 1902–1940s. In *Confronting the Bod,* ed. Mills, H James and Sen Satadru. London: Anthem Press.

Akhtar, Rais and Nilofar, Izhar. 1994. *On Primary Health Care in India.*

Aldridge, David. 2000. *Spirituality, Healing and Medicine—Return to the silence*. London: Jessica Kingsley Publishers Ltd.

Allsop, Judith. 1995. *Health Policy and the NHS Towards 2000*, 2nd ed. London and New York: Longman Publishing.

Alter, J.S. 2005. Ayurvedic Acupuncture: Transnational nationalism: Ambivalence about the origin and authenticity of medical knowledge". In *Asian Medicine and Globalization,* ed. Joseph S. Alter. Pennsylvania: University of Pennsylvania Press.

Anderson, Benedict. 1983. *Imagined Communities: Reflections on the Origins and Spread of Nationalism*. London: Verso.

Andrews, Bridie. 2014. *The Making of Modern Chinese Medicine, 1850–1960*. Vancouver: UBC Press.

Angrosino, Michael V. 1987. *A Health Practitioner's Guide to the Social and Behavioural Sciences*. Massachusetts: Auburn House Publishing Company.

Appadurai, Arjun. 1996. *Modernity at Large—Cultural Dimensions of Globalization*. Minnesota: The University of Minnesota Press.

Arnold, David. 1993. *Colonizing the Body—State Medicine and Epidemic Disease in Nineteenth-Century India*. Berkeley: University of California Press.

Arthur, J. Rubel and Michael R. Hass. 1990. Ethno medicine. In *Medical Anthropology-Contemporary Theory and Method,* ed. Johnson, Thomas M., and Carolyn F. Sargent. New York: Praeger.

Ashcroft, Bill, et al. 1995. *The Post-Colonial Studies Reader*. London: Routledge.

Asthana, Sheena. 1994. Primary health care and selective PHC: Community participation in health and development". In *Health and Development, ed.* Phillips, David R. and Yola Verhasselt. London: Routledge.

AYUSH. 2002. *National Policy on Indian Systems of Medicine & Homoeopathy (2002).* New Delhi: Department of Ayurveda, Yoga & Naturopathy, Unani, Siddha and Homoeopathy (AYUSH), Ministry of Health and Family Welfare, Government of India.

AYUSH. 2003. *AYUSH in India* 2003. New Delhi: Planning and Development Cell, Department of Ayurveda, Yoga & Naturopathy, Unani, Siddha & Homoeopathy, Ministry of Health and Family Welfare, Government of India.

AYUSH in India. 2012. *Annual Report.* New Delhi: Department of AYUSH, Ministry of Health and Family Welfare, Government of India.

M.N. Islam, *Chinese and Indian Medicine Today*,
DOI 10.1007/978-981-10-3962-1

Baer, Hans A., et al. 1997. *Medical Anthropology and the World System—A Critical Perspective*. USA: Bergin & Garvey Publishers.

Baggott, Rob. 2000. *Public Health: Policy and politics*. London: Macmillan Press Ltd.

Bala, Poonam. 1991. *Imperialism and Medicine in Bengal: A Socio-historical Perspective*. New Delhi: Sage Publications.

Barker, Philip. 1993. *Michel Foucault—Subversions of the Subject*. Hertfordshire: Harvester Wheatsheaf.

Barnard, Alan. 1998. Beliefs. In *Encyclopaedias of Social and Cultural Anthropology,* ed. Barnard, Alan, and Jonathan Spencer. London: Routledge.

Basham, A.L. 1976. The practice of medicine in ancient and medieval India. In *Asian Medical Systems: A contemporary Study,* ed. Leslie, Charles. Berkeley: University of California Press.

Beijing University of Chinese Medicine. 2014. Schools and Hospitals. Retrieved from the following link: http://www.bucm.edu.cn/portal/media-type/html/group/en/page/default.psml/js_pane/P-1270a6cdfd7-1000e. Accessed on 26 Dec 2014.

Bhatacharya, Sudindranath and Shapon Kuar Bhuiya. 1999. *A Sharok Pustika on the Famous Ayurvedic Practitioners in Sutanuti Onchal*. Calcutta: Sutanuti Porishad.

Bing, Wang. 2010. *Yellow Emperor's Canon of Internal Medicine (Huang Di Nei Jing)*, Translated by Wu Liansheng and Wu Qi. Beijing: China Science and Technology Press.

Bode, Maarten. 2002. Indian indigenous pharmaceuticals: Tradition, modernity, and nature". In *Plural Medicine, Tradition and Modernity, 1800–2000,* ed Waltraud, Ernst. New York: Routledge.

Bodeker, Gerard. 2002. A framework for cost-benefit analysis of traditional medicine and conventional medicine. In *Traditional Medicine in Asia*, ed. Chaudhury, Ranjit Roy and Uton Muchtar Rafei. World Health Organization (WHO): Regional Office for South-East Asia.

Bookman, Milica Z., and Karla. R. Bookman. 2007. *Medical Tourism in Developing Countries*. New York: Palgrave Macmillan.

Bordo, Susan. 1993. *Unbearable Weight*. Berkeley: University of California Press.

Bose, Sumantra. 2013. *Transforming India: Challenges to the world's Largest Democracy*. Cambridge: Harvard University Press.

Brass, P.R. 1972. The politics of ayurvedic education: A case study of revivalism and modernization in India. In *Education and politics in India*, ed. S.H. Rudolph and L.I. Rudolph, 342–371. Massachusetts: Harvard University Press.

Brown, Peter J. 1998. Belief and Ethnomedical Systems. In *Understanding and Applying Medical Anthropology*, ed. Peter J. Brown. California: Mayfield Publishers Company.

Brown, Peter J., and Marcia C. Inhorn. 1991. *The Anthropology of Infectious Disease—International Health Perspective*. The Netherlands: Gordon and Breach Science Publishers.

Brown, Peter J. et al. 1998. Medical anthropology: An introduction to the fields". In *Understanding and Applying Medical Anthropology,* ed. Brown, Peter J. California: Mayfield Publishers Company.

Caraka Samhita. 2003. ed. Nag, Brojendra Chandra, vol. 1–4. Calcutta: Nabopatro Prokashon.

Cavaye, Joyce. 2012. Does Therapeutic massage support mental well- Being? *Medical Sociology Online* 6, No. 2, 43–50.

Central Council of Indian Medicine. 2003–04. *B.A.M.S. Curriculum and Text Books*, No.3:3-56 (2003–04). Translated by Vd. Pawankumar R. Godatwar. New Delhi: Central Council of Indian Medicine.

Central Research Institute (Ayurveda). 2004. *Annul Progress Report 2003–04*. Calcutta: Dept. of AYUSH, Ministry of Health and Family Welfare, Government of India.

Chandra, Bipan. 1979. *Nationalism and Colonialism in Modern India*. New Delhi: Orient Longman.

Chandra, Shailaja. 2002. Role of traditional systems of medicine in national health care systems. In *Traditional Medicine in Asia,* ed. Chaudhury, Ranjit Roy and Uton Muchtar Rafei. World Health Organization (WHO): Regional Office for South-East Asia.

Chapman, J. 2007. *Growing Interest in Traditional Chinese Medicine Spa Therapy*. Retrieved from http://www.asiaone.com/Health/Alternative%2BMedicine/Story/A1Story20070625155533.html.
Charlie Changli, Xue, et al. 2006. Comparison of Chinese Medicine Education and Training in China and Australia. *Annals Academy of Medicine* 35(11): 775–779.
Chatterjee, Parta. 1994. Was there a Hegemonic Project of the Colonial State? In *Contesting Colonial Hegemony: State and Society in Africa and India,* ed. Engels, Dagmar and Marks, Shula. London: British Academy Press.
Chatterjee, Partha. 1986. *Nationalist Thought and the Colonial World: A Derivative Discourse*. London: Zed.
Chatterjee, Partha. 1995. Nationalism as a problem. In *The Post-Colonial Studies Reader,* ed. Ashcroft, Bill, et al. London: Routledge.
Chattopadhyaya, Debiprasad. 1977. *Science and Society in Ancient India*. Calcutta: Research India Publications.
Chen, Nancy N. 2005. Mapping science and nation in China. In *Asian Medicine and Globalization,* ed. Alter, Joseph S., 107–119. Philadelphia: University of Pennsylvania Press.
China Daily. 2011. Scam prompts health check for tourists' TCM visits. Retrieved from http://www.chinadaily.com.cn/china/2011-06/14/content_12687749.htmand. Accessed on 23 Dec 2013.
Chrisman, Noel J., and Arthur, Kleinman. 1983. Popular health care, social networks, and cultural meanings: The orientation of medical anthropology. In *Handbook of Health, Health Care, and the Health Professions,* ed. Mechanic, David. New York: Free Press.
Clay, Rotha M. 1966. *The Mediaeval Hospitals of England*. London: Yale University Press.
Cochrane, Allan and Kathy, Pain. 2004. A globalizing society? In *A Globalizing World?: Culture, Economics, Politics,* ed. Held, Devid. London: Routledge (in association with the Open University).
Cohen, Lawrence. 1995. The epistemological carnival: Meditations on disciplinary intentionality and Ayurveda. In. *Knowledge and the Scholarly Medical Traditions,* ed. Bates, Don. Cambridge: Cambridge University Press.
Cohen, H. 1961. The evolution of the concept of disease. In *Concept of Medicine,* ed. Lush, B. New York: Pergamon Press.
Comaroff, J. 1982. Medicine: Symbol and ideology. In *The Problem of Medical Knowledge: Examining the Social Construction of Medicine,* ed. Wright, P., and A. Treacher. Edinburgh: University of Edinburgh Press.
Connell, J. 2011. *Medical Tourism*. Oxon: CABI Publishing.
Connor, Linda H., and Samuel Geoffrey (eds.). 2001. *Healing Powers and Modernity: Traditional Medicine, Shamanism and Science in Asian Societies*. London: Bergin and Garvey.
Cook, Allan R. 1999. *Alternative Medicine Sourcebook*. United States: Frederick G. Ruffner, Jr. Publisher.
Coughlin, J. 2010. China's Gray Revolution: Why China May Invent the New Business of Aging. Retrieved from http://www.disruptivedemographics.com/2010/02/chinas-gray-revolutionwhychina-may_21.html. Accessed on March 2011.
Dabur India Limited. 2015. *Annual Report 2014–15*. New Delhi: Dabur India Limited.
D'anglure, Bernard Saladin. 1998. Shamanism. In *Encyclopedia of Social and Cultural Anthropology,* ed. Barnard, Alan and Jonathan, Spencer. London: Routledge.
Department of Resources, Energy and Tourism. 2011. Medical Tourism in Australia: A Scoping Study. A consultancy report prepared by the Deloitte Access Economics Pty Ltd.
Directorate of Health Service, Government of West Bengal. *Health on the March. West Bengal (2002–03)*. Calcutta.
Directorate of Health Service, Government of West Bengal. *Health on the March. West Bengal (2003–04)*. Calcutta.
Disch, Estelle. 2006. *Reconstructing Gender*. New York: McGrawHill.

Dong, Hongguang and Zhang, Xiaorui. 2002. An overview of traditional Chinese medicine. In *Traditional Medicine in Asia,* ed. Chaudhury, Ranjit Roy and Rafel Uton, Muchtar, 17–30. New Delhi: World Health Organization (WHO).

Dressler, William W. 1998. Case studies in explanatory models. In *Understanding and Applying Medical Anthropology,* ed. Brown, Peter J. California: Mayfield Publishers Company.

Dreyfus, Hubert L., and Paul Rabinow. 1986. *Michel Foucault—Beyond Structuralism and Hermeneutics*. Great Britain: The Harvester Press Limited.

Duara, Prasenjit. 1995. *Rescuing History from the Nation: Questioning Narratives of Modern China*. Chicago: University of Chicago Press.

Dunn, Fred L. 1976. Traditional Asian medicine and cosmopolitan medicine as adaptive systems. In *Asian Medical Systems: A Contemporary Study,* ed. Charles, Leslie. Berkeley: University of California Press.

Dutta, Arijita. 2009. Prospects of ancient medical systems in India and China in today's world. In *Economic Reforms in India and China,* ed. Reddy, B. Sudhakara, 375–390. New Delhi: Sage Publications India Pvt Ltd.

Elling, Roy H. 1981. The capitalist world system and international health. *International Journal of Health Services* 11: 21–51.

Engels, Dagmar and Marks, Shula. 1994. *Contesting Colonial Hegemony: State and Society in Africa and India (Introduction).* London: British Academy Press.

Featherstone, Mike, et al. 1991. *The Body—Social Process and Cultural Theory*. London: Sage Publications.

Fernandes, Leela. 2006. *India's New Middle Class*. Minneapolis: University of Minnesota Press.

Fields, Gregory P. 2001. *Religious Therapeutics: Body and Health in Yoga, Ayurveda, and Trantra*. New York: Albany State University of New York Press.

Frawley, David. 1997. *Ayurveda and the Mind: The Healing of Consciousness*. Winconsin: Lotus Press.

Geertz, Clifford. 1973. *The Interpretation of Cultures*. New York: Basic Books.

Gellner, Ernest. 1983. *Nations and Nationalism*. Oxford: Blackwell.

Giddens, Anthony. 1990. *The Consequences of Modernity*. Cambridge: Polity Press.

Giddens, Anthony. 1999. *Lecture 1—Globalization*. London: BBC Reith Lectures.

Goldie, Terry. 1995. The representation of the indigene. In *The Post-Colonial Studies Reader,* ed. Ashcroft, et.al. (Please give full name of primary editor—there are many Ashcrofts). London: Routledge.

Goldstone, L. 2000. Massage as an Orthodox medical treatment past and future. *Complementary Therapies in Clinical Practice* 6, No. 4, 169–75.

Good, Byron J. 1994. *Medicine, Rationality and Experience: An Anthropological Perspective*. Cambridge: Cambridge University Press.

Goodrich, J.N., and G.E. Goodrich. 1994. Health care tourism. In *Managing Tourism,* ed. Medlik, S. Oxford: Butterworth-Heinemann.

Gopinath, B.G. 2001. Foundational ideas of ayurveda. In *Medicine and Life Sciences in India,* ed. Subbarayappa, B.V. Volume iv part 2: History of Science, Philosophy and Culture in Indian Civilization series. New Delhi: Centre for Studies in Civilization.

Government of India. 1958. Ministry of Health. *Report of the Committee to Assess and Evaluate the Present Status of Ayurvedic System of Medicine,* 25. New Delhi: The Times of India Press.

Gramsci, Antonio. 1978. *Selections From the Prison Notebooks*. Edited and translated by Hoare Quintin and Smith Geoffrey Nowell. New York: International Publishers.

Gupta, Akhil. 1995. Blurred boundaries: The discourse of corruption, the culture of politics and the imagined state. *American Ethnologist* 22 (2): 375–402.

Gupta, Brahmananda. 1976. Indigenous medicine in nineteenth- and twentieth-century Bengal. In *Asian Medical Systems: A Contemporary Study,* ed. Charles, Leslie. Berkeley: University of California Press.

Habib, S. Irfan and Dhruv, Raina. 2005. Reinventing traditional medicine: Method, institutional change, and the manufacture of drugs and medication in late colonial India. In *Asian Medicine and Globalization,* ed. Alter, Joseph S. Pennsylvania: University of Pennsylvania Press.

Hahn, Robert A. 1999. Anthropology and the enhancement of public health practice. In *Anthropology in Public Health,* ed. Hahn, Robert A. Oxford: Oxford University Press.

Harris, M. 1966. The cultural ecology of India's sacred cattle. *Current Anthropology* 7: 51–66.

Health Statistics. 2009. National Health and Family Planning Commission of the People's Republic of China". Retrieved from the http://www.moh.gov.cn/publicfiles/business/htmlfiles/zwgkzt/ptjnj/year2010/index2010.html. Accessed on 30 March 2014.

Heelas, Paul. 1996. *The New Age Movement: The Celebration of the Self and the Sacralization of Modernity*. Oxford; Cambridge; USA: Blackwell.

Heelas, Paul. 2008. *Spiritualities in Life: New Age Romanticism and Consumptive Capitalism*. Malden, MA: Wiley-Blackwell.

Helman, Cecil G. 2001. *Culture, Health and Illness*, 4th ed. London: Arnold.

Hendry, Joy. 1999. *An Introduction to Social Anthropology: Other people's Worlds*. Hampshire: Macmillan Press.

Herrick, Devon M. 2007. Medical Tourism: Global Competition in Health Care. Policy report No. 304. Texas: National Center for Policy Analysis.

Herzberg, Larry, and Qin Herzberg. 2011. *China Survival Guide: How to Avoid Travel Troubles and Mortifying Mishaps*. Berkeley: Stone Bridge Press.

Heung, Vincent C.S., and Kucukusta, Deniz. 2012. Wellness Tourism in China: Resources, Development and Marketing International Journal of Tourism Research. *International Journal of Tourism Research*. Published online by Wiley Online Library (wileyonlinelibrary.com) doi: 10.1002/jtr.1880.

Holey, E. and E. Cook. 2003. *Evidence- based Therapeutic massage: A practical Guide for Therapists*. London: Elsevier Health Sciences.

Hollen, Cecilia Van. 2005. Nationalism, transnationalism, and the politics of traditional Indian medicine for HIV/AIDS. In *Asian Medicine and Globalization,* ed. Alter, Joseph S. Pennsylvania: University of Pennsylvania Press.

Hsu, Elisabeth. 1999. *The Transmission of Chinese Medicine*. Cambridge: Cambridge University Press.

Huang Di Nei Jing (The Medical Classic of the Yellow Emperor). 2009. *Translated by Zhu Ming*. Beijing: Foreign language Press.

Huard, P. 1970. Medical Education in South-East Asia. In *The History of Medical Education,* ed. O'Malley C.D.

Hyma, B., and A. Ramesh. 1994. Traditional medicine: Its extent and potential for incorporation into modern national health systems. In *Health and Development,* ed. Phillips, David R., and Yola, Verhasselt. London: Routledge.

Islam, M. Nazrul. 2008. *Repackaging Ayurveda in Post-Colonial India: Revivalism and Global Commodification.* Hong Kong: The University of Hong Kong.

Islam, M. Nazrul. 2010. Indigenous medicine as commodity: Local reach of ayurveda in modern India. *Current Sociology* 58(5): 777–798. London: Sage Publications.

Islam, M. Nazrul. 2012. New age orientalism: Ayurvedic 'wellness and spa' culture. *Health Sociology Review, published in association with The Australian Sociological Association,* 21 (2): 220–231. Oxfordshire: Routledge Journal, Taylor and Francis.

Islam, M. Nazrul. 2012. Repackaging ayurveda in post-colonial India: Revival or dilution? *South Asia: Journal of South Asian Studies by South Asian Studies Association of Australia*, 35(3): 503–519. Oxfordshire: Routledge Journal, Taylor and Francis.

Islam, M. Nazrul. 2013. The promotion of masculinity and femininity through ayurveda in modern India. *Indian Journal of Gender Studies* 20(3): 415–434. New Delhi: Sage Publication (Co-author Kuah-Pearce, K E).

Islam, M. Nazrul. 2014. Chinese Medicine as a product filling the wellness health tourism niche in China: Prospect and challenges. *International Journal of Tourism Sciences* 14(2): 51–69. Seoul: The Tourism Sciences Society of Korea and Backsan Publishing Company.

Islam, M. Nazrul. 2014. Medical secularism vs. religious secularism: New era of ayurveda in India. *Indian Journal of Social Work* 75(2): 575–616. Mumbai: Tata Institute of Social Sciences.

Islam, M. Nazrul. 2015. Massage and related services as popular culture: New consumption and fluid sex hierarchy in China. *International Journal of China Studies* 6, No. 1, 85–100. Kuala Lumpur: University of Malaya Press.

Islam, M. Nazrul. 2016. Integration of Chinese Medicine in public health: Current trend and challenges. In *Public Health Challenges in Contemporary China: An Interdisciplinary Perspective*, ed. Islam, M. Nazrul, 55–72. Heidelberg: Springer.

Jaggi, O.P. 1979. *History of Science, Technology and Medicine in India*, vol. 15. Delhi: Atma Ram & Sons.

Jaggi, O.P. 1981. Medicine in Medieval India. In *History of Science and Technology in India*, vol. 8. Delhi: Atma Ram & Sons.

Jaggi, O.P. 1979. Medical education and research. In *History of Science, Technology and Medicine in India*, ed. Jaggi, O.P. New Delhi: Atma Ram & Sons.

Jaggi, O.P. 2004. Medicine in India: Modern period. In *History of Science, Philosophy and Culture in Indian Civilization* Series, ed. Chattopadhyaya, D.P., vol. ix, part 1. New Delhi: Oxford University Press.

Jaspan, M.A. 1969. *Traditional Medical Theory in South-East Asia*. Hull: University of Hull.

Jayawardena, Kumari. 1995. *The White Woman's Other Burden*. New York & London: Routledge.

Jeffery, Roger. 1988. *The Politics of Health in India*. California: University of California Press.

Jeffreys, Sheila. 2005. *Beauty and Misogyny*. East Sussex: Routledge.

John, Comaroff and Comaroff, Jean. 1992. *Ethnography and the Historical Imagination*. Boulder: Westview Press.

Joshi, Sanjay. 2001. *Fractured Modernity: Making of a Middle Class in Colonial North India*. Oxford: Oxford University Press.

Joshi, Sunil V. 1997. *Ayurveda and Panchakarma: The Science of Healing and Rejuvenation*. Winconsin: Lotus Press.

Juah, Shan. 2011. Wealthy Chinese Spur Medical Tourism, November 7. Beijing: China Daily.

Kaviraj, Sudipta. 1994. On the construction of colonial power: Structure, discourse, hegemony. In *Contesting Colonial Hegemony: State and Society in Africa and India*, ed. Engels, Dagmar and Marks, Shula. London: British Academy Press.

Kennedy, Mark. 1988. An Inquiry into the role of the Nation state in development: Rethinking dependency. Paper prepared for the Tenth International Colloquium on the World Economy. Cairo, February 11–13.

Khan, Maryam. 2010. Medical tourism: Outsourcing of healthcare. A conference presentation in the International CHRIE conference. University of Massachusetts-Amherst.

King, Helen. 1999. Comparative perspectives on medicine and religion in the ancient world. In *Religion, Health and Suffering*, ed. Hinnells, John R., and Roy, Porter. London: Kegan Paul International.

Kohn, Livia. 2005. *Health and Long Life: The Chinese Way*, 1–8. Cambridge: Three Pines Press.

Kolodny, Robert C. 1987. Medicine and psychiatric perspectives on a healthy sexuality. In *Sexuality and Medicine: Conceptual Roots*, ed. Shelp, Earl E., vol. 1. Holland: D. Reidel Publishing Company.

Korde, Neelesh. 2016. The daily ayurvedic regimen. Retrieved from the following link https://www.youtube.com/watch?v=NGV2FT9zAvs&list=PLy6afWEJ8MGeww-CuDOikciNbz_FUkVc2. Accessed on 19 Dec 2016.

Kumar, Anil. 1998. *Medicine and the Raj: British Medical Policy in India, 1835–1911*. New Delhi: Sage Publications.

Kurup, P.N.V. 2002. Ayurveda. In *Traditional Medicine in Asia,* ed. Chaudhury, Ranjit Roy, and Uton, Muchtar Rafei. World Health Organization (WHO): Regional Office for South-East Asia.
Lambert, Helen. 1998. Medical anthropology. In *Encyclopaedia of Social and Cultural Anthropology,* ed. Barnard, Alan and Jonathan, Spencer. London: Routledge.
Langford, M.Jean. 2002. *Fluent Bodies: Ayurvedic Remedies for Postcolonial Imbalance*. Durham: Duke University Press.
Larson, D.B., et al. 1998. *Scientific Research on Spirituality and Health: A Consensus Report*. Rockville, MD: National Institute for HealthCare Research.
Laws, Eric. 1996. Health tourism: A business opportunity approach". In *Health and the International Tourist,* ed. Clift, Stephen and Stephen J. Page. London: Routledge.
Leslie, Charles. 1976. The ambiguities of medical revivalism in modern India. In *Asian Medical Systems: A Contemporary Study,* ed. Leslie Charles. Berkeley: University of California Press.
Levinson, Richard. 1998. Issues at the interface of medical sociology and public health. In *Modernity, Medicine and Health,* ed. Scambler, Graham and Paul, Higgs. London: Routledge.
Liebeskind, Claudia. 1996. Unani medicine of the subcontinent. In *Oriental Medicine,* ed. Van Alphen, Jan and Anthony, Aris. Boston: Shambhala.
Lin, Justin. January 1995. The needham puzzle: Why the industrial revolution did not originate in China. *Economic Development and Cultural Change* 43(2): 269–292. doi:10.1086/452150.
Lesa, Lockford. 2004. *Performing Feminity*. Lanham: Altamira Press.
Loustaunau, Martha O., and Elisa J. Sobo. 1997. *The Cultural Context of Health, Illness and Medicine*. Connecticut: Bergin & Garvey.
Lupton, Deborah. 1994. *Medicine as Culture—Illness, Disease and the Body in Western societies*. London: Sage Publications Limited.
Lupton, Deborah. 2003. *Medicine as Culture: Illness, Disease and the Body in Western Societies*. London: Sage Publications.
Magner, Lois N. 1992. *A History of Medicine*. New York: Marcel Dekker.
Majumdar, Boria. 2007. Cricket in India: Representative playing field to restrictive preserve. In *From the Colonial to the Postcolonial,* ed. Chakrabarty, Depesh (et al). Oxford: Oxford University Press.
Manohar, Ram and Darshan, Shankar. 1996. Ayurvedic medicine today—Ayurveda at the crossroads. In *Oriental Medicine—An Illustrated Guide to the Asian Arts of Healing,* ed. van Alphen, Jan and Anthony, Aris. Boston: Shambhala.
McCracken, David R. Phillips. 2012. *Global Health: An Introduction to Current and Future Trend.* London and New York: Routledge.
Mc Intyre Lisa, J. 2006. *The Practical Skeptics*. New York: McGrawHill Higher Education.
McElroy, Ann, and P.K. Townsend. 1996. *Medical Anthropology in Ecological Perspective*. Boulder, Colo: Westview Press.
Michel, George. 1994. *The Royal Palaces of India*. London: Thames and Hudson.
Ministry of Finance of the People's Republic of China Web page. Retrieved from the http://yss.mof.gov.cn/. Accessed on 22 March 2014.
Ministry of Health and Family Welfare, Government of India. 1983. National Health Policy. New Delhi.
Ministry of Health and Family Welfare, Government of India. Webpage (http://mohfw.nic.in/reports/Performance%20Bud0506.pdf).
Ministry of Health of People's Republic of China. 2007. *China Health Statistical Yearbook 2007*. Beijing: Peking Union Medical College Press.
Mondol, Anshuman A. 2003. *Nationalism and Post-Colonial Identity: Culture and ideology in India and Egypt*. London: RoutledgeCurzon.
Moore, L.Henrietta. 1988. *Feminism and Anthropology*. London: Polity Press.
Morgan, Lynn M. 1993. *Community Participation in Health: The Politics of Primary Care in Costa Rica*. Cambridge: Cambridge University Press.

Morsy, Soheir. 1990. Political economy in medical anthropology. In *Medical Anthropology: A handbook of theory and method,* ed. Johnson, Thomas M., and Carolyn F. Sargent. New York: Greenwood Press.

Mukhopadhyaya, Girindranath. 2003. *History of Indian Medicine*, vol. 1–3. New Delhi: Munshiram Monoharlal Publishers.

Nahrstedt, Wolfgang. 2004. Wellness: A new perspective for leisure centers, health tourism, and spas in Europe on the global health market". In *The tourism and Leisure Industry,* ed. Weiermair, Klaus and Mathies, Christine. New York: The Haworth Hospitality Press.

Nahrstedt, Wolfgang. 2004. Wellness: A new perspective for leisure centers, health tourism, and spas in Europe on the global health market. In *The Tourism and Leisure Industry,* ed. Weiermair, Klaus and Christine, Mathies. New York: The Haworth Hospitality Press.

National Bureau of Statistics of China. 2012. Statistical communiqué of the People's Republic of Chinaon the 2013 national economic and social development. P. 1. Retrieved from the http://www.stats.gov.cn/english/PressRelease/201402/t20140224_515103.html. Accessed on 30 March 2014.

National Bureau of Statistics of China. 2012. Statistical communiqué of the People's Republic of Chinaon the 2011 national economic and social development. P. 18.

Needham, Joseph, Lu, Gwei-djen and Nathan, Sivin (2000) *Science and Civilization in China. Biology and Biological Technology*, vol. 6, part vi, Medicine. Cambridge: Cambridge University Press.

Neil, Lunt, Stephen T. Green, Russell, Mannion and Daniel, Horsfall. 2013. Quality, safety and risk in medical tourism. In *Medical Tourism: The Ethics, Regulation, and Marketing of Health Mobility*, ed. Hall, C. Michael. Oxon: Routledge.

Nichter, Mark. 1992. *Anthropological Approaches to the Study of Ethnomedicine*. Switzerland: Gordon and Breach Science Publishers.

Nichter, Mark. 1996. Drinking boiled cooled water: A cultural analysis of a health education message. In *Anthropology and International Health—Asian Case Study,* ed. Nichter, Mark and Mimi, Nichter. The Netherlands: Gordon and Breach Publishers.

Nichter, Mark. 1996. Popular perception of medicine: A South Indian case study. In *Anthropology and International Health—Asian Case Study,* ed. Nichter, Mark and Mimi, Nichter. The Netherlands: Gordon and Breach Publishers.

Nichter, Mark. 1996. The primary health care centre as a social system: Primary health care, social status, and the issue of team-work in South Asia". In *Anthropology and International Health—Asian Case Study*, ed. Nichter, Mark and Mimi, Nichter. The Netherlands: Gordon and Breach Publishers.

Nichter, Mark. 1999. Project community diagnosis: Participatory research as a first step toward community involvement in primary health care". In *Anthropology in Public Health,* ed. Hahn, Robert A. Oxford: Oxford University Press.

Nichter, Mark. 2001. The political ecology of health in India: Indigestion as sign and symptom of defective modernization". In *Healing Powers and Modernity—Traditional Medicine, Shamanism, and Science in Asian Societies,* ed. Connor, Linda H., and Geoffrey, Samuel. London: Bergin & Garvey.

Ninivaggi, Frank John. 2001. *An Elementary Text Book of Ayurveda*. Medison, Connecticut: Psychosocial Press.

Ortner, Sherry B. 1974. Is female to male as nature is to culture?". In *Women, Culture and Society,* ed. Rosaldo, Michelle Zimbalist and Louise, Lamphere. California: Stanford University Press.

Ortner, Sherry, and Harriet Whitehead. 1981. *Sexual Meanings: The Cultural Construction of Gender and Sexuality*. Cambridge: Cambridge University Press.

Paramesh, Rangesh. 2001. The spread of ayurveda outside India". In *Medicine and Life Sciences in India,* ed. Subbarayappa, B.V., vol. iv, part 2. History of Science, Philosophy and Culture in Indian Civilization series. New Delhi: Centre for Studies in Civilization.

Pargament, K.I. 1999. Psychology of religion and spirituality. *International Journal for the Psychology of Religion* 9: 3–16.

Parsons, Talcott. 1966. Illness and the role of the physician: A sociological perspective. In *Medical Care: Readings in the Sociology of Medical Institutions,* ed. Scott, W.R., and E.H. Volkart. New York: Wiley.

Planning, Commission. 2003. *Five Year Plan 2002–2003*, vol. 2. New Delhi: Government of India.

Prasad, L.V. 2002. Indian system of medicine and homoeopathy. In *Traditional Medicine in Asia,* ed. Chaudhury, Ranjit Roy and Uton, Muchtar Rafei. World Health Organization (WHO): Regional Office for South-East Asia.

Quah, Stella R. 1989. *The Triumph of Practicality: Tradition and Modernity in Health Care Utilization in Selected Asian Countries*. Singapore: Social Issues in Southeast Asia, Institute of Southeast Asian Studies.

Rabinow, Paul. 1997. *Michel Foucault—Ethics, Subjectivity and Truth*. New York: The New Press.

Rahman, Syed Zillur. 2001. Unani medicine in India: Its origin and fundamental concepts. In *Medicine and Life Sciences in India,* ed. Subbarayappa, B.V., vol. iv, part 2. History of Science, Philosophy and Culture in Indian Civilizationseries. New Delhi: Centre for Studies in Civilization.

Ramachandrudu, G. 1997. *Health Planning in India*. New Delhi: A. P. H. Publishing Corporation.

Rawcliffe, Carole. 1999. Medicine for the soul: The medieval English hospital and the quest for spiritual health. In *Religion, Health and Suffering,* ed. Hinnells, John R., and Roy, Porter. London: Kegan Paul International. Retrieved from the following link http://english.jl.gov.cn/Investment/Opportunities/Industry/MedicineandBiotechnology/201208/t20120810_1256011.html. Accessed on 16 Feb 2016. Retrieved from the http://www.gfmer.ch/TMCAM/Hypertension/Education_Traditional_Chinese_Medicine_China.htm. Accessed on 11 Dec 2014.

Rhodes, Lorna Amarasingham. 1990. Studying bio-medicine as a cultural system. In *Medical Anthropology—Contemporary Theory and Method,* ed. Johnson, Thomas M., and Carolyn F. Sargent. New York: Praeger.

Romanucci-Ross, Lola. 1997. The impassioned knowledge of the Shaman. In *The Anthropology of Medicine: From Culture to Method,* ed. Romanucci-Ross, Lola et al. London: Bergin & Garvey.

Rosen, G. 1993. *A History of Public Health*. Baltimore: John Hopkins University Press.

Roy, Mira. 2001. Vedic medicine: Some aspects. In *Medicine and Life Sciences in India,* ed. Subbarayappa, B.V., vol. iv, part 2. History of Science, Philosophy and Culture in Indian Civilization series. New Delhi: Centre for Studies in Civilization.

Said, W. Edward. 1987. *Orientalism*. London: Penguin Books.

Saks, M. 2005. Political and historical perspectives. In *Perspectives on Complementary and Alternative Medicine*, eds. Heller, T., et al. Abingdon: Routledge.

Saks, Mike. 1998. Medicine and complementary medicine: Challenge and change. In *Modernity, Medicine and Health,* ed. Scambler, Graham and Paul, Higgs. Paul. London: Routledge.

Samson, Colin (ed.). 1999. *Health Studies—A Critical and Cross-Cultural Reader*. Oxford: Blackwell Publishers.

Schobersberger, Wolfganger, et al. 2004. Alpine health tourism: Future prospects from a medical perspective. In *The Tourism and Leisure Industry,* ed. Weiermair, Klaus and Mathies, Christine. New York: The Haworth Hospitality Press.

Schobersberger, Wolfganger et al. 2004. Alpine health tourism: Future prospects from a medical perspective. In *The Tourism and Leisure Industry,* ed. Weiermair, Klaus and Mathies, Christine. New York: The Haworth Hospitality Press.

Seal, Anil. 1973. *The Emergence of Indian Nationalism: Competition and Collaboration in the Later Nineteenth Century*. Cambridge: Cambridge University Press.

Selby, Martha Ann. 2005. Sanskrit gynecologies in postmodernity: The commoditization of Indian medicine in alternative medical and new-age discourses on women's health". In *Asian Medicine and Globalization,* ed. Alter, Joseph S. Philadelphia: University of Pennsylvania Press.

Selin, Helaine, and Hugh Shapiro (eds.). 2003. *Medicine across Cultures: History and Practice of Medicine in Non-Western Cultures*. Dordrecht: Kluwer Academic Publishers.

Sharma, Hari, and Christopher Clark. 1998. *Contemporary Ayurveda—Medicine and Research in Maharishi Ayur-veda*. Pannsylvania: Churchill Livingstone.

Sharma, Ursula. 1992. *Complementary Medicine Today—Practitioners and Patients*. London: Routledge.

Shinno, Reiko. 2013. Medical schools and the temples of the three progenitors, pp. 140-144. In *Chinese Medicine and Healing: An Illustrated History,* ed. Hinrichs, T and Barnes, Linda L., 140–144. Cambridge, Massachusetts: The Belknap Press of Harvard University Press.

Singer, Merrill and Hans, Baer. 1995. *Critical Medical Anthropology*. Critical Approaches in the Health Social Sciences series. New York: Baywood Publishing Company.

Sivin, Nathan. 1995. *Medicine, Philosophy and Religion in Ancient China*. Great Britain: Variorum Ashgate Publishing Limited.

Smith, William Roy. 1973. *Nationalism and Reform in India*. London: Kennikat Press.

Spector, Rachel E. 1991. *Cultural Diversity in Health and Illness*, 3rd ed. California: Appleton & Lange.

Spencer, John W. 1999. *Essential Issues in Complementary/Alternative Medicine—An Evidence Based Approach*. Missouri: Mosby.

Spencer, Jonathan. 1998. Modernism, modernity and modernization. In *Encyclopedia of Social and Cultural Anthropology,* ed. Barnard, Alan and Jonathan, Spencer. London: Routledge.

Spencer, Jonathan. 1998. Nationalism. In *Encyclopedia of Social and Cultural Anthropology,* ed. Barnard, Alan and Jonathan, Spencer. London: Routledge.

Standing, Hilary. 1991. *Dependency and Autonomy: Women's Employment and the Family in Calcutta*. London: Routledge.

State Administration of Traditional Chinese Medicine of the People's Republic of China (中华人民共和国国家中医药管理局). 2012. The statistics of Traditional Chinese Medicine. Retrieved from http://www.satcm.gov.cn/1999-2011/atog/2012/B02.htm. Accessed on 19 March 2014.

Strozier, Robert M. 2002. *Foucault, Subjectivity and Identity—Historical Construction of Subject and Self*. Michigan: Wayne State University Press.

Subbarayappa, B.V. 2001. A perspective. In *Medicine and Life Sciences in India,* ed. Subbarayappa, B.V., vol iv, part 2. History of Science, Philosophy and Culture in Indian Civilization series. New Delhi: Centre for Studies in Civilization.

Subedi, Janardan and Eugene B. Gallagher. 1996. *Society, Health, and Disease—Transcultural Perspectives*. Upper Saddle River, N.J.: Prentice Hall.

Sugich, Michael. 1992. *Palaces of India*. London: Pavilion Books Limited.

Susrut Samhita. 1999. ShenSharma, Baydacharjo Kalikinkor and Shatoshakhor, Ayurvedachanjo Bhattacharjo, vol. 1–3. Calcutta: Dipaon.

Svoboda, Robert. 1996. Theory and practice of ayurvedic medicine. In *Oriental Medicine—An Illustrated Guide to the Asian Arts of Healing,* ed. Van Alphen, Jan and Anthony, Aris. Boston: Shambhala.

Taylor, Carl E. 1976. The place of indigenous medical practitioners in the modernization of health services. In *Asian Medical Systems: A Contemporary Study,* ed. Leslie, Charles. Berkeley: University of California Press.

Thapan, Meenakshi. 1997. Introduction. In *Embodiment—Essays on Gender and Identity* (Introduction), ed. Thapan, Meenakshi. New Delhi: Oxford University Press.

Theertha, Swami Dharma. 1992. *History of Hindu Imperialism*. Madras: Dalit Educational Literature Centre.

Thoresen, Carl E. et al. 2001. Spirituality, religion, and health: Evidence, issues, and concerns. In *Faith and Health: Psychological Perspectives*, ed. Plante, Thomas G., and Allen C. Sherman. New York: The Guilford Press.

Trawick, Margaret. 1995. Writing the body and ruling the land: Western reflections on Chinese and Indian medicine. In *Knowledge and the Scholarly Medical Traditions*, ed. Bates, Don. Cambridge: Cambridge University Press.

Tsui, A. 2008. Asian wellness in decline: A cost of rising prosperity. *International Journal of Workplace Health Management* 1 (2): 123–135.

Tucker, Jim B. 2003. Religion and medicine. In *Medicine Across Cultures: History and Practice of Medicine in Non-Western Cultures*, ed. Selin, Helaine and Hugh, Shapiro. Dordrecht: Kluwer Academic Publishers.

Turner, Bryan S. 1996. *The Body and Society (second edition)*. London: Sage Publications.

Tylor, Edward B. 1891. *Primitive Culture*, vol. 1. London: John Murray.

United Nations. 2010. World Population Ageing 2009 Report. Retrieved from the http://www.un.org/esa/population/publications/WPA2009/WPA2009-report.pdf. Accessed on 23 Dec 2013.

Vagbhatas. 2009. *Astanga Hrdayam*. Translated by prof. K.R. Srikantha Murthy. Varanasi: Chowkhamba Krishnadas Academy.

Valiatham, M.S. 2003. *The Legacy of Caraka*. Hyderabad: Oriental Longman Private Limited.

Varma Pavan, K. 1998. *The Great Indian Middle Class*. New Delhi: Viking Penguin India.

Veer, Peter Van Der. 1998. Religion. In *Encyclopaedias of Social and Cultural Anthropology*, ed. Barnard, Alan and Jonathan, Spencer. London: Routledge.

Wajastyk, Dominik. 1996. Medicine in India. In *Oriental Medicine—An Illustration Guide to the Asian Arts of Healing*, ed. Van Alphen, Jan and Anthony, Aris. Boston: Shambhala.

Wangzhong, Qiao. 1996. *The Education of Traditional Chinese Medicine in China*. Geneva: Geneva Foundation for Medical Education and Research.

Wanli, Yang and Zhihua, Liu. 2012. Health Tourism can be a Dose of Good Medicine. 24 September. Beijing: China Daily.

Whitaker, Mark P. 1998. Relativism. In *Encyclopaedia of Social and Cultural Anthropology*, ed. Barnard, Alan and Jonathan, Spencer. London: Routledge.

World Health Organization. 2005. *National Policy on Traditional Medicine and Regulation of Herbal Medicines-Report of a WHO Global Survey*. Geneva: World Health Organization.

World Health Organization. 2000. *Legal Status of Traditional Medicine and Complementary/Alternative Medicine: A World Wide Overview. A Working Paper Produced by the Traditional Medicine Unit*. Geneva: WHO.

World Health Organization. 2001. *Report of the Inter-regional Workshop on Intellectual Property Rights in the Context of Traditional Medicine*. Bangkok: WHO.

Wujastyk, Dominik. 1996. Medicine in India. In *Oriental Medicine—An Illustrated Guide to the Asian Arts of Healing*, ed. Van Alphen, Jan and Anthony, Aris. Boston: Shambhala.

Xie, Zhu-fan. 2002. Harmonization of traditional and modern medicine. In *Traditional Medicine in Asia*, ed. Chaudhury, Ranjit Roy and Rafel, Uton Muchtar, 115–134. New Delhi: World Health Organization (WHO).

Xie, Zhu-fan. 2002. Harmonization of traditional and modern medicine. In *Traditional Medicine in Asia*, ed. Chaudhury, Ranjit Roy and Uton, Mucktar Rafei. World Health Organization (WHO): Regional Office for South-East Asia.

Xuefeng, Zhao. 2012. *Chinese Medicine Processing Project of Hunchun*. Jilin Daily.

Yeung, Agnes K.C. et al. 2003. *Prospect of Health Tourism Development in Hong Kong*. Hong Kong: Division of Social Studies, City University of Hong Kong.

Zhan, Mei. 2013. Get on track with sub-health: changing trajectories of preventive medicine. In *Chinese Medicine and Healing: An Illustrated History*, ed. Hinrichs, T., and Linda L. Barnes. Cambridge: Harvard University Press.

Zhang, Fan. 2012. Systemization of science and technology. In *The history of Chinese Civilization*, ed. Zhang, Chuanxi, vol. ii. Cambridge: Cambridge University Press.

Ming, Zhu. 2009. *The Medical Classic of the Yellow Emperor (Huang Di Nei Jing)*. Beijing: Foreign Language Press.

Zimmer, H.R. 1948. *Hindu Medicine*. Baltimore: John Hopkins Press.

Zimmermann, Francis. 1995. The scholar, the wise man, and universals: Three aspects of Ayurvedic medicine. In *Knowledge and the Scholarly Medical Traditions,* ed. Bates, Don. Cambridge: Cambridge University Press.

Zysk, Kenneth. 1991. *Asceticism and Healing in Ancient India: Medicine in the Buddhist Monastery*. New York and Oxford: Oxford University Press.

Index

M.N. Islam, *Chinese and Indian Medicine Today*,
DOI 10.1007/978-981-10-3962-1